MW01257163

SPIRITUAL LIVES

General Editor

Timothy Larsen

SPIRITUAL LIVES

General Editor

Timothy Larsen

The *Spiritual Lives* series features biographies of prominent men and women whose eminence is not primarily based on a specifically religious contribution. Each volume provides a general account of the figure's life and thought, while giving special attention to his or her religious contexts, convictions, doubts, objections, ideas, and actions. Many leading politicians, writers, musicians, philosophers, and scientists have engaged deeply with religion in significant and resonant ways that have often been overlooked or underexplored. Some of the volumes will even focus on men and women who were lifelong unbelievers, attending to how they navigated and resisted religious questions, assumptions, and settings. The books in this series will therefore recast important figures in fresh and thought-provoking ways.

Titles in the series include:

Woodrow Wilson
Ruling Elder, Spiritual President
Barry Hankins

Christina Rossetti
Poetry, Ecology, Faith
Emma Mason

John Stuart Mill

A Secular Life

TIMOTHY LARSEN

OXFORD
UNIVERSITY PRESS

Great Clarendon Street, Oxford, OX2 6DP,
United Kingdom

Oxford University Press is a department of the University of Oxford.
It furthers the University's objective of excellence in research, scholarship,
and education by publishing worldwide. Oxford is a registered trade mark of
Oxford University Press in the UK and in certain other countries

First Edition published in 2018

Impression: 1

Published in the United States of America by Oxford University Press
198 Madison Avenue, New York, NY 10016, United States of America

British Library Cataloguing in Publication Data
Data available

Library of Congress Control Number: 2017961364

ISBN 978–0–19–875315–5

Printed and bound by
CPI Group (UK) Ltd, Croydon, CR0 4YY

For Kevin Hoffman

Preface

There were, of course, no truly secular lives in nineteenth-century Britain. There were people who lost their faith and looked back wistfully upon their days of untroubled devotion. There were people who triumphantly threw off the faith of their fathers and mothers and then went on to taunt and mock those who still clung to traditional beliefs. There were sober souls who carefully calculated that religion was outmoded and sought to guide the ship of civilization in a sound and orderly way toward a future without it. There were nominal believers and nonchalant conformists. There were dutiful men and women saying their prayers without giving the whole thing much thought. There were pious rogues and oily hypocrites. There were fanatics who made one's blood chill, as well as some heart-warming ones. There were kind-hearted, religiously motivated social reformers. As has been the case from generation unto generation, there were saints and martyrs, prophets and preachers, mystics and visionaries. There were freethinkers, sceptics, unbelievers, infidels, blasphemers, agnostics, and atheists. There were even self-styled Secularists, who alternated between denouncing the old faith and seeking to craft an alternative view of life completely devoid of revelation and the supernatural. No one, however, simply floated along in a world without religion.

John Stuart Mill (1806–73) was the exception that proves this rule. Mill is one of the most prominent and well-respected public intellectuals in modern British history. He was a philosopher, a Member of Parliament, a passionate activist against many forms of injustice, a pioneering feminist. Many of his books have become classics, including *A System of Logic*, *Principles of Political Economy*, *On Liberty*, *Utilitarianism*, and *The Subjection of Women*. Not least in this impressive oeuvre is his posthumously published *Autobiography*. In it, Mill himself made the case that he was the exception. Others had either maintained or thrown off their childhood faith, he reflected, but he was an anomaly in nineteenth-century Britain: someone who had been raised without it. He had no religion to either reject or retain.

This book is a biography of John Stuart Mill. It will follow his life from birth to death. It will watch him in crisis and in love. It will listen to his public pronouncements and private musings. It will examine his major publications—and some minor ones as well. It will follow him into Parliament and the south of France. It will let him speak for himself. It will also, however, attend to religion throughout. Mill's life was impinged upon by religion at every turn. This is true both of the close relationships that shaped him and of his own, internal thoughts. Mill was a religious sceptic, but not the kind of person which that term usually conjures up in one's imagination. The unexpected presence and prominence of spirituality is not only there in Mill's late, startling essay, 'Theism', in which he makes the case for hope in God and in Christ. It is everywhere. It is there in his father, who tried to become a Christian minister in the Church of Scotland but could not find a congregation that would take him. It is there in his mother and sisters who maintained their Christian faith to the end. It is there in his best male friend, who was an ordained clergyman in the Church of England. It is there in his wife, whom he says became for him a religion. It is there in his commending of the Religion of Humanity. Mill rejected dogmatic religion and at various times in his life saw traditional, organized religion as a pernicious force that society would be better off without. On the other hand, he also praised works of orthodox theology, quoted the Bible to express his own thoughts, had his spirits uplifted by church services he attended, and viewed religion as a necessary feature for human flourishing. It is even there in such a seemingly unpropitious place as his *Logic*, which addresses religious themes over and over again. This is the Mill you never knew; the Mill that even some of his closest disciples never knew. This is John Stuart Mill, the Saint of Rationalism—a secular life and a spiritual life.

*

I am grateful to all those who helped me along the way, including librarians, archivists, and fellow scholars in multiple countries—some of whom are acknowledged by name in the endnotes. I am thankful for my time spent during this project at welcoming and supportive institutions: as a Visiting Fellow, All Souls College, Oxford; a Visiting Scholar, Northwestern University; at Trinity College, Cambridge—which has graciously extended accommodation and high table dining privileges to me; and my continuing collaboration with the University of Wales Trinity Saint David as an Honorary Research Fellow. My greatest institutional debt is to Wheaton College. In addition to all that the college continually and generously does to support my life and work year upon year, this project benefitted specifically through a grant from the G. W. Aldeen Memorial Fund. My faculty colleagues are a continual source of joy, encouragement, and intellectual and professional development. Dan Treier, Rick Gibson, Jim Beitler, and Matt Milliner have particularly attended with gracious and unfailing interest to the progress of this project, as have honorary colleagues Alan Jacobs and John Wilson. It is also my delight to mention the valuable and cheerful labour of postgraduate students who have served as my research assistants—Tyler Streckert, Daniel J. King, and, most especially on this project, David Monahan—as well as one undergraduate student, Morgan Rawlinson. PhD student Susanne Calhoun helped me clarify my thoughts by asking astute questions about Mill over the years. I am deeply, truly, continually thankful for the work of Tom Perridge and Karen Raith at Oxford University Press and my ongoing publishing partnership with them. My life is sustained by the wonderful presence and support of my wife Jane and our three children, Lucia, Theo, and Amelia—even the youngest of whom can now drive a car! My father has kindly asked after this project from his hospice bed, as has my mother, his full-time caregiver. I love them all dearly. Kevin Hoffman and I became friends when we were both teenagers in a blue-collar world. He went on to become a philosopher, and I a historian. This one is for you, Kev. Thanks for being my friend.

Table of Contents

1
All His Father's Sins

> 'Now, lo, if he beget a son, that seeth all his father's sins which he had done.'
>
> (Ezekiel 18:14)

John Stuart Mill, one of the most eminent philosophers in British history, was the firstborn son of Harriet Barrow Mill. She had married James Mill at St Pancras Old Church, London, on 18 June 1805. The exact date is not important, but it is telling that it has always been reported incorrectly.[1] Even the entry on James Mill in such an authoritative, meticulous source as the *Oxford Dictionary of National Biography* has the couple being joined together until death do them part almost a fortnight earlier—on June 5th.[2] Alexander Bain, who solicited information from the Mill children, gave this erroneous date, and it has just been recopied by scholars and writers ever since. It is tempting to read this false information regarding the nuptial day as indicative of the fact that James and Harriet Mill did not celebrate their wedding anniversary. Certainly the marriage was not a happy one.

In his posthumously published *Autobiography*, John recounted his secular childhood:

> I was brought up from the first without any religious belief, in the ordinary meaning of the term.... I am thus one of the very few examples, in this country, of one who has, not thrown off religious belief, but never had it: I grew up in a negative state with regard to it. I looked upon the modern exactly as I did upon the ancient religion, as something which in no way concerned me. It did not seem to me more strange that English people should believe what I did not, than that the men whom I read of in Herodotus should have done so.[3]

This is a much exaggerated and—especially for readers' today—a deeply misleading statement.[4] Concealing past religiosity, however, was a habit that John inherited from his father.

James Mill grew up in the county of Forfarshire in the north east of Scotland.[5] He was the namesake of his father, a shoemaker who was known for being a devout Christian who practised faithfully and impressively spiritual disciplines such as fasting. James's mother, Isabel, had been a servant. As a wife and mother, she had a local reputation for being haughty. Despite the family's lowly social position, Isabel was determined to raise her firstborn to be a gentleman. The only way up was through education. Fortunately, young James was a bright child and a pupil of much promise. He went to the parish school, then to Montrose Academy. James gained a crucial ally in the scramble of life in the parish minister. Some 'pious ladies' had created a scholarship fund for educating worthy young men for the Christian ministry, and James thereby had the good fortune to be able to attend university. Having pursued a course in divinity at Edinburgh, he became a ministerial candidate in the Church of Scotland in the Presbytery of Brechin. James's trial efforts included delivering a popular sermon on Revelation 22:14 ('Blessed are they that do his commandments, that they may have right to the tree of life') and a lecture on Galatians 2:20 ('I am crucified with Christ: nevertheless, I live; yet not I, but Christ liveth in me: and the life which I now live in the flesh I live by the faith of the Son of God, who loved me, and gave himself for me'). On 4 October 1798, James Mill was licensed to preach the Gospel of Jesus Christ.

At this point, his career stalled. His mother had instilled in him her own sense of superiority. James even looked down on his own siblings. His brother, not being the chosen one, was put to work in the shoe shop. Isabel managed to create a study room in the house for the exclusive use of her favoured son. Rather than join the family, James would take his dinner there alone. His sister was tasked with providing him with room service. She particularly resented an occasion when she brought him his meal and he returned the favour by mocking her common, colloquial manner of speech. Contrariwise, when James preached, ordinary folk complained that they could not follow what he was saying. Having still not secured a parish despite his fervent efforts, James took up tutoring as a stopgap. All the stories from this period of his life have the same theme: he thought of himself as a gentleman among gentlemen which caused him to clash with the families employing him who were apt to treat him as a servant amongst the servants. One anecdote is about James having the effrontery to try to offer a toast to a lady who was a relation of the wellborn family of the house. Another is that he resigned one appointment in anger when he learned that he was expected to leave the dining room along with the ladies after the evening meal. James learned to hate aristocratic airs. Indeed, that lesson had begun earlier in his life when he had fallen for a young woman who was unattainably above his station: Wilhelmina, the daughter of his patron, Sir John Stuart.[6] To rub fine, old brandy into the wound, James failed in his effort to receive a call to be the minister of a pleasant parish that he had set his heart on. It went instead to someone with better social connections. One might wonder if his inability to preach effectively was no less decisive, but James developed the deep-seated, lifelong conviction that aristocracy was merely a pernicious system for keeping those with exceptional talents and abilities from receiving their due rewards. His anti-aristocratic ally later in life, the Utilitarian philosopher Jeremy Bentham, would sharply observe of James Mill: 'His creed of politics results less from love of the many, than hatred of the few.'[7] Still, one thing was clear: James was falling between two stools in his efforts to become a minister of the established Church of Scotland, having the advantages of neither being highborn nor of a common touch. He decided that his humble origins were too well known and therefore he would always be a prophet without honour in his own country. He made up his mind to go to London. Perhaps he would try his hand at a literary life; men with less brains than him were making good money at it, he mused.

By his own candid admission, John Stuart Mill did not love either of his parents. As to his father, it was simply a case of the perfect fear that casteth out love. There was respect, but not affection; he believed his father to be a truly great man, but there was no confiding intimacy, no tenderness.[8] And, even in the category of being a great man, one thing John held against the patriarch of the family was his father's married life. Harriet was a beauty who brought some badly needed property with her into the union, but her husband soon came to despise her as a being contemptibly beneath him intellectually. Their son John—always a quick study—did not take long in learning to share this low opinion of his own mother. What he never could understand, however, was how his father's disdain for his wife as a silly and stupid woman could be coupled with continued coupling. To marry the wrong woman is a tragedy, but to go on to have nine children with her seemed like sheer carelessness. (James even named his first girl Wilhelmina, a bitter reminder of the true love that he could not obtain.) John himself was born on 20 May 1806. Then the Mill children kept coming in two-year intervals: Wilhelmina in 1808; Clara in 1810; Harriet in 1812; James Bentham in 1814; Jane in 1816; then a double gap before Henry in 1820; Mary in 1822; and the last of the lot also broke the pattern, George Grote in 1825.[9]

Throughout his adult life, John was passionately committed to the Malthusian belief that a key to increasing the happiness of the human race overall was to decrease the birth rate. This meant that contraception was to be preferred over excessive breeding. His youthful foray into criminality came when he was arrested for distributing a tract which expounded a sponge method of birth control, *To Married Working People*. Nevertheless, Mill's true and highest ideal was chastity. The atheist leader Charles Bradlaugh, knowing and sharing Mill's Malthusian views, was surprised and disappointed to learn that the philosopher really had condemned another birth control manual, *Elements of Social Science*. Mill had been outraged by its dismissive attitude towards abstinence, which he thought actually ought to be the preferred option and the one which would be adopted by any truly enlightened society. Defying a humanitarian wave that had overtaken even parts of officialdom, Mill was adamant that married couples confined to the workhouse should not be allowed to sleep together. This was not merely to prevent pregnancies, but to cultivate virtue: 'I consider it an essential part of the moral training.'[10] Mill thought that what it meant to reform society was to discover 'how to obtain the greatest amount of chastity'.[11] In 1854, he reflected in his diary: 'As I probably shall have no opportunity of writing out at length my ideas on this and other matters, I am anxious to leave on record at least in this place my deliberate opinion that any great improvement in human life is not to be looked for so long as the animal instinct of sex occupies the absurdly disproportionate place it does.'[12] Mill went so far as to chide the Church for being too pro-sex.[13] To have sex regularly—even within a good, loving marriage—a moralizing Mill pontificated, was to succumb to the vice of 'intemperance'.[14] What his father had done, however, was much more vile. In an article published in 1834 (that is, when his father was still alive), Mill fumed against the kind of low creature who would use the fact of being legally married to continue 'a merely animal connexion' when 'affection has never existed, or has ceased to exist'.[15] In defiance of all his high standards—not least his extolling of the classical virtue of temperance—James Mill had spent his adult life in a union that was not intellectual, but merely carnal. His son would spite him by dedicating himself for two decades to a relationship with the love of his life, Harriet Taylor, which was not carnal but was deeply intellectual. Only a true equal is a suitable romantic partner, Mill insisted. There can be no morganatic marriages in the intellectual aristocracy.

Mill acknowledged that his mother was a kind woman whose whole life was given over to serving her children. Nevertheless, unlike his siblings, he did not love her. Moreover, in a classic blaming-the-victim sort of way, he even faulted her—her kindness and self-sacrifice notwithstanding—for her inability 'to make herself loved'.[16] (Allowances should also be made, however, for the fact that Mill wrote this at a time in his life when he was exasperated with his family. There are a couple of accounts by visitors to the family in which John is witnessed being an affectionate son to his mother.)[17] Mill admitted that as a boy he developed an impertinent way of interacting with adults. His father could not correct this character flaw because John was too afraid of him to display it in his presence: 'My mother did tax me with it, but for her remonstrances I never had the slightest regard.'[18] We have a glimpse of their domestic life in the diary entry of Caroline Fox from the evening when she first visited the Mills at their home. Fox was charmed by Mrs Mill, but John seems ashamed of his mother, constantly assuming that she was boring their guest. And we glimpse Mrs Mill pathetically trying to find a bridge between her domestic life and John's intellectual world by observing that the pudding she had baked for them was a favourite of the Utilitarian philosopher Jeremy Bentham![19] After Mill had taken offence at his family, when writing to his own brother George, he could even refer to the woman who had brought him into the world and cared for him all his days as 'your mother'.[20]

One of the many ways that Mill was a great man and a benefactor of humanity was his brave, far-seeing, pioneering, large-hearted championing of the rights of women. To his credit, at his best, Mill could discern that his mother had been the victim of an oppressive patriarchal system in which he and his father had taken their part among the victimizers. In *The Subjection of Women*, he reflected that the legal power given to husbands 'causes them to feel a sort of disrespect and contempt towards their own wife . . . which makes her seem to them an appropriate subject for any kind of indignity'. And legally enforced gender inequality had a similar effect upon her son: 'how early the youth thinks himself superior to his mother, owing her perhaps forbearance, but no real respect'.[21] The teenage Mill was tutored in German by the erudite translator and author, Sarah Austin. He quickly came to see her as the kind of woman of intellectual substance that his mother so inexcusably was not. He started addressing Mrs Austin as his 'Mütterlein' (Mummy).

As Sarah Austin was his alternative mother, beginning already early in his childhood, Mill's secondary father figure was Jeremy Bentham. The earliest letter of John's that survives was written by him when he was six years old and it was in response to Bentham's paternal interest in the progress of his studies. James Mill was Bentham's most important disciple and one of his closest friends. The Mill family claimed that Bentham was the reason why James lost his faith. James E. Crimmins has demonstrated convincingly that Bentham himself had already adopted an irreligious stance early in life. He was 'an ardent secularist' and arguably the greatest 'intellectual force for secularization' in early nineteenth-century England. Still, a theme of this study of John Stuart Mill is that the contours of such a stance are very different when the person holding it is situated in a society in which religion is pervasive. Thus, Crimmins also observes that religion was 'never far from the centre' of Bentham's thoughts 'throughout his long and industrious intellectual career'.[22] Bentham wrote a handful of books (or manuscripts that his followers turned into books) on religious themes. The first to be published was *'Swear not at all': containing an exposure of the needlessness and mischievousness, as well as antichristianity, of the ceremony of an oath* (1817). Bentham's vexation stemmed from the fact that oaths such as requiring subscription to the Thirty-Nine Articles of the Church of England were a hindrance to free thought and a temptation to dishonesty or hypocrisy. Nevertheless, it is not incidental that the title comes from the very words of Jesus of Nazareth as recorded in the Sermon on the Mount (Matthew 5:34), and Bentham really did brandish his scriptural proof text triumphantly, remarking in private to a disciple a decade later: 'Was ever text more clear than that, "Swear not at all".'[23] In the same year as that tract was published, his *Church-of-Englandism and its Catechism Examined* was first printed. This tome was then published in 1818 with Bentham's name on the title page. *Church-of-Englandism* is a bizarre, prolix book of over 450 pages. Woven throughout is an unconvincing exposé of the National Society for Promoting the Education of the Poor in the Principles of the Established Church as not simply wrongheaded but sinisterly malfeasant. The ostensible argument is that the Bible is a better guide than the catechism and that Anglican doctrine and practice is not faithful to the true 'religion of Jesus'. Nevertheless, what the Church of England is said to get wrong are often matters that are considered major components of the faith across almost all varieties of Christianity. Notably, Bentham argued that Jesus did not intend to set up the Lord's Supper (Holy Communion) as a permanent institution and therefore Christians should eliminate the sacrament from their worship.

Bentham's greatest philosophical contribution to religious controversy was *Analysis of the Influence of Natural Religion on the Temporal Happiness of Mankind*, a book that had been constructed from Bentham's notes by George Grote (who would later achieve fame as the historian of ancient Greece), and which was published under a pseudonym in 1822. It purported not to be addressing revealed religion (that is, Christianity), but only natural religion (that is, what human beings think about religion on their own, without supernatural guidance). It argued that natural religion failed to pass the test of utility: it is actually 'the foe and not the benefactor of mankind'.[24] Despite its stated scope, the *Analysis* often used Christian examples to make its points and was clearly intended to shake the reader's confidence in revealed as well as natural religion.

If the theme of *Church-of-Englandism* was 'not Cranmer, but Christ', Bentham went much further than that in a volume published in 1823: *Not Paul, but Jesus*. A pseudonym was used for it as well; and it too was crafted with the help of a disciple. Another bulky volume—coming in at over 400 pages—it once again purports to be a defence of the 'religion of Jesus'. This time, however, it is not the Church of England which has departed from the true faith, but the apostle Paul himself. One might think it would be sufficient for any such polemical purpose to argue that Paul was a fanatic whose teaching is erroneous and dangerous. But no. Bentham insisted that St Paul was insincere, that he never did have a genuine conversion experience at all; he only feigned one. Paul turned to Christian ministry, Bentham averred, solely as a way of making money and accruing fame. There is a whole section in *Not Paul, but Jesus* titled, 'Motive: Temporal Advantage.' The driving force of Paul's supposed apostleship was exclusively 'his concupiscence'.[25] The accounts in the Acts of the Apostles of divine healing coming through Paul's ministry were actually con-tricks: he paid an accomplice to fake the scene. This unmeasured attack crescendoes in the final chapter, where Bentham sets out the claim that St Paul was himself the Antichrist.

One of the few things that many people know about Bentham today is that, in accordance with his own instructions, his body was made into an 'auto-icon' that is still in the possession of University College London. Icons, of course, are an important part of a life of worship for many Christians; and the bodily remains of saints are venerated by myriads of the faithful as relics. Bentham even suggested in his will that his followers might want to create a kind of annual feast day to commemorate their founder at which they would gather around his auto-icon. In a treatise, he went so far as to imagine a *cultus* which could accompany this liturgical calendar: 'On certain days the Auto-Icons might be exhibited, and their exhibition associated with religious observances.'[26] People could even make the journey to his earthly remains an act of pilgrimage, he mused. As with Henri de Saint-Simon, Auguste Comte, and even John Stuart Mill himself, so with Jeremy Bentham: despite a lifetime of kicking against the pricks, their late thoughts are less free of the stamp of the religious past than one might have supposed.

The mature James Mill was not merely unorthodox: his son was quite willing to declare flatly that his father did not believe in Christianity.[27] Rather, James was a bitterly anti-clerical religious sceptic. Still, as this volume is intended to drive home, a nineteenth-century sceptical identity did not exempt one from being enmeshed in tangled, theistic terrain. No straightforward secularity should be imagined. To wit, the mature, sceptical James wrote in his commonplace book: 'The first article of any religion is the belief of an all-perfect God. To that I stick. Whatever I cannot reconcile with that I reject.'[28] In his *Autobiography*, John goes into some detail regarding the precise nature of his father's unbelief. This is usually read as motivated simply by a desire to make the extent of his father's rejection of traditional religion clear. What is actually going on in that passage, however, is far more interesting. John was seeking to demonstrate that there was nothing in his father's thinking that ruled out the case for God that he would lay out in his essay 'Theism' (which, like the *Autobiography*, itself was only published posthumously): 'These particulars are important, because they shew that my father's rejection of all that is called religious belief, was not, as many might suppose, primarily a matter of logic and evidence: the grounds of it were moral, still more than intellectual.'[29] John solved the moral problem to his own satisfaction by eliminating omnipotence from God's attributes, thus his father's legacy—he is asserting in the *Autobiography*—does *not* include any logical or evidentiary argument against the kind of reverent, hope-filled religious possibilities presented in 'Theism'.

Very much in line with Bentham's *Church-of-Englandism* (which he cites), was James Mill's article, 'The Church, and Its Reform'. It was published in the second issue of the *London Review* and it so outraged even many people within the Mills' own radical milieu as to endanger the life of the young journal. The article's thesis was that 'the present ecclesiastical establishment in England is a perfect nullity in respect to good, but an active and powerful agent in the production of evil'.[30] That makes it sound like it could be a particularly full-blooded argument from the side of Protestant Dissent but, as was the case with Bentham's writings, James Mill's examples include practices and beliefs shared by all Christians. Many found particularly offensive his attack on prayer as a pointless activity that should be abandoned. Petitionary prayer is ridiculous because it is telling an all-wise being what to do; and praise is no less so, as it is informing an all-knowing being of his own attributes. Jesus discouraged prayer, James avers, but allowed it because of your hardness of heart. It was time to put a stop to prayer altogether. Nevertheless, old habits of the heart die hard. Some pages later in the very same article, in a weak moment, James himself lapses into prayer: 'Oh God! with what perseverance and zeal has this representation of thy Divine nature been maintained, by men who, with the same breath, and therefore in the spirit of base adulation, were calling thee the God of truth.'[31] James Mill had not only lost his old faith, he was preaching a crusade against it.

James dealt with his past life by burying it. John was in a claustrophobically close relationship with his father for thirty years: he was homeschooled by him and, even when he went out to work at the age of seventeen, his father was his immediate supervisor at the office. Nevertheless, in those three decades of continuous interaction, John never discovered that his father had been licensed to preach. He was left to learn it from others after his father's death. John knew his father had studied divinity, but he had somehow gained the erroneous impression that he had also pursued medicine. A friend from Scotland visited in 1810 and he observed that James Mill did not allow any discussion of his old life and acquaintances until after his wife and their son (John) had left the room. When, in the course of his research, Bentham wanted to know what the procedure for clerical subscription was in the Church of Scotland, he asked James, who replied that he would make inquiries with a Scottish minister that he knew. As Bain observed, this was a strange response, as James had himself subscribed and so ought to have been able to give the information from his personal experience. In his commonplace book, James makes a no less odd comment when reflecting on Christian doctrine: 'The time was when I would have very readily declared that I believe all this, and when I would have gone to death rather than have renounced it—but I am now aware that religion is not believed.'[32] It is as if he is trying to reconcile his current, sceptical self with his former one as someone so pious that he would have been willing to be a martyr for orthodoxy by deciding that he had always—in some mysterious, subterranean way—been an unbeliever without knowing it.

The change from believer to unbeliever was also slower in coming than, in James's later years, he would have liked people to realize. For years James Mill had been a Christian man about town in London. He successfully gained the help and support of Dr Henry Hunter, the minister of the Scotch Church, London Wall. James found work as the editor of the *St James's Chronicle*, a clerical paper later renamed the *English Churchman*. (Bain observed that this connection was one of the things that were firmly interred: 'the fact was never mentioned by himself'.)[33] In 1805 (that is, three years after he arrived in London), James published a translation 'with copious notes' of Charles Villers, *An Essay on the Spirit and Influence of the Reformation of Luther*. The notes were gratuitous, which makes all the more telling one that condemns

Hume and Gibbon as 'infidels'; and a long one which expresses how offended he was by an insufficiently reverent treatment of the sacred scriptures. Villers had highlighted the Bible's literary composition, but James countered with the vastly more important reality that it is a divine communication which, despite the varied circumstances of composition, comprises 'a perfect whole'.[34] Also in 1805 the *Eclectic Review* was founded as an organ of evangelical Dissenting Protestants, and James became one of its contributors. James Mill even wrote a letter in 1807 in which he was still scheming and hoping to secure a parish in the Church of Scotland and thus live out his days pursuing his holy calling to preach the Gospel of Jesus Christ.[35] As this was nine years after he first qualified to pursue Christian ministry, John's account of his father's biography erased a significant percentage of James's entire adult life, as well as anachronistically importing a reason that was not in operation during all those years: James Mill 'was licensed as a Preacher, but never followed the profession; having satisfied himself that he could not believe the doctrines of that or of any other church'. Even more chronologically misleading was John's opening summary: 'I was brought up from the first without any religious belief, in the ordinary acceptation of the term. My father, educated in the creed of Scotch presbyterianism, had by his own studies and reflexions been early led to reject not only the belief in revelation, but the foundations of what is commonly called Natural Religion.'[36] And James never could bring himself to throw out the sermons he had written in the zeal of his youth: the family found a saddlebag full of them in the attic. Based on statements regarding the influence of the death of Francisco de Miranda on his loss of faith, Packe calculated that James did not arrive at a thoroughgoing, unbelieving identity until 1816, by which time he was forty-three years old (and his eldest son was ten).[37] John reported that his father had told him that 'for some time' after he had begun to entertain sceptical thoughts he was able to continue to be a believer because his faith was shored up by the arguments in Bishop Butler's *The Analogy of Religion, Natural and Revealed, to the Constitution and Course of Nature*.[38] Moreover, all those years (and perhaps even some thereafter) James was attending Church of England worship services regularly. When in 'The Church, and Its Reform' he exercised his right to criticize a type of Anglican sermon on the grounds that he had 'heard a good many of that class', it was no idle assertion. Even more startlingly in that article is James's vision for a reformed future in which the clergy are forbidden to proclaim religious dogma but which nevertheless also includes mandatory Sabbath-day services for the entire populace: 'We think it of great importance, that all the families of a parish should be got to assemble on the Sunday.'[39] Even as an unbeliever, one of James's favourite sayings was the biblical admonition: 'The righteousness of the righteous man guideth his steps.'[40]

Harriet Mill's mother was a 'religious woman' who, as grandmothers are apt to do, helped with the spiritual formation of the Mill children. Harriet herself was a lifelong, practising Christian. All nine of the Mill children were baptized. As indicated by his name, John Stuart Mill's godparents were Sir John Stuart and Lady Jane Stuart. Later in life, Lady Jane wrote to James Mill (whose training for the Christian ministry she had helped to fund) in order to express her hope that now that he had become a prominent, well-respected figure he would not neglect to prioritize a life of faith in God. She also commended to him a volume of sermons by the evangelical minister Thomas Chalmers.[41] Of the nine Mill children, it seems possible that all of them were Christians in the usual, Victorian meaning of that appellation except for the first, John Stuart, and the last, George Grote. Certainly, the five girls were given a standard Christian spiritual formation. It is not clear if some of the sons joined them as well throughout their childhood and youth, but mother and daughters, at any rate, never gave up attending church regularly. Bentham was so hostile to Christian worship that he refused to allow his servants to use the chapel in Forde Abbey. Yet when the Mills stayed with him there, the women of the family (at the very least) worshipped faithfully at Thorncombe parish church. Moreover, the Mill children not only were taught to pray, but they even memorized the catechism (despite Bentham having so ridiculed and denounced it in *Church-of-Englandism*). Ironically, given his claim about his own case in his *Autobiography*, John himself once asserted in a letter to the *Morning Chronicle*: 'There is no place where religion does not form one of the most essential parts of education.'[42] Harriet (the third daughter and fourth child) testified that their father let all this religious practice carry on without the slightest attempt to curb it. As a woman in her sixties, Harriet proclaimed her faith in God confidently. The complete reverse of John's experience, sister Harriet remarked that it was her experience of injustice 'which first made me feel the utter necessity of God'. Even during her childhood, this daughter of James Mill found the thought that God is all-knowing a great comfort in times of trouble.[43] Harriet wrote these remarks to the Revd Joseph W. Crompton, who had been a close friend of her brother James, and who became a trustee of the property of another sister, Jane. Mary, the eighth child and youngest daughter—despite having been educated entirely at home by her father and her brother John—was a deeply devout Christian. She and her husband were zealous believers who dedicated their lives to good works.[44] In the midst of the parting of the ways in 1851, Mary confessed to John that she was 'striving each day to become more Christian', before adding wistfully: 'I have prayed that this letter may touch your heart.'[45] Seven years later (by which time John was fifty-one years old), sister Mary wrote to him declaring—much to his annoyance—that her greatest wish for her famous brother was that she might know that he was a Christian.[46]

One intriguing glimpse into the spiritual life of the Mill family comes during the final illness of Henry, the seventh child, who died of tuberculosis when just nineteen years old. There were nightly Bible readings at his bedside. Maria Fox, a recorded Quaker minister who was also a family friend, came and spoke to him: Henry reported afterwards that Fox's 'allusions to religious subjects quite overcame him, and he was on the point of bursting into tears'.[47] One of the Mill sisters, Clara, recommended to her dying brother that he meditate on the hymn 'As thy day, so shall thy strength be.' Its first stanza opens, 'Afflicted saint, to Christ draw near; The Saviour's gracious promise hear'; and its last, 'When death at length appear in view, Christ's presence shall thy fears subdue.'[48] Henry told his sister Harriet that he had 'certainty' that there was life after death awaiting him.[49] John was there when he breathed his last. The doctor remarked, 'This sort of scene puts an end to Reason, and Faith begins.' The Utilitarian philosopher agreed with an emphatic and earnest 'yes' and, rising to the occasion, began to discourse on the theme in a way that the devout Christian Caroline Fox, a friend of the family who was also present, found 'edifying'. Mill wrote to his friend Barclay Fox (Caroline's brother), reflecting that the lesson he had learned from his brother Henry's death was to be guided by Christ's admonition to work while it is day because 'the night cometh, when no man can work' (John 9:4).[50] (It is indicative of the need to take more seriously the religious milieu of Mill's life that good scholars writing for university presses have repeatedly attributed this saying to Thomas Carlyle! Carlyle did evoke it in *Sartor Resartus*; and he did not bother to put it in quotation marks because he could not imagine a reader who would not recognize a pronouncement by Jesus from the Gospels.)[51] Barclay himself died fifteen years later. His last words were: 'What a mercy it is that Christ not only frees us from the guilt of sin, but also delivers us from its power.' The scene was so inspiring that Caroline wrote a long letter to John Stuart Mill recounting the death of his friend as a way of commending the Christian faith to him. Caroline also wrote a conspiratorial letter to her fellow Christian, Mill's sister Clara, wondering at her own boldness in proclaiming the Gospel to the celebrated philosopher: 'Thanks be to God, who giveth us the victory through our Lord Jesus Christ!'[52] Mill was out of the country when his mother died. Knowing the end was near, she wrote him a note on her deathbed. Harriet Mill's last words to her firstborn, John, were a mother's prayer: 'God bless you my dear son.'[53]

Thus, one can hardly take literally Mill's assertion: 'I looked upon the modern exactly as I did upon the ancient religion, as something which in no way concerned me. It did not seem to me more strange that English people should believe what I did not, than that the men whom I read of in Herodotus should have done so.' His mother and sisters (whom he continued to live with well into his forties) were not perceived by him as engaging in activities that might as well have been offering sacrifices to Dionysus and, if they had been, as involving his closest relations and living companions, it could hardly be something that in no way concerned him. When his father was buried in Kensington church in a service during which his family could gain comfort from the reminder in a prayer, 'of whom may we seek for succour, but of thee, O Lord?', it is highly unlikely that Mill was thinking to himself that he might as well be witnessing a petition to Poseidon. And it is important to keep in mind that these are not two Mill families, but just one. The same sister, Mary, who longed to know that John was a Christian also wrote a review of a treatise on political economy; the same sister, Harriet, who found comfort in God's omniscience also excelled under John's tutelage at university-level mathematics. And this was a two-way bridge. John too went to church regularly when he was young and presumably was also taught to pray, and so on. An aunt recalled attending a church service with him and John enthusing afterwards 'that the two greatest books were Homer and the Bible'.[54] A letter John wrote from Forde Abbey when he was eight years old casually mentions in his general report of his activities that he too had been to Thorncombe parish church, so even when Bentham had home-field advantage, the boy was still receiving a Christian spiritual formation. Indeed, Mill occasionally attended Christian worship services during his teen years and thereafter for the rest of his life. The sea of faith was full and all around.

Notes

1. Scan of the original marriage record: accessed from www.familysearch.org on 8 April 2014.
2. Jose Harris, 'Mill, John Stuart (1806–1873)', *Oxford Dictionary of National Biography* (accessed online at www.oxforddnb.com).
3. John Stuart Mill, *Autobiography and Literary Essays* (Collected Works of John Stuart Mill I), ed. J. M. Robson, Indianapolis: Liberty Fund, 2006 (reprint of Toronto: University of Toronto Press, 1981), pp. 40, 45. (On second citation, all volumes in the Collected Works of John Stuart Mill will be given a short title using the abbreviation CWJSM.)
4. This was demonstrated long ago: Michael St. John Packe, *The Life of John Stuart Mill*, London: Secker and Warburg, 1954, p. 25. This chapter will provide substantial additional evidence, and further fill out, this observation.
5. The information in this section is primarily derived from Alexander Bain, *James Mill: A Biography*, London: Longmans, Green, and Co., 1882.
6. Nicholas Capaldi, *John Stuart Mill: A Biography*, Cambridge: Cambridge University Press, 2004, pp. 1–2.
7. Packe, *Life*, p. 101.
8. For a Freudian account of this relationship as an example of the Oedipus Complex, see Bruce Mazlish, *James and John Stuart Mill: Father and Son in the Nineteenth Century*, London: Hutchinson, 1975.
9. Capaldi, *John Stuart Mill*, p. 367.
10. John Stuart Mill to Edward Herford, 22 January 1850: Francis E. Mineka and Dwight N. Lindley (eds), *The Later Letters of John Stuart Mill, 1849–1873*

(Collected Works of John Stuart Mill XIV), Toronto: University of Toronto Press, 1972, p. 45.

11. John Stuart Mill to Lord Amberley, 2 February 1870: CWJSM XVII (*Later Letters*), p. 1693.
12. Diary entry for 26 March 1854: John M. Robson (ed.), *Journals and Debating Speeches* (Collected Works of John Stuart Mill XXVII), Toronto: University of Toronto Press, 1988, p. 664.
13. Packe, *Life*, p. 301.
14. John Stuart Mill to Harriet Taylor, n.d. [*c.*31 March 1849]: CWJSM XIV (*Later Letters*), p. 21.
15. John Stuart Mill, *Newspaper Writings (August 1831—October 1834)*, eds Ann P. Robson and John M. Robson (Collected Works of John Stuart Mill XXIII), Toronto: University of Toronto Press, 1986, p. 679.
16. CWJSM I (*Autobiography and Literary Essays*), p. 612.
17. For example, see the Statement from the Reverend Joseph W. Crompton, JMK\PP\87\20A, Keynes Papers, Archives Centre, King's College, Cambridge.
18. CWJSM I (*Autobiography and Literary Essays*), p. 36.
19. Horace N. Pym (ed.), *Memories of Old Friends: being extracts from the Journals and Letters of Caroline Fox of Penjerrick, Cornwall*, London: Smith, Elder, and Co., 1882, p. 99 (entry for 19 May 1840).
20. John Stuart Mill to George Grote Mill, 4 August 1851: CWJSM XIV (*Later Letters*), p. 74.
21. John Stuart Mill, *Essays on Equality, Law, and Education*, eds John M. Robinson and Stefani Collini (Collected Works of John Stuart Mill XXI), Toronto: University of Toronto Press, 1984, pp. 296, 324.
22. James E. Crimmins, *Secular Utilitarianism: Social Science and the Critique of Religion in the Thought of Jeremy Bentham*, Oxford: Clarendon Press, 1990, especially pp. 1, 17, 19.
23. Crimmins, *Secular Utilitarianism*, p. 130.
24. Jeremy Bentham, *The Influence of Natural Religion on the Temporal Happiness of Mankind*, introduction by Delos McKown, Amherst: Prometheus Books, 2003, p. 20. (Originally published as Philip Beauchamp [Jeremy Bentham and George Grote], *Analysis of the Influence of Natural Religion on the Temporal Happiness of Mankind*, 1822.)
25. Gamaliel Smith, Esq. [Jeremy Bentham], *Not Paul, But Jesus*, London: John Hunt, 1823, p. 156.
26. Crimmins, *Secular Utilitarianism*, p. 298.
27. John Stuart Mill to John Lalor, 27 June 1852: CWJSM XIV (*Later Letters*), p. 92.

28. 'Religion' in *James Mill's Common Place Books*, ed. Robert A. Fenn, vol. II, ch. 5 (2010), p. 24: accessed at http://intellectualhistory.net/mill/cpb2ch5.html
29. CWJSM I (*Autobiography and Literary Essays*), pp. 42–3.
30. [James Mill], 'The Church, and Its Reform', *London Review*, Vol. I, No. II (1835), pp. 257–95 (here 259).
31. Mill, 'The Church, and Its Reform', p. 281.
32. 'Religion' in *James Mill's Common Place Books*, p. 25.
33. Bain, *James Mill*, p. 53.
34. Charles Villers, *An Essay on the Spirit and Influence of the Reformation of Luther*, Translated and Illustrated with Copious Notes, by James Mill, Esq., London: C. and R. Baldwin, 1805, p. 304.
35. Bain, *James Mill*, p. 63.
36. CWJSM I (*Autobiography and Literary Essays*), pp. 6, 40.
37. Packe, *Life*, p. 25.
38. John Stuart Mill to William George Ward, n.d. [Spring 1849]: CWJSM XIV (*Later Letters*), p. 30.
39. Mill, 'The Church, and Its Reform', pp. 269, 299.
40. John Stuart Mill to John Elliot Cairnes, 26 December 1863: CWJSM XV (*Later Letters*), p. 912. This saying contains the substance but not the exact wording in the Authorized Version of both Proverbs 11:5 and Proverbs 13:6. It is likely he just did not remember one of these verses precisely, but James was trained in Old Testament Hebrew exegesis and therefore it is even possible that this version might have been his own translation.
41. Bain, *James Mill*, p. 201.
42. Letter to the *Morning Chronicle*, 12 February 1823: CWJSM XXII (*Newspaper Writings)*, p. 16.
43. Harriet I. Mill to the Revd Joseph W. Crompton, 26 October 1873: JMK\PP\87\20A, Keynes Papers, Archives Centre, King's College, Cambridge.
44. Mill later had reasons that cannot now be identified to distrust Mary's husband and the couple were separated, so it is possible that his religious zeal eventually cooled or was proved to be hypocritical, but nothing of the kind can be said about Mary herself.
45. Mary Elizabeth Colman (née Mill) to John Stuart Mill, 18 July 1851: Mill-Taylor Collection, London School of Economics, Vol. XLVIII.
46. CWJSM XV (*Later Letters*), p. 547.
47. Pym, *Memories*, p. 69.
48. Edward Davies and John A. Baxter, *A Selection of Psalms and Hymns, chiefly adapted for public worship*, third edition, London: Simpkin and Marshall, 1835, p. 225 (hymn 231).

49. Harriet I. Mill to the Revd Joseph W. Crompton, 26 October 1873: JMK\PP\87\20A, Keynes Papers, Archives Centre, King's College, Cambridge.
50. Pym, *Memories*, p. 91.
51. Capaldi's thorough and stimulating life of Mill has helped me much during this project, so I regret to point out that even he is amongst those who claim that Mill was quoting Carlyle: Capaldi, *John Stuart Mill*, p. 131. I owe the same acknowledgement to Reeves, and thus feel the same displeasure at pointing out that this lapse also occurs in his highly useful study: Richard Reeves, *John Stuart Mill: Victorian Firebrand*, London: Atlantic Books, 2007, p. 451.
52. Pym, *Memories*, p. 303 (she is quoting 1 Corinthians 15:57).
53. John Stuart Mill to John Elliot Cairnes, 26 December 1863: CWJSM XIV (*Later Letters*), p. 231.
54. Bain, *James Mill*, p. 90.

2

Train Up a Child in the Way He Should Go

'Train up a child in the way he should go: and when he is old, he will not depart from it.'

(Proverbs 22:6)

Always precocious, Mill was reading Greek at the age of three and by the time he was twenty-two he was already bald. A standard reminiscence of early education from nineteenth-century Britain would began with a sentimental scene of learning to read with a Bible on one's mother's knee. In Mill's account, there is an avalanche of titles, authors, and tomes, but the Book of Books is conspicuous by its absence; as are both his mother and his mother tongue. Mill's *Autobiography* does not acknowledge he had a mother and so he never learns English: he just begins his account at the age of three with Greek and his father. To put it another way, Mill's ability to understand written English developed before his ability to retain memories did: 'I myself cannot remember any time when I could not read with facility & pleasure.'[1] We do, however, have a *terminus post quem*, as James Mill wrote to Jeremy Bentham on 25 July 1809 (when John was three years and two months old), and told an anecdote about his son asking to see Bentham's recent letter (written in English, of course) and pretending to read it aloud by making up its contents.[2] It is hard to discern to what degree Mill internalized a report of his early progress that had been exaggerated. To wit, Bentham's nephew George was under this impression regarding Mill: 'at the age of six he was a Greek and Latin scholar and a logician and fond of shewing off his proficiency without the slightest reserve.' Yet Mill himself claimed: 'I learnt no Latin until my eighth year', and that he began studying logic at twelve.[3] There is also the question of to what extent he was mechanically reading material that he was too young to comprehend. Nevertheless, there is no doubt that Mill was attempting to chronicle his early education with scrupulous accuracy, and his adult account is confirmed by his letters reporting on his progress while still a youth. For instance, at the age of thirteen Mill provided a record of scholastic accomplishments over the past five years (since the time that his correspondent, Sir Samuel Bentham, had last seen him.) Here is his summary of what he studied during his ninth year of life:

> The Greek which I read in the year 1815 was, I think, Homer's Odyssey. Theocritus, some of Pindar, and the two Orations of Æschines, and Demosthenes on the Crown. In Latin I read the six first books, I believe, of Ovid's Metamorphoses, the first five books of Livy, the Bucolics, and the six first books of the Æneid of Virgil, and part of Cicero's Orations. In Mathematics, after finishing the first six books, with the eleventh and twelfth of Euclid, and the Geometry of West, I studied Simpson's Conic Sections and also West's Conic Sections, Mensuration and Spherics; and in Algebra, Kersey's Algebra, and Newton's Universal Arithmetic, in which I performed all the problems without the book, and most of them without any help from the book.[4]

In short, John Stuart Mill is one of the best documented cases of a child prodigy from the nineteenth century or earlier in history that exists. Indeed, after painstaking work, a study of the early mental abilities of 312 historical figures identified as geniuses was published in 1926. In its standard tabulation procedure, Mill was crowned the king of young geniuses in this pageant across the centuries. He was deemed to have possessed an IQ of 190, the highest of the lot. (By contrast, Mozart was 150; Michelangelo, 145; Charles Darwin and Alexander Hamilton were both 135; and Isaac Newton, 130.)[5] One of his father's concerns was to keep John from hearing himself praised.

If on the strength of *Genetic Studies of Genius*, a crass publicist might try to bill Mill as the smartest person in history, Mill himself made the even more improbable claim that his natural intellectual abilities were 'rather below than over par': 'What I could do, could assuredly be done by any boy or girl of average capacity and healthy physical constitution.'[6] No less remarkable is that in the first published volume of Mill's letters, the editor, Hugh S. R. Elliot, accepted this claim at face value, making a determined case for the thesis: 'Mill's success was due far more to the rigour of his father's education than to any inborn genius of his own.'[7] We will have to set Elliot's judgement aside as an inscrutable mystery, but the reasons for Mill's own modest self-assessment are more readily discernible. One motive was presumably simply an admirable desire to foster the virtue of humility. Related to this was his sense that the kinds of gift he possessed were not what made for true genius, which he saw as being more about creating meaning than cramming memorization. The main reason, however, was that James Mill had intended his son's case to vindicate a particular theory of education and John was keen in his *Autobiography* to credit his father with having been proven right. Moreover, even as an adult, John himself adhered to Claude Adrien Helvétius's theory that all human beings have roughly equal natural capacities. Differences arose, its proponents insisted, primarily as a matter of circumstances, influences, opportunities, and training. In other words, James saw the education of his son as a vindication of nurture over nature. And, as Macaulay would later point out, James had a weakness for not letting the findings of actual, lived experience undermine his pure, abstract positions. John must have been able to perceive that his eight siblings—all of whom he homeschooled personally—even when given the same attention on that particular lesson in the same environment, were not able to master all of their studies with the same rapidity and profundity. Indeed, John having set the standard for what was ostensibly possible, the younger children often had the vexing experience of being punished for not having learned something that was hopelessly beyond their grasp in the time frame that had been allotted.

But there is more than one way to excel or fail, and what nature gave John in intellectual capacity, it withheld when it came to physical prowess and practical sagacity. He learned an ancient language earlier than any of his siblings, but they all mastered the life skill of changing their own clothes before he did. At the age of thirty-six, Mill confessed to the French thinker Auguste Comte: 'I lack mechanical aptitude, and my incapacity in all operations that require manual dexterity is really prodigious.'[8] On a walking tour with Henry Cole in 1832, the two men decided to take a boat down the river. Cole would later grumble in his journal that he had to do all the work as Mill was 'but a tyro in rowing' and, yet worse, 'frequently just but skimmed the surface of the water'.[9] Mill's companions quickly learned that he was an ineffectual ally in the ordinary battles of daily life. Despite having home field advantage, here is Caroline Fox's record of how a visit at his own house to the thirty-four year old philosopher ended: 'We asked for a hackney coach, but J. S. Mill was delightfully ignorant as to where such things grew, or where a likely hotel was to be found.'[10] Long past the stage of finding this trait endearing, Mill's wife Harriet, who is sometimes described as an invalid, complained to her daughter about what it was like to travel on the continent with her husband: 'the fact is we always get the last seats in the railway carriages, as I can not run on quick, & if he goes on he never succeeds, I always find him running up & down & looking lost in astonishment.'[11]

The great reprieve of John's youth came when he turned fourteen and was sent to live in France for a year as the guest of Sir Samuel Bentham (Jeremy Bentham's brother) and his family. While Mill never suspected it—and as far as I can tell no scholar has hitherto commented upon it—there clearly was a benevolent conspiracy afoot amongst the Benthams to get this clumsy, overeducated boy to live in his body rather than his books. Here are some excerpts from Mill's reports from the first month:

> June 12: . . . the greater part of Sir S. B.'s books, indeed all except two or three, are packed up, not to be unpacked till we arrive at the house near Montpellier . . .
>
> June 14: Could not get into the library, before breakfast, the door being locked . . .
>
> June 22: . . . the stay here begins now to be very tiresome to me, on account of the confusion of my being obliged to pack up my books so early, thinking we were to set off the very next day, etc. especially now, when I am excluded from the library.
>
> June 23: I understand that my truck is not to go till evening. As all my books are locked up in the trunk, all Sir Samuel's also packed up, and all M. de Pompignan's locked up in the library, I am afraid I shall be a little troubled with ennui to-day but I must do my best to avoid it.[12]

Instead, the family filled Mill's days with a homeschooling curriculum that prioritized sinews rather than scholastics. It began with learning how to drive and how to swim ('I believe it is intended that we should go every morning'). A procession of masters were coming and going all week long, giving Mill regular lessons in dancing, singing, piano, fencing, and riding. The closest to traditional, academic subjects that came at the family's initiation were biology and botany, and these were taught by sending the boy out into a forest to collect specimens of insects and plants. Mill's book learning was therefore squeezed toward the margins of his days: 'Before breakfast, read the remainder of the treatise on Indefinite Pronouns.'[13] It was the happiest year of his youth.

From his childhood onwards, Mill's formidable reading regime included significant quantities of religious literature. This is not generally understood because in what was the first, proper biography of Mill, his disciple and friend Alexander Bain made the false assertion that Mill 'scarcely ever read a Theological book'.[14] This statement has misled students of John Stuart Mill ever since. Leslie Stephen, in his entry on Mill for the *Dictionary of National Biography*, even intensified Bain's claim into an absolute one: 'he had never read a book upon theology'.[15] One explanation for this misleading statement is that Bain had a tendency to downplay or ignore those parts of Mill's thinking with which he did not agree. As Nicholas Capaldi has astutely observed, Bain failed 'to recognize the Romantic influence on Mill (Coleridge, for example, is never mentioned)'.[16] Moreover, Bain made his statement about his lack of theological reading in his discussion of Mill's late essay on 'Theism'. That composition annoyed the disciple-biographer because Bain vehemently rejected its openness to God and to Jesus Christ. Claiming that Mill did not read theology was Bain's polite way of saying that Mill was wrong and that the best sceptical authors explain why. Bain explicitly mentioned David Hume as a case in point—Hume being an anti-theological rather than a theological author—and who, of course, Mill had read: he even cites Hume in 'Theism'. Again, Bain is essentially saying that one need not be persuaded by Mill's arguments and affirmations in 'Theism' because there are other authors one can read which (if one thinks like Bain) ought to lead one to reject them. In truth, Mill was particularly well versed in anti-theological literature. To take a title we have already discussed, while it was still in manuscript form, his father had John read, mark, and inwardly digest Bentham's *Analysis of the Influence of Natural Religion on the Temporal Happiness of Mankind*—a book that Mill singled out for its deep impact on him.[17]

And all the evidence indicates that Mill read a great deal more theological than anti-theological literature. Given his references to books he had already read in statements made in his youth, it is apparent that Mill read a lot more religious titles in the first two decades of his life than just the ones mentioned in his *Autobiography*. What he lists in the *Autobiography* are works in the field of church history: 'Mosheim's *Ecclesiastical History*, McCrie's *Life of Knox*, and even Sewell's and Rutty's Histories of the Quakers'.[18] The reason for this list, once again, was that he was illustrating his father's theory of education and James Mill's idea was that this was the right kind of reading as it would foster (in today's language) a religious studies approach rather than a catechetical, confessional one. Mill himself advanced this view in his address as Lord Rector of the University of St Andrews. He argued that rather than 'being taught dogmatically the doctrines of any church or sect', there was another, better way to include religion in the curriculum: 'Christianity being a historical religion, the sort of religious instruction which seems to me most appropriate to an University is the study of ecclesiastical history.'[19] Mill was also reading Paley and Butler and collections of sermons and so on—this is evident from the way that he quotes from them as a teenager—but he did not mention these in his *Autobiography* because such books were what everyone read so it would not have served the purpose of illustrating his father's distinctive pedagogical plan.

Most of Mill's serious theological reading happened throughout the course of his adult life. One of the most famous passages in all of Mill's writings is his outburst against that 'detestable, to me absolutely loathsome book' arising from the Bampton divinity lectures delivered by the Reverend H. L. Mansel, *The Limits of Religious Thought Examined* (1858).[20] As a famous religious sceptic, however, what is more striking is how often Mill read volumes of Christian theology—many of them even of the orthodox or supernatural variety—and made sympathetic comments about them. In April 1840, he was enthralled with the spiritual journal of a Quaker minister and mystic: 'Last night John Mill sat for hours . . . expatiating on the delights of John Woolman (which he is reading) and on spiritual religion, which he feels to be the deepest and trustiest'; Mill 'then dilated on the different Friends' books he was reading: on John Woolman he philosophised on the principle that was active in him—that dependence on the immediate teaching of a Superior Being'.[21] Towards the end of that same year, Mill read a sermon by an evangelical Methodist, apparently from the labouring classes, which he praised as 'a really admirable specimen of popular eloquence . . . well calculated to go to the very core of an untaught hearer'. Mill distanced himself from some of the more conservative doctrinal claims made by the preacher but, fascinatingly, in their stead, offered a learned theological reflection in which he dissented from a classic, substitutionary theory of the atonement (Anselm) in favour of the Moral Influence Theory (Abelard).[22] In 1842, Mill wrote to the Anglican clergyman F. D. Maurice, informing him that he had read with pleasure his *The Kingdom of Christ*: 'I agree to a much greater extent than you would perhaps suppose, in your view.'[23] In 1859, Mill boasted that he had read almost all of the books of the Reverend Charles Kingsley, and that he was planning to read them all. (Most of Kingsley's books up to that date had been collections of sermons: the one for that year was *The Good News of God.*)

Mill declared (to Alexander Bain!) that the Tractarian the Reverend W. G. Ward's *The Idea of a Christian Church* (1844) was 'a remarkable book in every way'. Once Ward had become a Roman Catholic, Mill was even more delighted with his *On Nature and Grace: A Theological Treatise* (1860).[24] When seven years later Ward wrote 'Science, Prayer, Free Will, and Miracles' for the Roman Catholic *Dublin Review*, Mill enthused:

> I have read your article with very great interest. You are the clearest thinker I have met for a long time who has written on your side of these great questions. And I quite admit that your theory of divine premovement is not on the face of it inadmissible.[25]

Mill's general comment to this Roman Catholic theological writer was: 'I never read anything of yours in which I have not found much more to sympathise with than to dislike.'[26] Returning to 1860—and again writing to Bain—Mill judged the Reverend Baden Powell's *The Order of Nature considered in Reference to the Claims of Revelation* to be 'a wonderful book for a clergyman & an Oxford professor to write, & remarkable as an exemplification of one form of modern theism'.[27] Mill also read in draft Florence Nightingale's theological *magnum opus*, *Suggestions for Thought to the Searchers After Truth Among the Artizans of England*, which was essentially a work of Christian apologetics arguing for the credibility of belief in God. Mill responded enthusiastically: 'few books have a better chance than this of doing *some* good, and that too in a variety of ways. . . . I have seldom felt less inclined to criticize than in reading this book.'[28] And yet again writing to Bain—the very man who set going the rumour that Mill did not read theology—Mill reflected in 1863 on the contemporary state of the study of the synoptic gospels, mentioning knowingly authors from France, Britain, and Germany ('Baur & the Tubingen school').[29] In 1865, Mill reported that he had read one of the *Tracts for Priest and People*, the Reverend William Henry Lyttelton's *The Testimony to the Authority of Conscience and Reason*, 'with very great pleasure & sympathy'.[30] My own little discovery is that Mill annotated his copy of William Paley's *Evidences of Christianity*, writing at the top of the opening page of chapter IX his own connections to biblical texts which are not mentioned there: '53d Chapter of Isaiah. 10 1st verses 1st Chapt. of St John'.[31] This list of Mill's theological reading is far from exhaustive: it is only illustrative. In particular, there are many more religious books, not least volumes of sermons, that we know Mill must have read at least in part because he quotes from them in his published writings. Mill was the kind of 'secular' figure who read theological treatises appreciatively.

His father's educational plan included purging away everything that was sentimental and replacing it with the analytical. John was not allowed to have friends so that they would not contaminate the purity of the experiment. He related even to his own siblings as their tutor rather than playmate. Mill observed poignantly in his *Autobiography* that he never had any toys. To Caroline Fox, he lamented, 'I was never a boy.'[32] Instead, Mill excelled at logic: 'The first intellectual operation in which I arrived at any skill was dissecting a bad argument and finding in what part the fallacy lay.'[33] Everything was dissected. The Benthamites were on a crusade against 'feeling' which they saw as the refuge of bad arguments and the prop of bad politics. As a young adult, Mill would come to find this ruthless approach a burden greater than he could bear. He had been warped, he decided in despair at his lowest moment, into someone who was now 'irretrievably analytic'. The Benthamite method was 'a perpetual worm at the root both of the passions and of the virtues'.[34] It was a worm that dieth not; it was hell.

A common human trait is something that I will call a 'devotional sense'. A devotional sense is a way of fostering one's own identity and sense of self through one's loyalty and emotional connection to another entity. This loyalty is marked by a delight in praising that entity in unmeasured ways. What Mill was reporting is that, as a result of his unusual, taxing education, this way of being human had been thoroughly stifled and blocked for him. As my choice of the word 'devotional' implies, this blockage had major implications for Mill's relationship to religion. Nevertheless, it is helpful to see the love of God as just one member of this set. For many people, an early expression of their devotional sense is the cult of motherhood. Myriads of boys have proudly declared, 'My mother is the best mother in the world!' Not only did Mill harbour no such thought in his own breast, but he would have treated such a statement analytically as an unsubstantiated and improbable claim. As with his mother, so with his mother-country. Mill remembered his embarrassment as a child when he saw his error in assuming that a side in a conflict was the right one because it was the English one. He never made that mistake again. Instead, in his war against the unwarranted pronouncements of patriotism, he overcompensated. Mill's favourite adjective for English people was 'stupid'. Throughout his life, he took perverse delight in declaring that other countries—especially France, Germany, Italy, and America—were much better than Britain. In his annoyance at the unstinted praise of patriots, Mill was apt to make assertions that were just as improbable in the opposite direction: that the history of England, for instance, was 'one of the least interesting of all histories'.[35] And as with mother and mother-country, so also Mill was baffled by that other nourishing mother which some people possessed, *alma mater*. It is striking how often Mill went out of his way to attack by name the schools of Eton and Westminster and the universities of Oxford and Cambridge and to give vent to his 'contempt' and 'utter abhorrence' of them.[36] In one series of letters to an Old Etonian, Mill seemed determined to puncture and to wound. If asked why, Mill would have legitimately given political, religious, social, and pedagogical reasons for his opposition, but I am putting forward the possibility of an additional, subterranean factor: it got up his nose that old boys would so over-praise these foundations and he therefore felt an urge to set the record straight and give the world a more critical assessment of their worth. The only possible exception from Mill's childhood to this lack of a devotional sense was his attitude towards his father, whom he always did over-praise (even claiming he was the 'greatest philosophical genius' in 'the world'), and who became a kind of substitute god for him.[37] Nevertheless, James Mill was a god of fear rather than a god of love, and a god whose iron law was logic *contra* sentiment. Still, John tended toward thinking of his father as infallible: 'If I could not convince him I was right I always supposed I must be wrong.' Dying to self-assertion, John made the will of his father all in all. The word of his father even became a sort of replacement for the promptings of the Spirit: 'my conscience never speaking to me except by his voice'.[38] In other words, the way that his father loomed large for him did nothing to cultivate in John an unhindered devotional sense that could readily find other outlets.

A devotional sense can be a great bond among people. A shared love can open the door of friendship. Moreover, people often respect someone for their devotion even when the object of that loyalty is different from their own. That is why—to take a twentieth-century example—people from other countries who are inordinately proud of their own nation can find it deeply moving when the French patriots sing *La Marseillaise* in the film *Casablanca.* Such feelings and attachments burst forth in extravagant praise. Mill, however, could only hear a claim such as that God is all-powerful as a didactic rather than a devotional one. People typically believe in and defend the truthfulness of their devotional claims—they really do believe that their nation is the greatest nation on earth—but outsiders tend to hear and understand such statements more indulgently if they are themselves at ease with the contours of an inner life of devotion. The heart has its reasons of which reason knows nothing.

James Mill and Jeremy Bentham both failed to understand and completely ignored the devotional aspect of Christianity. It is indicative of this spiritual unmusicality that Bentham could only find the apostle Paul's ministry explicable on the assumption that he was in it for the money. Alas for these Utilitarian philosophers, however, for many believers a heart overflowing with devotion is actually at the centre of why their faith is vital to them. Both James Mill and Bentham proposed plans for reforming the Church that eliminated altogether worship, prayer, and praise. James Mill seriously imagined that people would come to church every Sunday year in and year out for a service that consisted merely of hearing didactic discourses on themes such as political economy and jurisprudence! Having a blocked devotional sense, John likewise could not truly grasp what their faith meant to the faithful. As a teenager in the height of his Benthamite zeal, Mill wrote an article which addressed the subject of Christianity in the analytical, defining, dissecting method in which he had been so thoroughly trained. He pronounced that Christianity consisted entirely of two elements, morality and dogma: 'This division appears to me to be complete. No one can mention any thing connected with Christianity, which is not either matter of precept, or matter of opinion.'[39] One wonders where devotion belongs in that analysis.

Notes

1. John Stuart Mill to Edward Jones, 19 January 1869: Francis E. Mineka and Dwight N. Lindley (eds), *The Later Letters of John Stuart Mill, 1849–1873* (Collected Works of John Stuart Mill XVII), Toronto: University of Toronto Press, 1972, p. 1550.
2. Alexander Bain, *James Mill: A Biography*, London: Longmans, Green, and Co., 1882, p. 100.
3. John Stuart Mill, *Autobiography and Literary Essays* (Collected Works of John Stuart Mill I), ed. J. M. Robson, Indianapolis: Liberty Fund, 2006 (reprint of Toronto: University of Toronto Press, 1981), pp. 8, 21, 556.
4. John Stuart Mill to Samuel Bentham, 30 July 1819: Francis E. Mineka (ed.), *The Earlier Letters of John Stuart Mill, 1812–1848* (Collected Works of John Stuart Mill XII), Toronto: University of Toronto Press, 1963, p. 7.
5. Catharine Morris Cox, *Genetic Studies of Genius: Volume II: The Early Mental Traits of Three Hundred Geniuses*, Stanford: Stanford University Press, 1926. (I am, of course, not suggesting that the results of this study should be accepted as valid. Moreover, this study itself offered various adjustments and qualifications that cannot be gone into here. In particular, however, it should be noted that they conceded that the greater amount of records regarding Mill's early life gave him an advantage in their calculations.)
6. CWJSM I (*Autobiography and Literary Essays*), p. 32.
7. Hugh S. R. Elliot (ed.), *The Letters of John Stuart Mill*, 2 vols, London: Longmans, Green, and Co., 1910, I, p. xxx.

8. John Stuart Mill to Auguste Comte, 9 June 1842: Oscar A. Haac (translator and editor), *The Correspondence of John Stuart Mill and Auguste Comte*, New Brunswick, NJ: Transaction Publishers, 1995, p. 75.
9. John M. Robson (ed.), *Journals and Debating Speeches* (Collected Works of John Stuart Mill XXVII), Toronto: University of Toronto Press, 1988, p. 599.
10. Horace N. Pym (ed.), *Memories of Old Friends: being extracts from the Journals and Letters of Caroline Fox of Penjerrick, Cornwall*, London: Smith, Elder, and Co., 1882, p. 107 (entry for 3 June 1840).
11. Harriet Taylor Mill to Helen Taylor, 18 October 1858: Jo Ellen Jacobs (ed.), *The Complete Works of Harriet Taylor Mill*, Bloomington, IN: Indiana University Press, 1998, p. 581.
12. CWJSM XXVI (*Journals and Debating Speeches*), pp. 19–30.
13. CWJSM XXVI (*Journals and Debating Speeches*), p. 35.
14. Alexander Bain, *John Stuart Mill: A Criticism: with personal recollections*, London: Longmans, Green, and Co., 1882, p. 139.
15. Leslie Stephen, 'Mill, John Stuart (1806–1873)', in *Dictionary of National Biography*, Vol. XIII, Sidney Lee (ed.), New York: Macmillan, 1909, pp. 390–9 (here 397).
16. Nicholas Capaldi, *John Stuart Mill: A Biography*, Cambridge: Cambridge University Press, 2004, p. xiv.
17. CWJSM I (*Autobiography and Literary Essays*), p. 73.
18. CWJSM I (*Autobiography and Literary Essays*), p. 11.
19. John Stuart Mill, *Essays on Equality, Law, and Education*, ed. John M. Robinson and Stefani Collini (Collected Works of John Stuart Mill XXI), Toronto: University of Toronto Press, 1984, p. 249.
20. CWJSM XV (*Later Letters*), p. 817.
21. Pym, *Memories*, pp. 82–3 (entries for 1 and 7 April 1840). (And that Benthamite tick of using an indefinite pronoun, 'a Superior Being', provides evidence that Fox reported Mill's words accurately.)
22. John Stuart Mill to Barclay Fox, 23 December 1840: CWJSM XIII (*Earlier Letters*), pp. 452–3.
23. CWJSM XVII (*Later Letters*), p. 1997.
24. John Stuart Mill to Alexander Bain, [March 1845]: CWJSM XIII (*Earlier Letters*), p. 662; John Stuart Mill, *An Examination of Sir William Hamilton's Philosophy and of the Principal Questions Discussed in his Writings*, ed. J. M. Robson (Collected Works of John Stuart Mill IX), London: Routledge, 1996, pp. 164–5.
25. John Stuart Mill to W. G. Ward, 14 February 1867: CWJSM XVI (*Later Letters*), p. 1238.
26. CWJSM XVI (*Later Letters*), pp. 1041–2.

27. CWJSM XV (*Later Letters*), pp. 695–6.
28. John Stuart Mill to Florence Nightingale, 4 October 1860: CWJSM XV (*Later Letters*), pp. 711–12.
29. CWJSM XV (*Later Letters*), p. 903.
30. CWJSM XVI (*Later Letters*), p. 1080.
31. The Library of John Stuart Mill, the Archives, Somerville College, Oxford. (I will leave the attribution as my own responsibility, but an expert on the library who looked at it with me was confident that this annotation was in Mill's handwriting.)
32. Pym, *Memories*, p. 85.
33. CWJSM I (*Autobiography and Literary Essays*), p. 22.
34. CWJSM I (*Autobiography and Literary Essays*), p. 143.
35. CWJSM XIV (*Later Letters*), p. 6.
36. John Stuart Mill, *Essays on Politics and Society*, ed. J. M. Robson (Collected Works of John Stuart Mill XIX), New York: Routledge, 1977, pp. 138–9; CWJSM I (*Autobiography and Literary Essays*), p. 336.
37. CWJSM XII (*Earlier Letters*), p. 312.
38. CWJSM I (*Autobiography and Literary Essays*), pp. 32, 613.
39. John Stuart Mill, *Newspaper Writings (December 1822—July 1831)*, ed. Ann P. Robson and John M. Robson (Collected Works of John Stuart Mill XXII), Toronto: University of Toronto Press, 1986, p. 7.

3
More Exceedingly Zealous

'Being more exceedingly zealous of the traditions of my fathers.'

(Galatians 1:14)

John was raised a Benthamite of the Benthamites. The *Edinburgh Review* acknowledged in 1829 that his father was 'by far the most distinguished' of Bentham's followers.[1] The eponymous patriarch arranged for the Mills to reside nearby him in London and, for some years, to live with him in the same country house for a period during every summer. John thus grew up with Jeremy Bentham as a close, personal presence. Bentham took a keen interest in the progress of the boy's education. After a health scare, James even asked Bentham to agree to become his eldest son's guardian in the event of his own death or incapacitation. (One is only left to wonder what was supposed to happen to the other children!) Bentham accepted this bequest in high spirits. Aware that this role normally fell to a child's godfather—whose primary task was to ensure a sound, religious upbringing—Bentham promised with mock solemnity that he would 'do whatsoever may seem most necessarily and proper, for teaching him to make all proper distinctions, such as between the Devil and the Holy Ghost'.[2] John imbibed Benthamism with the summer air of Forde Abbey. The right standard of morality was the greatest happiness of the greatest number. By the time he was a teenager, John knew the principles of Utilitarianism the way that other boys knew the rules of cricket.

Nicholas Capaldi has observed that a genre informing Mill's *Autobiography* was the German *Bildungsroman*, a coming-of-age story that is an account of self-discovery and self-fashioning.[3] There is also, however, another more homegrown genre that informs Mill's life writing: the evangelical conversion narrative. Mill actually recounts two, distinct 'conversion' experiences. For the second—which happened at the start of his twenties—he made the genre connection himself, observing that he was then in 'the state, I should think, in which converts to Methodism usually are, when smitten by their first "conviction of sin"'.[4] The first conversion, however, happened around five years earlier. Many evangelical conversion stories highlight turning points in the lives of people who have been raised in the faith and—to both outward appearances and their own self-perception—have been faithfully adhering to its formal requirements. Typically, a dutiful Christian youth—perhaps even the son of a clergyman or preacher—suddenly has the faith come alive to him in a dramatic moment. David Bebbington has calculated that in the nineteenth century the mean age for the conversion of future Methodist ministers was fifteen or sixteen years old.[5] Mill's original conversion thus came right on time—when he was fifteen and a-half years old. As with a typical such event for evangelicals, it was a moment that made the faith of his father, which he had already formally accepted, an existentially alive, inward reality of transforming power. Evangelical conversation narratives standardly involve reading as a key trigger. The decisive textual encounter on this first occasion for John was with *Traité de Législation* by the interpreter of Bentham, Étienne Dumont. Bruce Hindmarsh has observed: 'This experience of a text of Scripture being made personal ("applied to me") recurred frequently in evangelical conversions.'[6] So Mill testified exuberantly: 'My previous education had been, in a certain sense, already a course of Benthamism. The Benthamic standard of "the greatest happiness" was that which I had always been taught to apply: I was even familiar with an abstract discussion of it... Yet in the first pages of Bentham it burst upon me with all the force of novelty.'[7] What had once been a formal faith was now a living one. Again, Mill himself makes explicit that the only fitting analogy to his experience at this moment is the discovery of a religious faith: 'I now had opinions; a creed, a doctrine, a philosophy; in one among the best senses of the word, a religion.'[8] In the middle of his teens, John Stuart Mill had become a true believer.

The trope of Benthamism as akin to a faith such as Methodism was evoked on all sides. Bentham himself had written to Dumont, rejecting the term Benthamite, but suggesting Utilitarian in its place, as 'a new religion would be an odd sort of thing without a name'. And again: 'I dreamt t'other night that I was a founder of a sect, of course a person of great sanctity and importance: it was called the sect of the Utilitarians.'[9] T. B. Macaulay would use this rhetorical move as a sneer, dismissing James Mill as 'the zealot of a sect'.[10] John himself would later come to accept this reproach, frequently confessing that he had once been a narrow, Benthamite sectarian. By 1842, Mill could even list Puseyism (the Anglo-Catholic, Tractarian movement also identified at that time with John Henry Newman) alongside Benthamism both as attempts to reform the world that are partial and insufficient to the task.[11]

But how was Mill to make his way in the world? More than one person—including his godfather, Sir John Stuart—wanted him to attend the University of Cambridge. Oxford insisted that students subscribe to the Thirty-Nine Articles of the Church of England at the beginning of their studies, ruling it out for conscientious dissenters. Cambridge, on the other hand, only required subscription at the end of one's studies and therefore a young man could gain an education (but not a degree) there without swearing his conformity to the doctrines of the Church of England. With good reason, James Mill judged that the state of John's academic accomplishments was already far ahead of what was provided by a standard undergraduate education. The counter argument was made that attending a leading university would allow John to forge strategic relationships with other men of his generation who would also rise to lead the country in due course, but to no avail. His father thought that the law might be the right profession for him and thus, when he was fifteen years old, John began to be tutored in that subject by John Austin (the *Ehemann* of his *Mütterlein*, Sarah Austin). Instead, however, James Mill ended up getting his firstborn son into his own department at the India House at the earliest possible age, the day after his seventeenth birthday. Having skipped university and the bar, John went straight from being homeschooled by his father to his father obtaining for him an appointment with the East India Company which was, in John's oppressive phrase, 'immediately under himself'.[12]

The India House was merely a way to make a living. Mill's real object in life was 'to be a reformer of the world', and his true goal was 'the regeneration of mankind'. He went about this work, he later recalled, with 'youthful fanaticism'.[13] One concrete way for him to further radical reform was to be a good lieutenant. John put years of painstaking work into preparing Bentham's *Rationale of Judicial Evidence* for publication as an eight-volume work. (He would later apologize for the too-dogmatic tone of the notes he wrote for that publication.) Bentham—knowing how much of the final achievement was John's—insisted, to the young man's surprise, that his name also appear on the title page. When John reluctantly acquiesced, Bentham replied in that playful way which this unbelieving set had of feigning ignorance about religious matters: 'Dear John / Amen. If you know not what that means send to the Booksellers for a Hebrew Dictionary.'[14] John also served as his father's research assistant. When James Mill was writing an attack on the Whig *Edinburgh Review* he had his son systematically read through its back issues. James was the animating spirit of the *Westminster Review*, founded in 1823 as a radical alternative to the existing reviews and, although he was only seventeen years old when he started writing for it, in the *Westminster Review*'s first year of publication (1824), John Stuart Mill promptly became its most frequent contributor.

And John himself developed a passion for founding things. When he was sixteen years old, he founded the Utilitarian Society. Mill therefore took credit for having thereby introduced that appellation into general circulation. It has long been pointed out that Bentham himself used the word Utilitarian in a private letter as far back as 1802. Mill claimed that he had borrowed it from *Annals of the Parish* (1821), a novel which was written as if it was the autobiography of a Scottish minister. This fictional pastor was disturbed by the introduction into his parish of young men attracted to 'infidel philosophy'. Although Mill does not quote it, the passage he is referring to in his *Autobiography* is where the minister recalls: 'I told my people that I thought they had more sense than to secede from Christianity to become Utilitarians.'[15] This genesis is telling as it highlights a fact that was no doubt true at that time, namely, that Mill viewed organized Christianity as a rival that he wanted to see supplanted by Utilitarianism. While Mill thereby found a fitting linguistic replacement for 'Benthamite', the Utilitarian Society nevertheless enjoyed the honour of meeting in Bentham's own house. Mill also launched a self-improvement club to study important subjects by reading and discussing common texts, and a speculative society. He became a leading voice in and the treasurer of the London Debating Society.

During his teenage years, Mill emerged as the leader of a band of likeminded enthusiasts who were all around his own age. His two best friends and co-belligerents at this time were George John Graham and John Arthur Roebuck. Befitting Mill's passion to belong to groups during this period of his life, this too took on a kind of corporate identity. They called themselves the 'Trijackia'—a neologism which played on the fact that the three of them all happened to share in common the name John.[16] Despite these young men being zealous radicals and Benthamites, James Mill was frosty about his son's friendships. For John, it was a rare—if not singular—moment when he stood up to his forbidding father. The rest of the family watched the scene unfold with awe. The patriarch was told in no halting terms that the Trijackia was not to be frowned away. Another early friend was Charles Austin, a younger brother of Mill's law tutor, John Austin. Mill remembered Charles as his first adult relationship which felt like it was among peers. Nevertheless, in retrospect, Mill blamed Charles for bringing their radical and Utilitarian movement into disrepute and makings its adherents likely to abandon it after a season by his tweaking tendency to state its principles in the most stark and obnoxious manner, offensively desecrating all that others held sacred. This seems to be a classic case of the zeal of a new convert; of trying to be more Roman than Rome. Perhaps only a year before he joined their band, Charles Austin had won a prize at the University of Cambridge for his defence of an orthodox doctrine of scripture: *The Argument for the genuineness of the Sacred Volume, as generally received by Christians, stated and explained (The Hulsean Prize Essay for 1822)* (1823). Later in life, Mill was greatly surprised to hear a report of a dinner party at which Austin—whom he remembered as the most iconoclastic and taunting of radicals—enthused about his admiration for the contents of the New Testament.[17] Likewise, Mill was disgusted that Roebuck, so long a champion of radical politics, in the end became 'a conformist to the Church'.[18] Such men carried inside them the imprint and resources from their youthful Christian spiritual formation that had an enduring influence, even if sometimes only by way of reaction or negation. These latent beliefs and resources were harder for Mill to take into account because he did not have a *status quo ante* to return to in the same manner.

Mill could be hot-headed when it came to his fiery commitment to radical politics, and this tendency continued long after he was less of a sectarian partisan in other ways. When the Second French Revolution unfolded in July 1830, Mill was so excited that he went straight off to Paris to witness the glorious triumph of progress and freedom first-hand. As the fight for a Reform Bill in his own country grew increasingly bitter and enraging to radicals in the following year, Mill worked himself up into a Francophile frenzy: 'I should not care though a revolution were to exterminate every person in Great Britain & Ireland who has £500 a year.'[19] Curiously, a couple of decades on, Mill would decide that he could not afford to retire on less than £500 per annum! His actual, annual pension—awarded when he retired at the congenial age of fifty-two—ended up being exactly three times that amount. Mill literally became part of the 1 per cent.[20] But, to return to the revolutionary warpath, in 1840 Mill passed his sentence of death on Lord Palmerston, then foreign secretary in a Liberal government: 'For my part, I would walk twenty miles to see him hanged.'[21] Even as late as 1847, Mill was still half hoping for an armed uprising: 'In England on the contrary I often think that a violent revolution is very much needed, in order to give that general shake-up to the torpid mind of the nation which the French Revolution gave to Continental Europe. England has never had any general break-up of the old associations & hence the extreme difficulty of getting any ideas into its stupid head.'[22] Perhaps without the shedding of blood there is no regeneration of the world.

Meanwhile, Mill was doing his best to foment change through his writing and debating. He saw himself a 'member of the only Church which has now any real existence, namely that of the writers and orators'.[23] And he was enjoying himself. The texts of his debate speeches from the 1820s show him forcefully championing Utilitarianism and other radical positions. Here he is, for example, propagating (as it were) Malthusianism: 'If the gentleman says that the principle is repulsive to his feelings, I answer, that this is the first time I ever heard that feeling is the test of truth'; 'I have heard, and believe that feeling ought to be subordinate to reason, and not supreme over her, and that the province of feeling commences where that of reason ends.'[24] Mill could take an ironic, mocking tone, as in this attack on Oxford and Cambridge:

> The system moreover of theological instruction at our Universities is all bottomed upon the Thirty-nine Articles, a subject on which I should be

> extremely sorry to observe any scepticism, as I am informed that society would be in danger of dissolution if there were only thirty-eight, or if any one of the thirty-nine were altered from what it now is.[25]

Early on, Mill was more intent on winning arguments than winning friends, and he seemed surprised to learn by experience that getting the better of a debate did not appear to change anyone's mind, let alone lead on to the reformation of Britain. He had hoped to create a Utilitarian society, but had to settle for founding the Utilitarian Society. Mill does not seem to have behaved himself badly at all—and his large-hearted side could not have been too far in abeyance—but he did make some enemies. Abraham Hayward would nurse a grudge for decades regarding the way Mill treated him in one of these debates, waiting to serve his revenge up cold over Mill's cold corpse in the obituary he wrote for *The Times*. Mill had aroused sufficient personal dislike that there was an attempt to blackball him from membership in the Athenaeum Club, despite his radical, Benthamite father being quite acceptable there. Mill would later regret his 'dogmatic disputatiousness' during this phase of his life but, again, this probably says more about the nobility of his mature nature than the inappropriateness of his youthful conduct.

Mill recalled that Malthusianism was as much the rallying banner of his band of youthful radicals as Benthamism, and this was the cause that briefly placed him on the wrong side of the law. In his first year in the India Office, on his walk to work Mill discovered a dead baby in St James's Park. It was a case of infanticide. Longing to make the world a better place, he started distributing a birth control tract. Mill was arrested for obscenity, found guilty, and sentenced to fourteen days (but released after only two). The pamphlet in question, *To Married Working People*, had Richard Carlile for its publisher. Carlile was a political radical, an atheist, and a prominent leader among plebeian infidels. Uncowed by the conservative establishment, Carlile chose prison over compliance. Mill observed that Carlile's so-called crime was publishing material 'hostile to Christianity', and thus the young Utilitarian philosopher began to defend the infidel publisher as a martyr for free speech. Mill recalled that it was through the prompt of this cause that he first began writing for newspapers. He wrote a series of letters advocating for Carlile and 'free discussion of religious subjects', the first three of which were published in the *Morning*

Chronicle, but the paper became nervous of Mill's increasingly radical claims and declined the subsequent offerings. Mill chose for his pseudonym the name of an early English church reformer, which he spelled as 'Wickliff'. The most fascinating letter from this period, however, is one that Mill sent to Carlile's own paper, the *Republican*. It was published in the 3 January 1823 issue, when Mill was still sixteen years old. In it, Mill tried to position himself as even more thoroughly and completely irreligious than the editor himself, accusing Carlile (incorrectly apparently) of holding to a view of nature that gave it a quasi-divine quality. Mill's own religious unbelief is unequivocal and resolute. He insisted not only that theism had been completely discredited as a viable belief, but that any such substitute had been as well: 'Of course, the arguments which serve to explode the belief in an ante-material and intelligent Being, will also suffice to destroy the unmeaning word *Nature*.'[26] Mill signed this letter 'An Atheist'. Many years later, when he was running for Parliament, Mill would claim that there was not a single passage supporting atheism in any of his writings and he challenged his critics to prove this statement wrong. If his authorship of this letter had been known, he could have lost that challenge.

As we have now reached the high-water mark of Mill's irreligion and hostility to organized Christianity, it is worth demonstrating here a remark that was made earlier in this volume, namely that Mill continued to attend Christian worship occasionally across the decades of his life. Once again, this fact has been obscured by a false claim by Bain, who erroneously reported in his biography of Mill: 'He absented himself during his whole life, except as a mere child, from religious services.'[27] The actual case was quite different. We have already glimpsed John still attending a parish church at the age of eight. When in France at the age of fourteen, he attended Mass at the principal church in Toulouse. His interest on that occasion was such that he was frustrated by the fact that he did not have a very good view. At the age of sixteen, he had gone with John and Sarah Austin for a stay in Norwich, during which time Mr Austin continued to guide Mill's legal studies. The Austins were Unitarians and a letter home incidentally reveals that Mill was attending Octagon Chapel with them.

Mill had a lifelong passion for touring churches. Buildings consecrated for Christian worship were always a high-priority site for him to visit wherever he went. The earliest walking tour journal of his is from his Sussex trip in July 1827, when he had just reached his majority having turned twenty-one exactly two months earlier. Mill inspected at least one church every day for the first five days and sometimes more than one. Thus it went on; and thus it always was. In fact, if anything, this ecclesiastical commitment was even deeper when he was abroad. In Italy, for instance, nary a day would go by without him finding his way into yet another church. One might falsely assume that churches were pretty much the only sites that there were to see in the mid-nineteenth century, so nothing much should be made of this habit. That would be to mis-state the case, however. Even when Mill was staying at the Chatsworth Hotel and had plenty of free time on his hands, he made a point of saying that he had no interest in touring Chatsworth House, one of the most impressive stately homes in all of England.[28]

Even more to the point, Mill was often keen to attend a Christian worship service. He obviously was not there to worship in a traditional, dogmatic sense, but he certainly was not there to mock. For one, he found the music moving. He also had a sense of the atmosphere created by sacred space: 'I much prefer seeing pictures in churches to the way one sees them in the private galleries.'[29] Other features could also touch him. He wrote of one service he attended: 'The church was lighted with candles which looked like so many stars. Altogether the effect was fine.'[30] No doubt Mill was also glad for opportunities to understand better the devotional lives of others. Far from merely wanting to see the interior of the building, in 1855 he wasted a lot of time in Palermo Cathedral, hoping (in vain, as it turned out) that if he stayed long enough he would eventually be able to attend Mass. When he arrived in Peterborough in 1857, he rushed straight to the cathedral (Church of England, of course), hoping—this time successfully—to be in time to hear the service. In March 1856, Mill left his wife Harriet at home and went to live in Birmingham for at least six days so that he could attend the Holy Week services at the Catholic cathedral, St Chad's.[31] On that occasion, his stepdaughter Helen was not with him, but Mill and Harriet attended innumerable Masses at her prompting as Catholic worship was central to Helen's spiritual life.[32] Again seeking out corporate worship while travelling alone, when Mill attended Mass at St Agnes in Rome in 1855, he observed that the use of the organ reminded him of 'Warwick Street or Moorfields'.[33] We know of several, specific Catholic churches in London that Helen would attend, and sometimes her mother and Mill would join her for Mass at these places (the Spanish Ambassador's chapel, the French Ambassador's chapel, and the chapel to Our Lady at St John's Wood)—but were it not for this chance comparison in a surviving letter—we would not have otherwise known that any of them had ever attended Mass at these two particular Catholic churches: the Bavarian Ambassador's chapel in Warwick Street and St Mary's, Moorfields. The Saint of Rationalism could sometimes be found taking delight in the gathering of the saints.

While researching this book, it occurred to me at one point to wonder what Wikipedia, that great repository of current, conventional wisdom, had to say about my chosen subject. In the entry on John Stuart Mill, there appeared this bald statement: 'In his views on religion, Mill was an atheist.'[34] 'Atheist' is a slippery term with many accruing assumptions that were affirmed or eschewed by religious sceptics who accepted or rejected it as a fitting label in their particular case, especially in the context of the nineteenth century. Nevertheless, when it comes to some of his teenage years, in at least one common way in which that word was used in that time period, it is true enough to say that in his views on religion, Mill was an atheist.

Notes

1. [Thomas Babington Macaulay], Review of James Mill, *Edinburgh Review*, 49, 97 (March 1829), pp. 159–89 (here 159).
2. Hugh S. R. Elliot (ed.), *The Letters of John Stuart Mill*, 2 vols, London: Longmans, Green, and Co., 1910, I, p. xvi.
3. Nicholas Capaldi, *John Stuart Mill: A Biography*, Cambridge: Cambridge University Press, 2004, p. xiii.
4. John Stuart Mill, *Autobiography and Literary Essays* (Collected Works of John Stuart Mill I), ed. J. M. Robson, Indianapolis: Liberty Fund, 2006 (reprint of Toronto: University of Toronto Press, 1981), p. 137.
5. D. W. Bebbington, *Evangelicalism in Modern Britain: A History from the 1730s to the 1980s*, London: Unwin Hyman, 1989, p. 7. (For this paragraph, I am drawing upon Richard Hughes Gibson and Timothy Larsen, 'Nineteenth-century spiritual autobiography: Carlyle, Newman, Mill,' in Adam Smyth

(ed.), *A History of English Autobiography*, Cambridge: Cambridge University Press, 2016, pp. 192–206.)

6. D. Bruce Hindmarsh, *The Evangelical Conversion Narrative: Spiritual Autobiography in Early Modern England*, Oxford: Oxford University Press, 2005, p. 27.
7. CWJSM I (*Autobiography and Literary Essays*), p. 67.
8. CWJSM I (*Autobiography and Literary Essays*), p. 69.
9. James E. Crimmins, *Secular Utilitarianism: Social Science and the Critique of Religion in the Thought of Jeremy Bentham*, Oxford: Clarendon Press, 1990, p. 288; Richard Reeves, *John Stuart Mill: Victorian Firebrand*, London: Atlantic Books, 2007, p. 37.
10. [Thomas Babington Macaulay], Review of James Mill (Cont.), *Edinburgh Review*, 50, 99 (October 1829), pp. 99–125 (here 124).
11. Francis E. Mineka (ed.), *The Earlier Letters of John Stuart Mill, 1812–1848* (Collected Works of John Stuart Mill XIII), Toronto: University of Toronto Press, 1963, pp. 563–4.
12. CWJSM I (*Autobiography and Literary Essays*), p. 83.
13. CWJSM I (*Autobiography and Literary Essays*), pp. 168–9.
14. CWJSM XII (*Earlier Letters*), p. 18.
15. The Revd Micah Balwhidder, *Annals of the Parish*, Edinburgh: William Blackwood, 1821, p. 286. (The actual author, as Mill knew, was John Galt.)
16. Robert Eadon Leader, *Life and Letters of John Roebuck*, London: Edward Arnold, 1897, p. 28.
17. Alexander Bain, *James Mill: A Biography*, London: Longmans, Green, and Co., 1882, p. 368.
18. CWJSM I (*Autobiography and Literary Essays*), p. 158.
19. CWJSM XII (*Earlier Letters*), p. 84.
20. Reeves, *Mill*, p. 140. Indeed, in this book, Reeves has helpfully emphasized the degree to which Mill was a 'firebrand' throughout his entire life. Already in the Victorian age, W. L. Courtney had presented Mill in his early phase of his life as 'a revolutionary firebrand': W. L. Courtney, *Life and Writings of John Stuart Mill*, London: Walter Scott, n.d. (preface dated 1888), p. 54.
21. CWJSM XIII (*Earlier Letters*), pp. 459–60.
22. CWJSM XIII (*Earlier Letters*), p. 713.
23. CWJSM XII (*Earlier Letters*), p. 87.
24. John M. Robson (ed.), *Journals and Debating Speeches* (Collected Works of John Stuart Mill XXVII), Toronto: University of Toronto Press, 1988, pp. 296, 306–7.
25. CWJSM XXVII (*Journals and Debating Speeches*), p. 355.
26. John Stuart Mill, *Newspaper Writings (December 1822–July 1831)*, ed. Ann P. Robson and John M. Robson (Collected Works of John Stuart Mill XXII), Toronto: University of Toronto Press, 1986, p. 9.
27. Bain, *John Stuart Mill*, p. 139.

28. Francis E. Mineka and Dwight N. Lindley (eds), *The Later Letters of John Stuart Mill, 1849–1873* (Collected Works of John Stuart Mill XV), Toronto: University of Toronto Press, 1972, p. 565.
29. CWJSM XIV (*Later Letters*), p. 283.
30. CWJSM XIV (*Later Letters*), p. 393.
31. Harriet Taylor Mill to her son Algernon Taylor, 16 March 1856: Jo Ellen Jacobs (ed.), *The Complete Works of Harriet Taylor Mill*, Bloomington, IN: Indiana University Press, 1998, p. 427. (It is printed here as 'St Charles' but either it was transcribed incorrectly or Harriet did write this but she presumably meant St Chad's.)
32. Timothy Larsen, 'The Catholic Faith of John Stuart Mill's Stepdaughter: A Note on the Diary and Devotional Life of the Feminist Activist Helen Taylor (1831–1907)', *Catholic Historical Review*, 103, 3 (Summer 2017), pp. 465–81.
33. CWJSM XIV (*Later Letters*), p. 302.
34. en.wikipedia.org/wiki/John_Stuart_Mill, accessed on 10 November 2015. (At the time of writing, this stand-alone sentence appears in exactly the same form except that 'atheist' has been replaced by 'agnostic'.)

4

Vanity and Vexation of Spirit

'Then I looked on the works that my hands had wrought, and on the labour that I had laboured to do: and behold, all was vanity and vexation of spirit, and there was no profit under the sun.'

(Ecclesiastes 2:11)

In the autumn of 1826, Mill found himself in the Slough of Despond. It was one of the most distressing periods of his entire life. He lost his purpose and joy in living. He later recalled that his state at this time is depicted in the Coleridge poems, 'Dejection' and 'Work without Hope'. Befitting the fact that his *Autobiography* was an account of his intellectual development, Mill spoke of this time of personal trial as a mental crisis. And as the story being told in this volume is also in large measure tightly entwined with what Mill did or did not believe and how he came to believe or disbelieve it, the contours of this turning point at the start of his adult life that he himself stressed will likewise be central to this discussion. Nevertheless, it is quite possible to argue that the primary driving force of this frightening episode might have been something other than a search for intellectual coherence. Given the theme of this study, one might be tempted to argue that it was a spiritual crisis. There certainly were religious believers in the nineteenth century who leapt to the conclusion that this dark page in Mill's life could best be interpreted as arising from the sceptical philosopher's need for a living relationship with the living God. And there is actually more warrant for such a reading than one might suppose. 'Spiritual' was almost invariably a positive and useful—even essential—word for Mill, one which evoked the totality of one's being and the profoundest depths of the truest self. Mill himself certainly would not have found any incongruity in his own story being included in a biography series of Spiritual Lives. He even referred to the mental changes being discussed in this chapter as 'my spiritual history'.[1] When Mill went through another period of depression or uneasiness in 1833 he described it as a 'difficulty or perplexity of a spiritual kind' and as something being 'spiritually wrong' with him.[2] Moreover, as has already been pointed out, in his *Autobiography* Mill set the crisis that begins in the last half of 1826 within the context of the evangelical conversion narrative, observing that he was in 'the state, I should think, in which converts to Methodism usually are, when smitten by their first "conviction of sin"'.[3] The wind bloweth where it listeth, and the young Utilitarian thinking machine would discover that even he had a heart that could be strangely warmed.

It is worth taking a moment to explore that literary connection. The historian Bruce Hindmarsh has observed that descent into madness and the confession of suicidal urges were 'typical, if not universal, features' of the evangelical conversion narrative.[4] A number of well-known figures made such confessions, including John Newton, the 'wretch' famously saved by 'Amazing Grace'. Mill's friend Thomas Carlyle also invoked this convention in *Sartor Resartus* in stressing the despair that precedes the fictitious Teufelsdröckh's conversion (as it did in Carlyle's own). In his *Autobiography*, Mill followed suit. Before narrating his spiritual breakthrough, he intimates that he had become suicidal: 'I seemed to have nothing left to live for . . . I did not think I could possibly bear it beyond a year.'[5] If such spiritual depths might seem extreme or peculiar to modern readers, Hindmarsh reminds us that this kind of despair was not only familiar, or even normal, for Mill's nineteenth-century readers, it was to some extent even necessary—part of the traditional redemptive plot. Hindmarsh also notes that the turning point of the convert's story generally comes through an encounter with a text. While the Bible is the quintessential such text, it is by no means the only one, and this is true even among the classic conversion accounts. The conversion of John Wesley, the father of evangelicalism, occurred through an encounter with Martin Luther's preface to St Paul's epistle to the Romans. The textual encounter thus became fundamental to Victorian accounts of self-interpretation, even in its ostensibly non-religious forms. Thomas Scott, the evangelical who wrote a classic of spiritual life writing, *The Force of Truth* (1779), served as a prototype: his conversion is facilitated by reading Bishop Burnet's *History of His Own Times*. As for Mill himself, he records that 'a small ray of light' penetrated his despair while 'reading, accidentally, Marmontel's *Memoirs*'.[6] Perhaps it is not overstraining to hear even in that brief statement an invocation of the tradition of 'accidental' reading that reaches back to the *tolle, lege* ('take up and read') episode in Augustine's *Confessions* in which he randomly opens his Bible to the thirteenth chapter of Romans and this serves to disperse the gloom of perplexity. The more decisive textual encounter for Mill, however, came when he read the 1815 edition of William Wordsworth's poems. Not only was his despair dispelled and he was thereby born again to a new life, but he then goes on to say that he had joined a new spiritual fellowship: he was now to be numbered amongst the 'Wordsworthians'.[7] All of this matters. It is not insignificant that Mill was never seeking to eliminate spirituality, but only to find a way for it to be expressed that was not an offence to reason. Still, it would distort far more than it illuminated to take any of these statements and connections too literally. Mill's crisis at the start of his twenties is *not* best understood as a religious one.

The reference to Marmontel's *Memoirs* leads on to another explanation, namely, that Mill's crisis is best understood as being driven by Oedipal urges. With touching naivety, Mill recounts for all the world to know that he had become resigned to the assumption that his emotional life was buried beyond resurrection, but he found hope when he was moved to tears by the scene in which the author's father dies and Marmontel vows that he would replace him as the head of the family. It is unquestionably the case that John found the paternal yoke oppressive. Not only did he testify to this directly, he even assumed that his experience, though more extreme than most, was universal. Writing, for instance, in *The Subjection of Women*:

> Let any man call to mind what he himself felt on emerging from boyhood—from the tutelage and control of even loved and affectionate elders—and entering upon the responsibilities of manhood. Was it not like the physical effect of taking off a heavy weight, or releasing him from obstructive, even if not otherwise painful, bonds? Did he not feel twice as much alive, twice as much a human being, as before?[8]

The relationship between a father and a son is such an unequal one, he reflected in the same treatise, that it is highly unlikely that the latter can conduct himself in it with sincerity and openness. Others noticed

Mill's confined condition as well. Harriet Grote was willing to recall in print before the *Autobiography* had been published and, indeed, while Mill was still alive, that 'John was, as a boy, somewhat repressed by the elder Mill.'[9] During his father's lifetime, Mill wrote a critique of Bentham that he insisted could only be published anonymously. Once James Mill was dead, John expanded it into his famous 'Bentham' article—an essay that did not pull any punches and was felt to be a betrayal by his old gang of Philosophical Radicals. It does not seem too much of a stretch to wonder if this was a surrogate way of releasing some of his suppressed wish to attack his biological father. In any event, it is reasonable to suspect that perhaps Mill would not have been in such an extreme state in the winter of 1826–7 if his father had been an affectionate, easy-going, doting Utilitarian philosopher.

Mill himself spoke of his mental crisis as a 'depression', and it is also legitimate to ask to what extent what he was experiencing was depression in the clinical sense. In other words, perhaps it is best viewed as a psychological rather than an intellectual episode. Certainly, there was a dark cloud over him that cannot be reduced to the uncertainty of being at an ideological crossroads. He recalled, for instance, that his mind was 'tormented' by the thought that pleasing sequences of musical notes were finite and therefore the world could soon exhaust them and there would never again be any new music worth hearing.[10] Another significant piece of evidence is that Mill continued to have periods of depression even after his intellectual life become one much more marked by continuity than disruption. He wrote to Thomas Carlyle in 1833: 'At all events I will not if I can help it give way to gloom and morbid despondency, of which I have had a large share in my short life... nevertheless I will and must, though it leaves me little enough of energy, master it, or it will surely master me. Whenever it has come to me it has always lasted many months, and has gone off in most cases very gradually.'[11] To give another example, Mill had a 'dreadful depression' in the summer of 1843.[12] And to include just one more theory, Alexander Bain maintained that Mill's 1826–7 crisis was physical in origin, the result of overwork, insisting that this diagnosis 'may I think be certified beyond all reasonable doubt'.[13] As it is quite possible for a single event to have multiple contributing factors, there is no need to select just one of these theories as the only correct one.

Whatever non-intellectual factors might have been in play, the crisis of 1826–7 resulted in Mill adjusting his ideological positioning. He was tired of being a sectarian Benthamite. On the other side of this change in his approach to life, he explained to Carlyle in 1834: 'I am still, & am likely to remain, a utilitarian; though not one of "the people called utilitarians"; indeed, having scarcely one of my secondary premisses in common with them; nor a utilitarian at all, unless in quite another sense from what perhaps any one except myself understands by the word.'[14] The phrase Mill put in quotation marks was evoking John Wesley's *A Plain Account of the People called Methodists* (1748) which is, once again, Mill's way of saying that the Benthamites were akin to a religious sect. Now seeing through that dogmatic fraternity, Mill would condemn George Grote, for instance, as 'hard and mechanical . . . with much logical and but little aesthetic culture; *narrow* therefore . . . more a disciple of my father than of any one else'.[15] If that was harsh, Mill did not soften the blow when it came to self-reproach. Confessing that the caricature of a Benthamite as 'a mere reasoning machine' had actually been true of him during the two or three of his teenage years when he was most a zealot,[16] Mill indicted himself for having understood logic, but not 'reality'. He had been trained to look down on most of his contemporaries as blindly following dogma and tradition, but he was disconcerted to learn that, in their eyes, he was the manufactured man, the prefabricated result of a thorough course of indoctrination from his father and Bentham. In his inaugural address as Lord Rector of the University of St Andrews, Mill generalized his experience: 'Look at a youth who has never been out of his family circle: he never dreams of any other opinions or ways of thinking than those he has been bred up in; if he has heard of any such, attributes them to some moral defect, or inferiority of nature or education.'[17] Mill met the enemy and was rattled to discover that they were not just uniformed, unreflective, or second-rate minds. Sometimes they even seemed to be on to something. He gave up debating altogether. It was time to prioritize learning, growing, and befriending over winning.

So many things that he had been taught to view with suspicion now turned out to have more to them than he had been led to believe: poetry, feeling, history, tradition, the constitution, the Church, religion. Mill would illustrate this difference by pointing to Macaulay's critical review of his father James Mill's *Essays on Government* in the *Edinburgh Review*. John himself previously had championed the Benthamite party line that one must decide what was right for a society by deductive reasoning rather than being guided by historical experience: 'it is my decided opinion formed on mature consideration, that the importance of history as a source of political knowledge has been greatly overrated'.[18] He had signed a letter to the *Morning Chronicle* which was making the case for radical reform as 'No Worshipper of Antiquity'.[19] Macaulay mocked this approach as obscurantist, a willful disregard of the relevant empirical evidence: 'We have here an elaborate treatise on Government, from which, but for two or three passing allusions, it would not appear that the author was aware that any governments existed among men.'[20] Against all of his ideological coaching, John could not help but think that Macaulay had a point. He was disappointed, however, when his father's own response to the review was to treat 'Macaulay's argument as simply irrational'.[21] That would not do anymore.

There also might be a natural fraternity amongst prodigies. Bentham had been a child prodigy, which partially explains his attentiveness to John; and so was Macaulay. Another was Connop Thirlwall, who would go on to become a bishop in the Church of England. When Mill was nineteen he debated Thirlwall: 'it has remained impressed upon me ever since as the finest speech I ever heard'.[22] Mill always spoke well of Thirlwall thereafter. Even if their ideological positions were wrong, these were worthy opponents who could not be dismissed as uneducated, irrational, or anti-intellectual. Mill once remarked that around the age of twenty-two he saw the luminous truth that the only thing to learn to imitate from any writer is his or her earnestness.[23] By this somewhat cryptic observation, he was apparently marking the point at which he learned how to admire and respect an author with whose views he did not agree. The dismissive rhetoric of his Utilitarian set had started to ring hollow. In his essay on Coleridge, Mill averred that radicals needed to grasp that 'the Constitution and Church of England... are not mere frauds, nor sheer nonsense'.[24] In the parallel article to that one, Mill reflected on Bentham's limitations: 'Knowing so little of human feelings, he knew still less of the influences by which those feelings are formed... Man is never recognised by him as a being capable of pursuing spiritual perfection.' Mill even conceded that 'religious writers' had far superior knowledge to Bentham of 'the profundities and windings of the human heart'.[25] His best male friend, the Reverend John Sterling, reported in 1840 that Mill was recovering from his anti-religious phase: 'It is a new thing for John Mill to sympathise with religious characters; some years since, he had so imbibed the errors which his father instilled into him, as to be quite a bigot against religion.'[26] Mill had stood for progress and a better future unshackled by the past, but he came to see that in a curious, ironic way this was an old-fashioned view: his father was an eighteenth-century Enlightenment man dragging his moribund, passé stances into the nineteenth. The latest intellectual current was Romanticism, and thus to value the traditional, even the medieval, was paradoxically to be keeping up with the times. Mill became embarrassed by his former self. He burned the manuscript of an essay he had written which attacked sentiment. He came to see: 'Feeling at least as valuable as Thought, & Poetry not only on a par with, but the necessary condition of, any true & comprehensive Philosophy.'[27] Romanticism was giving him a way of intellectualizing the conviction that life is more than intellect: 'Much of this, it is true, consisted in rediscovering things known to all the world, which I had previously disbelieved, or disregarded. But the rediscovery was to me a discovery.'[28] The sealed springs of his emotional life were finding a way to break forth.

The particular intellectual problem with Utilitarianism that he was hitting up against in the crisis of 1826–7 was a version of the paradox of hedonism. Bentham taught that the ultimate good was happiness, but Mill found that the pursuit of happiness was not conducive to his happiness. Here is his account of how he resolved this conundrum:

> I never, indeed, wavered in the conviction that happiness is the test of all rules of conduct, and the end of life. But I now thought that this end was only to be attained by not making it the direct end. Those only are happy (I thought) who have their minds fixed on some object other than their own happiness. . . .[29]

Always fond of quoting the sayings of Christ, Mill had learned that those who try to save their own life will lose it and those who are willing to lose their life shall find it.

One bridge between Mill's sectarian youth and his broader life thereafter is the Unitarian world. For some decades now too many scholars have had an unfortunate habit of treating nineteenth-century Unitarianism as if it were a way of being or becoming secular when, of course, it was actually a way of being or staying religious. Mill himself was clear on this point. He not only personally liked the Unitarian minister James Martineau, but judged him to be 'one of the best metaphysicians of the day'.[30] When Martineau applied for a professorship at the University of London, however, Mill opposed his candidacy because he did not want a clergyman teaching at a secular institution. Nevertheless, Utilitarians and Unitarians were thoroughly and happily cross-pollinating and overlapping throughout the nineteenth century. For instance, John Bowring was one of Bentham's closest disciples and companions.[31] They arranged to live next door to each other and Bentham died in Bowring's arms. When the *Westminster Review* was launched to propagate the views of his circle, Bentham soon had Bowring established as its editor. Bentham even made Bowring his literary executor. Moreover, all of this was true despite the fact that Bowring was a devout Unitarian Christian. Far from his religious faith being a nominal or fading identity, several years after he became Bentham's disciple Bowring published *Matins and Vespers: with hymns and occasional devotional pieces* (1824). This volume, he explained, was intended to promote 'the cause of religion and virtue at home' and to cultivate 'the devotional spirit'; Bowring's prayer was that it would also serve 'to renew or to create confidence in heaven'.[32] Some of his hymns simply had a text of scripture for their title as well as theme: 'Psalm xc.', 'Habakkuk, chap. iii', and '1 Corinthians, chap. xiii'. Therefore, when Bowring edited for publication *The Collected Works of Jeremy Bentham*, he left out Bentham's anti-religious writings. When Bowring himself died, a line from one of his hymns was inscribed on his gravestone: 'In the cross of Christ I glory.'

One of James Mill's dearest friends was James Lindsay, a Presbyterian minister with Unitarian views. The political economist David Ricardo, who was James Mill's closest friend—and who was another prominent member of their cohort—also attended a Unitarian congregation. As we have seen, John's substitute mother, Sarah Austin, was a pious Unitarian, as was her husband, John Austin—both of whom were also members of the Benthamite circle. Again, this identity was sufficiently strong and enduring that when John Mill was twenty-seven years old, Sarah Austin's *Selections from the Old Testament: or the*

Religion, Morality, and Poetry of the Hebrew Scriptures, arranged under heads (1833) was published. This work was a biblical anthology designed for the education of children. Its goal was to bring the Old Testament into young lives because 'the sacred writings' are 'persuasive, consolatory, or elevating'.[33] The introductory part was titled, 'On the Excellency of the Holy Scripture', and the first main part was the 'Attributes of God', including a section on 'almighty'. The part on the duties of human beings included a section on 'Trust in God'.

By far the most important bridge figure was the Unitarian minister William Johnson Fox. To him went the honour of having written the first article published in the first issue (January 1824) of the mouthpiece of these Philosophical Radicals, the *Westminster Review*. John Mill saw Fox through the lens of his religious calling, referring to him in 1831, for instance, as 'the Rev. W. J. Fox, the enlightened and eloquent Unitarian preacher'.[34] Likewise, Mill would refer to the journal that Fox edited—which Mill praised in print—as 'the Monthly Repository, the Unitarian periodical'.[35] Fox introduced Mill to the Unitarian couple John and Harriet Taylor. She would become the most important person in his life. Harriet's closest female friend was Eliza Flower, another Unitarian whose faith was devotional and not merely social. Flower was a musical composer who created a Unitarian hymnal 'for congregational purposes': *Hymns and Anthems. The Words chiefly from Holy Scripture and the Writings of the Poets* (1842).[36] Her sister Sarah, who was also friends with Mill and Harriet Taylor, wrote sacred lyrics, including a hymn widely cherished by Christians from a wide range of denominations for generations, 'Nearer, my God, to Thee'. Another song for Christian worship with lyrics by Sarah Flower in Eliza's hymnal is 'Darkness shrouded Calvary'. The Reverend W. J. Fox himself became one of Mill's closest friends. Apart from the occasional visitor from abroad, Fox was the only person that John and Harriet Mill invited to their marital home. (Mill himself once observed: 'I often think one never knows one's friends or rather they are not properly one's friends until one has seen them in their home.')[37]

No attempt will be made to measure how many Unitarian laymen and women there were with whom Mill was in warm contact. He was friends with William Benjamin Carpenter, for example, a devout Unitarian who wrote a handbook on psalmody, describing him as 'a man whom I have a great esteem for'.[38] This friend's sister, the Unitarian social reformer Mary Carpenter, signed Mill's petition for women's suffrage. Another correspondent was John Lalor, the editor of the Unitarian *Inquirer.* Mill chaired the Jamaica Committee, a pressure group which existed to attempt to achieve the goal of the prosecution of Governor Eyre, and he worked closely with Unitarians on it, including its treasurer (P. A. Taylor), and its solicitor (William Shaen). The ordained men are a bit easier to quantify. A particularly frequent and congenial connection was with John Hamilton Thom, pastor of Renshaw Street Chapel, Liverpool. All told, Mill was in correspondence with over a dozen Unitarian ministers. To take an extreme example, once on the very same day (21 May 1841) Mill wrote friendly letters to two different Unitarian ministers on completely unrelated matters. When Bain wanted to discredit Mill's 'Theism' essay, he dismissed it as just a rehashed offering of the well-rehearsed Christian theology of the Unitarians.[39]

Notes

1. Francis E. Mineka (ed.), *The Earlier Letters of John Stuart Mill, 1812–1848* (Collected Works of John Stuart Mill XII), Toronto: University of Toronto Press, 1963, p. 224.
2. CWJSM XII (*Earlier Letters*), p. 154.
3. John Stuart Mill, *Autobiography and Literary Essays* (Collected Works of John Stuart Mill I), ed. J. M. Robson, Indianapolis: Liberty Fund, 2006 (reprint of Toronto: University of Toronto Press, 1981), p. 137.
4. D. Bruce Hindmarsh, *The Evangelical Conversion Narrative: Spiritual Autobiography in Early Modern England*, Oxford: Oxford University Press, 2005, p. 276. Once again, for these comments, I am drawing upon Richard Hughes Gibson and Timothy Larsen, 'Nineteenth-century spiritual autobiography: Carlyle, Newman, Mill', in Adam Smyth (ed.), *A History of English Autobiography*, Cambridge: Cambridge University Press, 2016, pp. 192–206.
5. CWJSM I (*Autobiography and Literary Essays*), pp. 139, 145.
6. CWJSM I (*Autobiography and Literary Essays*), p. 145.
7. CWJSM I (*Autobiography and Literary Essays*), p. 153.
8. John Stuart Mill, *Essays on Equality, Law, and Education*, ed. John M. Robinson and Stefani Collini (Collected Works of John Stuart Mill XXI), Toronto: University of Toronto Press, 1984, p. 337.
9. Mrs Grote [Harriet Grote], *The Personal Life of George Grote*, second edition, London: John Murray, 1873, p. 25.

10. CWJSM I (*Autobiography and Literary Essays*), p. 149.
11. John Stuart Mill to Thomas Carlyle, 11 and 12 April 1833: CWJSM XII (*Earlier Letters*), p. 149.
12. Alexander Bain, *John Stuart Mill: A Criticism: with personal recollections*, London: Longmans, Green, and Co., 1882, p. 78.
13. Bain, *John Stuart Mill*, pp. 37–8.
14. John Stuart Mill to Thomas Carlyle, 12 January 1834: CWJSM XII (*Earlier Letters*), p. 207.
15. CWJSM XII (*Earlier Letters*), p. 170.
16. CWJSM I (*Autobiography and Literary Essays*), p. 111.
17. CWJSM XXI (*Essays on Equality, Law, and Education*), p. 226.
18. John M. Robson (ed.), *Journals and Debating Speeches* (Collected Works of John Stuart Mill XXVII), Toronto: University of Toronto Press, 1988, p. 392.
19. John Stuart Mill, *Newspaper Writings (December 1822–July 1831)*, ed. Ann P. Robson and John M. Robson (Collected Works of John Stuart Mill XXII), Toronto: University of Toronto Press, 1986, p. 74.
20. [Thomas Babington Macaulay], Review of James Mill, *Edinburgh Review*, 49, 97 (March 1829), pp. 159–89 (here 161–2).
21. CWJSM I (*Autobiography and Literary Essays*), p. 165.
22. CWJSM XIII (*Earlier Letters*), p. 442.
23. R. L. Brett (ed.), *Barclay Fox's Journal*, Fowey: Cornwall Editions, 2008, p. 183.
24. John Stuart Mill, *Essays on Ethics, Religion and Society* (Collected Works of John Stuart Mill X), ed. J. M. Robson, Indianapolis: Liberty Fund, 2006 (reprint of Toronto: University of Toronto Press, 1969), p. 146.
25. CWJSM X (*Essays on Ethics, Religion and Society*), pp. 93, 95, 109.
26. Horace N. Pym (ed.), *Memories of Old Friends: being extracts from the Journals and Letters of Caroline Fox of Penjerrick, Cornwall*, London: Smith, Elder, and Co., 1882, p. 111.
27. CWJSM XII (*Earlier Letters*), p. 312.
28. CWJSM I (*Autobiography and Literary Essays*), p. 175.
29. CWJSM I (*Autobiography and Literary Essays*), p. 145.
30. CWJSM XII (*Earlier Letters*), p. 236.
31. These comments on Bowring are primarily derived from Gerald Stone, 'Bowring, Sir John (1792–1872)', *Oxford Dictionary of National Biography*. Accessed online at oxforddnb.com.
32. John Bowring, *Matins and Vespers: with Hymns and Occasional Devotional Pieces*, second edition, London: Printed for the Author (sold by G. and W. B. Whittaker), 1824, pp. iii–vi.
33. Sarah Austin (ed.), *Selections from the Old Testament: or the Religion, Morality, and Poetry of the Hebrew Scriptures, arranged under heads*, London: Effingham Wilson, 1833, pp. iii–iv.

34. CWJSM XII (*Earlier Letters*), p. 92.
35. CWJSM XII (*Earlier Letters*), p. 104.
36. *Hymns and Anthems. The Words chiefly from Holy Scripture and the Writings of the Poets. The Music by Eliza Flower*, Vol. I, London: Cramer Addison & Beale, 1842. (Vol. II was released by the same publisher in 1846.)
37. CWJSM XIII (*Earlier Letters*), p. 441.
38. CWJSM XIII (*Earlier Letters*), p. 423.
39. Bain, *John Stuart Mill*, p. 138.

5
The Lion Shall Lie Down With the Lamb

> 'The wolf also shall dwell with the lamb, and the leopard shall lie down with the kid; and the calf and the young lion and the fatling together.'
>
> (Isaiah 11:6)

In 1828, Mill began fraternizing with the enemy. John Sterling and F. D. Maurice joined him in debates, taking an opposing side to his as disciples of Coleridge and foes of Bentham. Both men would go on to be ordained in the Church of England. Maurice would become one of the most important Anglican theologians of the nineteenth century, arguably of that Communion's entire history. Mill was enchanted. It was love at first fight. Even with Maurice, he became much more intimate than scholars have realized. This oversight is attributable both to the fact that Mill himself later denied that they had been very close and because his last word on Maurice ended on a deprecatory note. Mill wrote in his *Autobiography*:

> I have so deep a respect for Maurice's character and purposes, as well as for his great mental gifts, that it is with some unwillingness I say anything which may seem to place him on a less high eminence than I would gladly be able to accord to him. But I have always thought that there was more intellectual power wasted in Maurice than in any other of my contemporaries. Few of them certainly have had so much to waste. Great powers of generalization, rare ingenuity and subtlety, and a wide perception of important and unobvious truths, served him not for putting something better in place of the worthless heap of received opinions on the great subjects of thought, but for proving to his own mind that the Church of England had known everything from the first,

> and that all the truths on the ground of which the Church and orthodoxy have been attacked (many of which he saw as clearly as any one) are not only consistent with the Thirty-nine articles, but are better understood and expressed in those articles than by any one who rejects them. I have never been able to find any other explanation of this, than by attributing it to that timidity of conscience, combined with original sensitiveness of temperament, which has so often driven highly gifted men into Romanism from the need of a firmer support than they can find in the independent conclusions of their own judgment.[1]

While this qualification does not rule out Mill's theory as to what motivated Maurice, it should be noted that Maurice had refused his Cambridge degree because he could not in good conscience affirm the Thirty-Nine Articles, so his subsequent theological convictions were not the complacent result of a life spent floating along with the currents of society. More to the point, every single reference to Maurice in Mill's private letters was entirely laudatory. Mill observed in 1859, for instance, that he respected Maurice highly.[2] And they were friends. In addition to corresponding, they often met in person and had long and stimulating conversations together. While it is hard for readers today to feel the import of his Victorian conventions, Mill would only omit a formal title when addressing family members or his most intimate, personal friends. After an estrangement from George and Harriet Grote, Mill expected this change in how he styled him to do all of the work of a full reconciliation scene: 'I do not, & have not for years, addressed him as *Mr*—& it is very dull of him not to have taken the hint.'[3] Even someone as close to Mill in his later years as John Morley never was graduated beyond 'Dear Mr Morley'. The chaplain of Guy's Hospital, however, warranted the rare and precious 'My dear Maurice'.[4]

John Sterling was the greatest male friendship of Mill's life. He freely acknowledged this in his *Autobiography*: 'With Sterling I soon became very intimate, and was more attached to him than I have ever been to any other man. He was indeed one of the most loveable of men.'[5] (Mill is using 'man' in a gender-specific sense here so as to reserve for his wife Harriet the pre-eminent place of friendship in his life.) Mill openly acknowledged this uniquely close bond while Sterling was still alive. He wrote to another friend, Barclay Fox, in 1841: 'none of my friends have heard of me for months past; not even Sterling, who of all men living had the strongest claim not to be so treated'.[6] His fate already clear, a month before Sterling died of tuberculosis at the age of thirty-eight, Mill poured his deep emotions into a farewell letter: 'I have never so much wished for another life as I do for the sake of meeting you in it. . . . I shall never think of you but as one of the noblest, & quite the most lovable of all men I have known or ever look to know.'[7]

Sterling was a staunch Churchman even at their first acquaintance. Indeed, they first met when Sterling spoke in a debate in defence of the Church of England. John Sterling had a gift for friendship, and Mill soon had someone he could confide in, respect, trust, and love. Sterling was ordained in June 1834. Mill, of course, knew of his friend's intention. He wrote to Carlyle some months earlier, reflecting that Sterling was a sincere man who would never make a dishonest confession. His best male friend's theological convictions, therefore, were held with intellectual integrity and it was 'happy' for Sterling that his conscience could align with the historic Christian faith as by law established, Mill reflected.[8] The Victorians were fascinated by Sterling's religious doubts later in life. Scholars have ceaselessly followed and strengthened this ant trail to Doubting Castle. They have also tended to conflate questioning orthodox doctrine with abandoning the Christian faith. Sterling not only lived and died a Christian, but even a clergyman. Just before he departed this life he wrote a poem which ended, 'Thy will be done in earth and heaven / And Thou my sins forgive!', lines he said to himself over and over again during his final hours.[9] Again, scholars today might like to see Sterling primarily as a religious sceptic, but his contemporaries generally saw him primarily as a clergyman. When Barclay Fox first met him, that was the key identifying noun: 'I had a call from a very superior intelligence in the person of a consumptive clergyman called Sterling, who came on behalf of a Mrs. Mill.'[10] When William Tait wanted to invite Sterling to contribute to his *Tait's Magazine*, he asked Mill for his contact details. The philosopher replied that he should address his correspondence to 'Rev. John Sterling, Falmouth'.[11] Mill's old sectarian cohort was outraged when he allowed a clergyman (Sterling) to write for the *London and Westminster Review*, which was supposed to be the organ of their radical views, including religious scepticism. This identity was maintained right to the end of his life. It was 'the Rev. John Sterling' in his obituary notices.[12] Even when Mill confided to Auguste Comte that he was grieving the loss 'of one of the very small numbers of persons for whom I felt a live friendship and the highest esteem', he identified him, not as an author, but as 'an Anglican clergyman'.[13]

The irony that the best male friend of the Saint of Rationalism was a priest in the established Church is lessened when one realizes that Mill had chosen him precisely because he was, at that period in his life, in a mood for opposites to attract. He wrote to Sterling in April 1828, confessing that he hoped to gain 'a still greater portion of your intimacy—which I value highly for this reason among many others, that it appears to me peculiarly adapted to the wants of my own mind; since I know no person who possesses more, of what I have not, than yourself, nor is this inconsistent with my believing you to be deficient in some of the very few things which I have'.[14] Mill was tired of the echo chamber that was his sectarian solidarity with figures such as Roebuck, Graham, and Charles Austin. He was developing a new theory of friendship, one based on complementarity. As he later articulated it: 'the greatest source of friendship between two minds of any capacity' is not '*equality*, for nothing can be so little interesting to a man as his own double; but *reciprocal superiority*'.[15]

John Stuart Mill was a young prince in the Benthamite sun, but he now had an irresistible urge to frolic in the Coleridgian moonlight. By 1834, he was testifying: 'Few persons have exercised more influence over my thoughts and character than Coleridge has . . . I consider him the most systematic thinker of our time, without excepting even Bentham . . . On the whole, there is more food for thought—and the best kind of thought—in Coleridge than in all other contemporary writers.'[16] For a time, it was as if Mill had simply defected to the opposing camp. He wrote to Sterling in 1831:

> Wordsworth seems always to know the pros and cons of every question: & when you think he strikes the balance wrong, it is only because you think he estimates erroneously some matter of fact. Hence all my differences with him, or with any other philosophic Tory, would be differences of matter-of-fact or detail, while my differences with the radicals & utilitarians are differences of principle . . .[17]

Likewise in 1838 Mill was indignant that anyone would still align him with his old comrades-in-arms:

> I expected no better from the Chronicle but what is the meaning of *your* insisting upon identifying me with Grote or Roebuck or the rest? Do

> you in your conscience think that my opinions are at all like theirs? Have you forgotten, what I am sure you once knew, that my opinion of their philosophy is & has for years been *more* unfavourable by far than your own? & that my radicalism is of a school the most remote from theirs, at all points, which exists? *They* knew this as long ago as 1829, since which time the variance has been growing wider & wider.... [They are] a set from whose opinions I differ more than from the Tories.[18]

It is hard not to read that as hyperbolic. Closer to the precise truth is Mill's confession to Carlyle that when they had met in 1831: 'I was then, and had been for some years, in an intermediate state—a state of *reaction* from logical-utilitarian narrowness of the very narrowest kind, out of which after much unhappiness and inward struggling I had emerged, and had taken temporary refuge in its extreme opposite.'[19] There was a synthesis yet to come.

Meanwhile there were more opposites to attract in the moonlight. Another was the heralds of a French visionary movement, the Saint-Simonians. Mill mitigated this enthusiasm in his *Autobiography* by observing that they 'had not yet dressed out their philosophy as religion'.[20] That is an observation that is getting at a truth, but it is also true that before he died in 1825 Comte de Saint-Simon had signalled a religious trajectory in his *The New Christianity*, and that Mill responded with remarkable indulgence when the group did evolve more and more into a new religious movement. Moreover, already in 1833 Mill himself was referring to them as a 'political and religious sect'. In the following year, Mill spoke in print of 'the St. Simonian religion'.[21] The Saint-Simonian Gustave d'Eichthal became one of Mill's cordial friends. As ever during this phase of his life, Mill's high-spirited flirtations were mistaken for a willingness to love and obey as long as he should live. He wrote to the Frenchman in October 1829: 'I have not even left myself space to tell you with how much pleasure I have read your pamphlet, which has made almost an entire convert of me.'[22] Before four months had passed, d'Eichthal was ready to rush across the Channel and perform the ceremony. Mill had to admit that his 'entire conversion' was 'extremely unlikely' and that it would be a mistake for his friend to make a journey 'with a view to my complete initiation in the St Simonian doctrine'.[23] On the other hand, approaching two years thereafter Mill was still a sympathetic fellow traveller, praising d'Eichthal for 'the great, and truly apostolic work in which you are engaged'.[24] One year on from that Mill was obliged to report to Carlyle that some of the St Simonians were now as millenarian a religious cult as one could imagine: 'the sea I believe is ultimately to consist not of salt water but lemonade; I understand this is no joke'.[25] Yet another year on, Mill could still write for publication, doing his best to see things through the eyes of at least the best of the movement: 'An arrangement, which, viewing it as St. Simonians, you cannot but regard as providential.'[26] Mill would refer to their leader respectfully by his spiritual title, 'Father Enfantin'.[27] He even expressed his goodwill by agreeing to translate for the British press the apostolic charge Enfantin delivered before retreating to his monastic calling: 'I, The Father of the new Family—Before I impose silence on the voice . . . God has given me a mission to call the poor, and women, to a new destiny; To give admittance into the sacred Family of Man . . .'[28] The sea may not have been lemonade, but neither was it withdrawing. Spirituality was all around.

One of the things that Mill valued most about the St Simonians was their view of the unfolding of history. They envisioned a rotation across the ages between organic and critical periods. This gave Mill a more compelling way to evade the standard critique of radicals and sceptics that they could only tear down but not build up and thus, if they had their way, they would just leave people huddling in ruins. The critical period, St Simonism allowed Mill to see, was temporary. It was only because the last unifying creed was no longer viable that it was being uprooted. This would not lead on to endless destruction—the St Simonian scheme gave Mill the faith to believe—but rather a new unifying creed would emerge around which a new organic period would flourish. This vision was augmented by the insight that he gained from Coleridge that one needed to balance the interest of 'permanence' with that of 'progression'.[29] Even more important in this regard, however, was the thought of a disciple of Saint-Simon who graduated to founding a movement—and eventually a religion—of his own, Auguste Comte. For a time, Comte too mistook Mill's exuberant praise for total discipleship. Mill gushed in a letter to Sir Edward Lytton Bulwer in 1843 that Comte 'seems to me by far the first speculative thinker of the age'.[30] As to a theory of history, Comte believed he had found a Casaubon-like key to all human progress, a law of three stages: 'the Theological, or fictitious; the Metaphysical, or abstract; and the Scientific, or positive'.[31] In his *Logic*, Mill enthused about Comte's stadial scheme: 'what a flood of light it lets in upon the whole course of history'.[32] Mill was now able to overcome the negative view of history that he had received from his Benthamite upbringing in two different ways. As to the first, he no longer believed that abstract theory was all that mattered and therefore there was little value in approaching a problem by viewing historical circumstances as impinging upon it and as serving as experimental data to illuminate it. Mill had once argued against the import of history himself in this manner (writing as 'No Worshipper of Antiquity'), but he started defending the forces of permanence in print (namely, 'Puseyism'—the Anglo-Catholic Tractarian movement in the Church of England!)—and signed these articles 'Historicus'.[33]

As to the second, it allowed Mill to praise rather than censure institutions as having served humanity well in their time, even while maintaining that they had had their day and needed to be set aside and replaced. This was very different from his father and Bentham just sneering at these institutions as shams and frauds. Even the Roman Catholic Church could now be extolled as a mighty force for good within its own organic period. Mill thought that the editor of the *Edinburgh Review* might not take an article of his because he had so taken this lesson to heart that he ended up praising Pope Gregory VII for strengthening the power of the papacy. Again, this approach was dramatically more respectful and affirming than the way that radicals had hitherto viewed matters. Nevertheless, stadial thinking tends to be patronizing. It is a way of telling your opponents that they are hopelessly out-of-date, that they are not keeping up with the times, that their ideas are now discredited. Comte's scheme did this explicitly with orthodox Christian doctrine: to be part of the modern era is to stop thinking theologically and to start thinking purely scientifically. In a long correspondence with Comte beginning in 1841, 'the first speculative thinker of the age' sometimes turned this condescending feature of stadialism on Mill himself. Most galling of all, Comte insisted that a belief in gender equality was an old-fashioned eighteenth-century crotchet, now overturned by contemporary research which has proven scientifically that women are inherently inferior to men: 'For a long time I was myself steeped in the sociological stage where you still are in this matter'; 'I am so much more confident here, as I have myself once passed through a rather analogous mental situation, although perhaps my studies in biology moved me faster away from it'; 'I had at first thought like you, before completing my philosophical education.'[34] Stadial schemes are often a kind of sleight of hand that makes assertions appear to be arguments. For Mill, however, these theories of history were primarily a way to be less dismissive than he had hitherto been about traditional institutions, practices, and beliefs.

At the height of the Saint-Simonian influence upon him, Mill wrote a series of articles in early 1831 for the *Examiner*. They were titled, 'The Spirit of the Age'. The terms he used for the historical rotation of periods were the natural and the transitional states. He pronounced the current moment to be an age of transition: 'Mankind have outgrown old institutions and old doctrine, and have not yet acquired new ones.'[35] In his stark seclusion on an isolated farm in Dumfriesshire, Scotland, Thomas Carlyle read these articles and thought to himself: 'here is a new Mystic'.[36] The Scotsman was in the midst of writing *Sartor Resartus* and therefore it must have seemed a particularly promising omen that the author in the *Examiner* had hit upon the very same metaphor he was fervently unfolding: 'When we say outgrown, we intend to prejudge nothing. A man may not be either better or happier at six-and-twenty, than he was at six years of age: but the same jacket which fitted him then, will not fit him now.'[37] Contrariwise, Carlyle was not only vehemently anti-Benthamite but in *Sartor Resartus* he could not resist larding his ridicule with prose punning on the surname of the Utilitarian father-and-son duo:

> 'Shall your Science', exclaimed he, 'proceed in the small chink-lighted, or even oil-lighted, underground workshop of Logic alone; and man's mind became an Arithmetical Mill, whereof Memory is the Hopper, and mere Tables of Sines and Tangents, Codification, and Treatises of what you call Political Economy, the Meal?'
>
> ...
>
> Foolish Wordmonger and Motive-grinder, who in thy Logic-mill hast an earthly mechanism for the Godlike itself, and wouldst fain grind me out Virtue from the husks of Pleasure,—I tell thee, Nay!
>
> ...
>
> O, the vast, gloomy, solitary Golgotha, and Mill of Death![38]

Likewise, one suspects that Charles Dickens later named his cold man of facts, Mr Gradgrind, in *Hard Times* (1854) as a dig at James Mill, and perhaps his son as well. He was the grand grinder. A grinder, according to one of its definitions in the *Oxford English Dictionary*, is 'a person who grinds anything in a mill'.[39] Mill was sufficiently sensitive to such possibilities that he corrected the manuscript of his *Principles of Political Economy* so as to ward them off: changing 'upper millstone' to 'upper stone', 'windmill or watermill' to 'machine' and 'in four other cases within five pages the possible pun is deleted'.[40] The closest John Mill came to expressing annoyance at these passages in *Sartor Resartus* was to ask Carlyle 'whether that mode of writing between sarcasm or irony and earnest, be really deserving of so much honour as you give it by making use of it so frequently'.[41] Nevertheless, the book rapidly grew on him, and his final judgement was that it was Carlyle's 'best and greatest work'.[42] In October 1831, Mill reported to Sterling that he now read Carlyle with 'very keen relish', although he used to think his writings were 'such consummate nonsense'.[43] Carlyle sought out the apparent mystic when he came to London in August 1831, and soon they were fast friends. Mill would tell the Scotsman that he considered him one of his teachers; and he told Barclay Fox that Carlyle should be acknowledged as a Hebrew Prophet. In 1842, Mill confessed to Comte that Carlyle was the only other person beside himself whose writings had given him such a 'jolt', the shock that comes through the disruptive force of 'sudden insight into a great and luminous new idea'.[44] Harriet Taylor eventually would convince Mill to rate Carlyle less highly. His mature view would defend Carlyle in his place through stadial condescension: 'It is only at a particular stage in one's mental development that one benefits much by him.'[45] Nevertheless, in his *Autobiography* Mill did not attempt to downplay the intensity or persistence of Carlyle's influence on him: 'I was during a long period one of his most fervent admirers.'[46] The author of *Sartor Resartus* tried to draw the young philosopher out more and more. He pressed Mill to confide his deepest feelings. Mill replied forlornly that when he gave him his analytical thoughts he really was giving all he had to give. As with Comte, Mill eventually had to confess that he was not as much a disciple of Carlyle as he had inadvertently made himself appear to be. He still believed quite differently from the Scotsman on various substantive issues, and that was unlikely to change. It was just that he was prioritizing learning from him and so was in no mood to contradict the Sage of Chelsea when he disagreed with him.

So what did Mill see, or think he saw, in Thomas Carlyle? He glimpsed a complementary partner for himself with which to forge his ideal relational model of reciprocal superiority. It is important to grasp how Mill outlined this division of a labour of love, as Carlyle was merely the forerunner: Mill would find his true intellectual soulmate and partner in Harriet Taylor. Mill's relationship with the woman who would become his wife was very much patterned on the plan that he imagined for his friendship with the Scottish author. It went thus: Carlyle was the Genius, the Artist, the Poet. He grasped truths intuitively and thus could make imaginative breakthroughs; could see the whole rather than just a part; could discern and declare the true meaning of things. Mill, on the other hand, was a logician and a reasoner. His sphere was method, not meaning. If a true Poet would but pronounce, Mill could come alongside him or her and work out the logical argumentation that supported their intuitive insights. Writing to Sterling, Mill described his own particular contribution:

> the only thing that I believe I am really fit for, is the investigation of abstract truth, & the more abstract the better. If there is any science which I am capable of promoting, I think it is the science of science itself, the science of investigation—of method. I once heard Maurice say (& like many things which have dropped from him, its truth did not strike me at first but it has been a source of endless reflexions since) that almost all differences of opinion when analysed, were differences of method.[47]

With sincere and poignant—even if arguably misplaced—modesty, Mill insisted that the 'artist's is the highest part', while his own role was 'the humbler part'. His task, he generously informed Carlyle, was 'to supply a logical commentary' on his intuitive truths, and 'to make those who are not poets, understand that poetry is higher than Logic, and that the union of the two is Philosophy'.[48] A true mysticism was a mysticism that could be translated into logic, he averred, and Mill would provide this service for the prophet. Part of his mission was to bear witness to the fact that there are more things in heaven and earth than were dreamt of in his father's philosophy: 'I believe if I have done any good a large share of it lies in the example of a professed logician & political economist who believes there are other things besides logic & political economy.'[49] Nocturnal creatures have their own insights and knowledge of the world: it takes both the sun by day and the moon by night to make the whole.

Wordsworth. Maurice. Sterling. Coleridge. Gustave d'Eichthal and the Saint-Simonians. Comte. Carlyle. The scholar Nicholas Capaldi has helpfully emphasized the degree to which Mill was permanently transformed into a Romantic at this stage in his life, a change that Mill himself somewhat obscured, Capaldi argues, out of a disinclination to make the break with his father's way of seeing things appear to be as decisive as it actually was.[50] Nevertheless, it is also true (as Capaldi would agree) that Mill pulled back from the extremes of this reactionary phase. Mill pointedly chose not to reprint his mystically tinged, Saint-Simonian-inspired 'Spirit of the Age' articles when he gathered his essays together. Likewise, by 1840 he was embarrassed by his essay on 'Genius' which had been published in 1832 in W. J. Fox's *Monthly Repository*: 'It was written in the height of my Carlylism', he apologetically explained.[51] Instead of merely switching sides, Mill came to champion the conviction that both sides were standing for valuable, but partial, truths. This was behind his surprisingly positive comments on Puseyism, a movement which even many orthodox Christians regarded as a pernicious force. Mill, however, saw the Tractarians not as an irrational, retrograde force *against* progress but as a thoughtful, current force *for* permanence, the other essential half of the whole. He predicted that in ten years' time a middle way would have been found between the two extremes of Oxford's Anglo-Catholicism, on the one hand, and Germany's irreligious rationalism, on the other.[52] 'Halfness is the great enemy of spiritual worth', was his new creed.[53]

Mill's resonant articulation of this philosophy of wholeness was his essays on 'Bentham' (1838) and 'Coleridge' (1840). The Romantic critique of Bentham was valid, Mill argued, but only to the extent that it was limited to what Bentham failed to see and understand. To become a thoroughgoing disciple of Coleridge instead would be thereby to let go of the 'half the truth' that Bentham understood and Coleridge, in his turn, lacked. Our task is to combine 'the points of view of all the fractional truths'.[54] In the Coleridge article this plea swelled into a manifesto: 'Whoever can master the premises and combine the methods of both, would possess the entire English philosophy of their age.'[55] Mill was not defecting after all. Rather, he was seeking the blessedness of the peacemaker: 'We hold that these two sorts of men, who seem to be, and believe themselves to be, enemies, are in reality allies.'[56] Mill had served as a vital intermediary between his father and his siblings on the domestic front and thus he had in some sense been trained in his private life for this new role he was seeking to take on in the public sphere. And like his father before him in James Mill's own passionate article in the *London Review*, John Mill's deep yearning to see this reconciliation achieved crescendoes into prayer: '"Lord, enlighten thou our enemies," should be the prayer of every true Reformer.'[57] He told Sterling that it felt like this message of reconciliation and wholeness was the Gospel that he was now called to proclaim: 'I sometimes think that if there is anything which I am under a special obligation to preach, it is the meaning & necessity of a catholic spirit in philosophy.'[58]

Hereafter, Mill would often be looking for a *via media* between seemingly incompatible opposing views. He longed, for instance, to find a course to steer between the Scylla of the doctrine of Necessity and the Charybdis of Free Will. He wanted to be a fox, not a hedgehog—let alone a porcupine:

> Whether men adhere to old opinions or adopt new ones, they have in general an invincible propensity to split the truth, and take half, or less than half of it; and a habit of erecting their quills and bristling up like a porcupine against any one who brings them the other half, as if he were attempting to deprive them of the portion which they have.[59]

One-sidedness was the chief vice; there was a lush plentitude of many-sidedness to inhabit. One did not need to choose between Bentham and Coleridge, between James Mill and Auguste Comte, between Ricardo and Carlyle, between Wordsworth and Shelley, and on and on across the philosophical, political, religious, and literary landscapes. Mill would contain multitudes.

Mill's disciples later in life such as Alexander Bain and John Morley found his open and sympathetic comments on the questions of God and Jesus Christ in his posthumously published essay, 'Theism', to be a surprising (and unwelcome) departure from the position of unequivocal religious scepticism which they assumed he had hitherto occupied. It is closer to the truth, however, to observe that Mill held key components of those more open views consistently throughout his adult life. What changed was that he had finally decided to articulate those views for publication. Mill had expressed them, however—especially to more religiously minded correspondents—across the decades of his adult life. As figures such as Bain were settled unbelievers, they were never the recipients of Mill's theistic musings.

In January 1834, Mill laid out his views on religion to Carlyle fully and frankly. He recognized that many people believed that they apprehended God intuitively, mystically, spiritually, or experientially—that many others had a devotional sense which served as an overflowing fount of confidence when it came to their belief in God. Mill lacked this: 'there is wanting something positive in me, which exists in others'.[60] One possibility, therefore, was that Mill had the spiritual equivalent to being tone deaf or colour blind. In his *Autobiography*, he conceded that it was possible that Carlyle not only could make a poetic breakthrough which it would take Mill a long time before he could doggedly work it out in logic, 'but that it was highly probable he could see many things which were not visible to me even after they were pointed out'.[61] And Mill confessed at the time to the Sage of Chelsea: 'many things which I once thought I understood—I now believe cannot be known with true Insight but by means of faculties which cannot be acquired and which to me have not been given, save in most scanty measure'.[62] The alternative theory, however, was that religious people had been socialized to have these feelings and experiences and therefore they did not have a genuine sense akin to sight or hearing which was actually apprehending a spiritual reality, but they were merely exhibiting 'an acquired association'. Mill did not know any way to adjudicate which of those two possibilities—an authentic perception of the existence of God or merely a cultivated, imitation one—was correct. This was an impasse. All he knew was that the existence of God did not come to him as a matter of faith, or intuition, or experience, or apprehension. Therefore, Mill was left to see to what degree he could obtain a belief in God that was derived purely from argument, reason, logic, and proof. When he undertook this task the result was that the existence of God was probable but not proven: he must make his way in life the best he could with 'a merely probable God'.[63] This is precisely what he taught in 'Theism' and he reiterated this position several times with various correspondents across the decades. Harry Settanni has convincingly demonstrated that Mill's religious stance should not be thought of as blank scepticism, let alone atheism, but rather 'probabilist Theism'.[64]

Mill's position was therefore a far cry from militant, self-satisfied, or sneering unbelief. Quite to the contrary, Mill longed to be a true religious believer. He wrote wistfully to Carlyle: 'As this is my condition in spite of the strongest wish to believe, I fear it is hopeless; the unspeakable good it would be to me to have a *faith* like yours, I mean as firm as yours...'[65] Moreover, Mill was attracted to the Christian faith in particular. Even Carlyle was surprised to learn that Mill was reading deeply and sympathetically in the New Testament, specifically, the Gospels. Mill replied that this disposition towards the founder of Christianity was not a new development; that 'for years' now he had had 'the same unbounded reverence' for Jesus Christ. Mill's own ideal was the imitation of Christ; he was seeking for the example of Jesus to become 'a living principle in my character'.[66] The praise for Christ in 'Theism' that so startled a generation later was already a part of Mill's thinking in the early 1830s. And he reiterated these affirmations at various times across his life. For instance, Mill made both points in 1861. As to his probabilist theism, he observed that the belief that 'the world was made, in whole or in part, by a powerful Being who cared for man, appears to me, though not proved, yet a very probable hypothesis'. And as to the second, he spoke of how 'I myself very strongly participate' in 'reverence for Christ'.[67]

Mill later admitted candidly that he had hidden from his father how much he was departing from the Benthamite party line in which he had been raised. He also frankly acknowledged that his father's death on 23 June 1836 was a release which freed him to pursue his more catholic approach openly. In the following year, he became the proprietor of the *London and Westminster Review*. Mill's vision for this journal was that it would still be radical in orientation, but no longer sectarian. He would leaven it with voices such as those of Carlyle and Sterling. He would make 'the public see that the review has ceased to be Benthamite'.[68] Mill's 'Bentham' article in 1838 was intended to be a declaration of independence, and his old cohort felt it as such. In 1840, Caroline Fox recorded a visit from John Bowring:

> He spoke of Mill with evident contempt as a renegade from philosophy, Anglicé—a renouncer of Bentham's creed and an expounder of Coleridge's. S. T. Coleridge's mysticism Dr. Bowring never could understand, and characterises much of his teaching as a great flow of empty eloquence, to which no meaning was attachable. Mill's newly-developed

> 'Imagination' puzzles him not a little; he was most emphatically a philosopher, but then he read Wordsworth and that muddled him, and he has been in a strange confusion ever since, endeavouring to unite poetry and philosophy.[69]

Mill was pouring a vast amount of his personal savings into keeping the *London and Westminster Review* afloat. Bain estimates that Mill might have expended £2,000 of his own money. This could not go on for long, but the philosopher was determined to keep the review alive until he could get his 'Coleridge' essay in print in 1840. By then, he not only was no longer a sectarian Benthamite, but he had also lost faith in the Radical party in politics. Mill had done his best to give it life, but 'there was no making those dry bones live' (Ezekiel 37).[70] When he shed his sectarianism in 1829, Mill confided to Sterling that the price of his freedom was isolation and loneliness: 'There is now no human being (with whom I can associate on terms of equality) who acknowledges a common object with me.'[71] Despite generous and heroic efforts at fraternity, this difficulty had not been satisfactorily overcome. The peacemaker is out in the middle, on his own. Recurringly, Mill reflected that there was no existing audience of likeminded thinkers to receive his ideas, that he must send them out into the unknown. He consoled himself with a biblical promise: 'cast ye your bread on the waters, & ye shall find it after many days' (Ecclesiastes 11:1).[72] Moreover, as events would prove, he did not really need a new sect, or a new party, or a new cohort. It would be more than sufficient to just have one true Poet by his side.

Notes

1. John Stuart Mill, *Autobiography and Literary Essays* (Collected Works of John Stuart Mill I), ed. J. M. Robson, Indianapolis: Liberty Fund, 2006 (reprint of Toronto: University of Toronto Press, 1981), p. 161.
2. Francis E. Mineka and Dwight N. Lindley (eds), *The Later Letters of John Stuart Mill, 1849–1873* (Collected Works of John Stuart Mill XV), Toronto: University of Toronto Press, 1972, p. 615.
3. CWJSM XIV (*Later Letters*), p. 133.
4. CWJSM XVII (*Later Letters*), p. 1997.
5. CWJSM I (*Autobiography and Literary Essays*), p. 161.
6. CWJSM XIII (*Earlier Letters*), p. 480.

7. John Stuart Mill to John Sterling, 16 August 1844: CWJSM XIII (*Earlier Letters*), p. 635.
8. CWJSM XII (*Earlier Letters*), p. 225.
9. Julius Charles Hare (ed.), *Essays and Tales by John Sterling, With a Memoir of His Life*, 2 vols, London: John W. Parker, 1848, I, p. ccxviii.
10. R. L. Brett (ed.), *Barclay Fox's Journal*, Fowey: Cornwall Editions, 2008, p. 178. (Entry for 8 February 1840.) (The Mrs Mill was John's mother, Harriet Mill.)
11. John Stuart Mill to William Tait, 17 August 1842: CWJSM XIII (*Earlier Letters*), p. 541.
12. See, for instance, *Gentleman's Magazine*, October 1844, p. 438.
13. Oscar A. Haac (translator and editor), *The Correspondence of John Stuart Mill and Auguste Comte*, New Brunswick, NJ: Transaction Publishers, 1995, pp. 257–8.
14. John Stuart Mill to John Sterling, 15 April 1829: CWJSM XII (*Earlier Letters*), p. 29.
15. John Stuart Mill to William Bridges Adams, 20 October 1832: CWJSM XII (*Earlier Letters*), p. 123.
16. CWJSM XII (*Earlier Letters*), p. 221.
17. John Stuart Mill to John Sterling, 20–2 October 1831: CWJSM XII (*Earlier Letters*), p. 81.
18. CWJSM XIII (*Earlier Letters*), pp. 370–1.
19. CWJSM XII (*Earlier Letters*), p. 205.
20. CWJSM I (*Autobiography and Literary Essays*), p. 171.
21. John Stuart Mill, *Newspaper Writings (August 1831–October 1834)*, ed. Ann P. Robson and John M. Robson (Collected Works of John Stuart Mill XXIII), Toronto: University of Toronto Press, 1986, pp. 442, 675.
22. John Stuart Mill to Gustave d'Eichthal, 8 October 1829: CWJSM XII (*Earlier Letters*), p. 38.
23. John Stuart Mill to Gustave d'Eichthal, 9 February 1830: CWJSM XII (*Earlier Letters*), p. 46.
24. John Stuart Mill to Gustave d'Eichthal, 30 November 1831: CWJSM XII (*Earlier Letters*), p. 88.
25. John Stuart Mill to Thomas Carlyle, 27 December 1832: CWJSM XII (*Earlier Letters*), p. 134.
26. CWJSM XXIII (*Newspaper Writings*), p. 443. (John Stuart Mill, 'Comparison of the Tendencies of French and English Intellectuals', *Monthly Repository*, November 1833.)
27. CWJSM XII (*Earlier Letters*), p. 109.
28. CWJSM XXV (*Newspaper Writings*), p. 1257. (It appeared in the *Morning Chronicle*, 27 April 1832.)

29. CWJSM XIII (*Earlier Letters*), p. 409.
30. CWJSM XIII (*Earlier Letters*), p. 579.
31. Harriet Martineau (trans. and ed.), *The Positive Philosophy of Auguste Comte*, 3 vols, London: George Bell & Sons, 1896, I, pp. 1–2.
32. John Stuart Mill, *A System of Logic, Ratiocinative and Inductive, being a connected view of principles of evidence and the methods of scientific investigation*, ed. J. M. Robson (Collected Works of John Stuart Mill VIII), Toronto: University of Toronto, 1974, p. 928.
33. CWJSM XXIV (*Newspaper Writings*), pp. 811–22. (These articles appeared in the *Morning Chronicle* in January 1842.)
34. Haac, *Mill and Comte*, pp. 105, 171, 359.
35. CWJSM XXII (*Newspaper Writings*), p. 230.
36. CWJSM I (*Autobiography and Literary Essays*), p. 181.
37. CWJSM XXII (*Newspaper Writings*), p. 230.
38. Thomas Carlyle, *Sartor Resartus*, London: Chapman & Hall, n.d. (originally serialized in 1833–4), pp. 46, 112, 115.
39. Accessed at www.oed.com
40. John Stuart Mill, *Principles of Political Economy with some of their applications to social philosophy* (Collected Works of John Stuart Mill II), ed. J. M. Robson, Indianapolis: Liberty Fund, 2006 (reprint of Toronto: University of Toronto Press, 1965), p. lxxi (from the 'Textual Introduction' by J. M. Robson).
41. John Stuart Mill to Thomas Carlyle, 5 September 1833: CWJSM XII (*Earlier Letters*), p. 176.
42. CWJSM I (*Autobiography and Literary Essays*), p. 183.
43. CWJSM XII (*Earlier Letters*), p. 85.
44. Haac, *Mill and Comte*, p. 109.
45. CWJSM XVII (*Later Letters*), p. 1657.
46. CWJSM I (*Autobiography and Literary Essays*), p. 183.
47. CWJSM XII (*Earlier Letters*), pp. 78–9.
48. John Stuart Mill to Thomas Carlyle, 5 July 1833: CWJSM XII (*Earlier Letters*), pp. 162–3.
49. John Stuart Mill to Barclay Fox, 23 December 1840: CWJSM XIII (*Earlier Letters*), p. 453.
50. Nicholas Capaldi, *John Stuart Mill: A Biography*, Cambridge: Cambridge University Press, 2004.
51. CWJSM XIII (*Earlier Letters*), p. 449. (Admittedly, he is saying here that he regrets its Carlylean style, but the earlier quotation on Carlyle being a phase that he outgrew makes the broader point clear.)
52. CWJSM XIII (*Earlier Letters*), p. 497.
53. CWJSM XII (*Earlier Letters*), p. 171.

54. John Stuart Mill, *Essays on Ethics, Religion and Society* (Collected Works of John Stuart Mill X), ed. J. M. Robson, Indianapolis: Liberty Fund, 2006 (reprint of Toronto: University of Toronto Press, 1969), pp. 93–4.
55. CWJSM X (*Essays on Ethics, Religion and Society*), p. 121.
56. CWJSM X (*Essays on Ethics, Religion and Society*), p. 146.
57. CWJSM X (*Essays on Ethics, Religion and Society*), p. 163.
58. John Stuart Mill to John Sterling, 4 November 1839: CWJSM XIII (*Earlier Letters*), p. 411.
59. CWJSM XXII (*Newspaper Writings*), p. 234.
60. John Stuart Mill to Thomas Carlyle, 12 January 1834: CWJSM XII (*Earlier Letters*), p. 206.
61. CWJSM I (*Autobiography and Literary Essays*), p. 183.
62. John Stuart Mill to Thomas Carlyle, 18 May 1833: CWJSM XII (*Earlier Letters*), pp. 154–5.
63. CWJSM XII (*Earlier Letters*), p. 206.
64. Harry Settanni, *The Probabilist Theism of John Stuart Mill*, New York: Peter Lang, 1991.
65. CWJSM XII (*Earlier Letters*), p. 206.
66. CWJSM XII (*Earlier Letters*), pp. 208–9.
67. John Stuart Mill to Arthur W. Greene, 16 December 1861: CWJSM XV (*Later Letters*), p. 754.
68. CWJSM XII (*Earlier Letters*), p. 382.
69. Horace N. Pym (ed.), *Memories of Old Friends: being extracts from the Journals and Letters of Caroline Fox of Penjerrick, Cornwall*, London: Smith, Elder, and Co., 1882, p. 113.
70. John Stuart Mill to Barclay Fox, 16 April 1840: CWJSM XIII (*Earlier Letters*), p. 426.
71. John Stuart Mill to John Sterling, 15 April 1829: CWJSM XIII (*Earlier Letters*), p. 30.
72. John Stuart Mill to Gustave d'Eichthal, 14 September 1839: CWJSM XIII (*Earlier Letters*), p. 404. (Also, John Stuart Mill to Barclay Fox, 6 May 1841, p. 474.)

6
Many Waters Cannot Quench Love

> 'Many waters cannot quench love, neither can the floods drown it.'
>
> (Song of Solomon 8:7)

John Taylor was a prosperous wholesale druggist. Living and working in London, he was also a radical who was active in reforming and philanthropic causes. Taylor was a founding member of the Reform Club (where a fellow member was John Stuart Mill). He was on the board of directors of the Society for the Diffusion of Useful Knowledge (as was James Mill). In March 1826, John Taylor married Harriet Hardy. Both families were Unitarians. John and Harriet Taylor set up house in Finsbury, just a short distance away from the Reverend W. J. Fox's South Place (Unitarian) Chapel, where they both were members. Taylor was very active in the life of the chapel. He became a leading member of the congregation's council and appears to have acted as the chapel's treasurer. He gained some visibility in the Unitarian body more widely, including being a main speaker at an annual meeting of the denomination, the British and Foreign Unitarian Association. Harriet's parents also made South Place Chapel their spiritual home, and her social circle consisted of this Unitarian fraternity, especially figures that gathered around Fox and an official journal of the denomination that he edited, the *Monthly Repository*.

Given subsequent events, people have looked for clues that this marriage might not have been built on a solid enough foundation. Taylor was eleven years older than Harriet, and she was only eighteen when they married. Harriet's father had been having financial troubles, and Taylor was well off. Those facts combined have caused some speculation that perhaps Harriet was not in love with him but felt driven by practical realities into the match. If that were true, however, all the evidence nevertheless indicates that she did come to love him. She wrote to him, for instance, a couple years after their marriage, when she and their young son had gone ahead of him for some days for their summer seaside holiday: 'I knew that my dear husband loves me, as I have loved him, with my whole heart... Oh my dear John... I think from my present feelings that I shall never again consent to our parting.'[1] Still, Harriet was a person of tremendous intellectual vitality, and she became dissatisfied with the level of mental culture on offer in her life and marriage. Harriet Grote's unsympathetic summary of what became Harriet Taylor's attitude towards her husband was that 'she was tired of him & cared for clever people'.[2] In a critique she wrote of the institution of marriage, Harriet condemned a system in which a woman promises 'to honour a being, mentally & morally her inferior—to obey a lesser intellect'.[3] Harriet was a co-author or executive editor of Mill's *Autobiography* with full veto power over every word, and how they explained the situation in it was to observe that her first husband was 'without the intellectual or artistic tastes which would have made him a companion for her'.[4] Harriet confided her frustrations to her pastor, W. J. Fox, and the minister's solution was to introduce her to a brilliant and intellectually occupied man who was only a year older than her, John Stuart Mill.

In 1830 a dinner party was arranged at the Taylor's home. Those present were John Taylor, Harriet Taylor, W. J. Fox, John Stuart Mill, John Roebuck, George John Graham, and Harriet Martineau.[5] As if to prove he was not quite up to grade, John Taylor is the only person besides Graham in that list who would not warrant an entry in the *Oxford Dictionary of National Biography*. Fox must have been able to visualize the affinity because Mill and Harriet were immediately attracted to each other. Mill would soon become a new and disruptive force in this family. The Taylors' firstborn, Herbert, was born in 1827. Their second child was also a son, Algernon, born in 1830 (the year Mill and Harriet met). Finally, a girl, Helen, followed in 1831. Mill was a twenty-four year old bachelor at the time of the dinner party that would change the shape of the rest of his life. He had pursued other women, but without much success. The best known of these adventures was his unreciprocated infatuation for Lady Harriet

Baring, the wife of the Member of Parliament, Bingham Baring (who later became Baron Ashburton). As others have noticed, it seems psychologically significant that Mill was interested in married women with the same name as his mother. Like some kind of Shakespearean comedy, the doubling of names keeps recurring in this story. W. J. Fox fell in love three times over the course of his life, all with women named Eliza. The last two—his wife and the woman he left his wife for—even had eerily similar last names: Eliza Florance and Eliza Flower.[6] And Harriet Taylor herself ended up with two men named John sharing her affection.

Mill and Harriet were soon giving themselves over to an ever-deepening emotional affair. Much was at stake for everyone concerned. They destroyed most of their correspondence, so we only get glimpses of the early years of this relationship. She sent him a packet of minerals as a token of her ardour. They arranged assignations at the London Zoo. Both intellectuals, the question naturally arose: What were they thinking? It was vital to find out. Probably in 1832, Harriet set Mill the task of writing a treatise exclusively for her, expounding his convictions on the questions of marriage and divorce. She, in turn, would simultaneously do the same for him, and they would then swap manuscripts. This was a delicate assignment for Mill. He was passionately consumed by this relationship with Harriet, yet it would be easy for him to offend, alienate, or otherwise mis-step in such an essay. He opened his treatise with an unequivocal declaration of his commitment to her: 'She to whom my life is devoted.'[7] He then astutely insisted that he anticipated being guided by her wisdom and therefore his ideas would no doubt be modified once he had been taught better by reading her essay, capping that sentiment with a biblical proof text: 'it is not good for man to be alone' (Genesis 2:18). This was a rather daring appropriation of a verse about marriage to their own relationship rather than to her relationship with her lawfully wedded husband.

Mill then argued that there might be rules about marriage which would be generally useful for guiding ordinary people towards what is best for all, but that 'higher natures' are a law unto themselves: 'If all resembled you, my lovely friend, it would be idle to prescribe rules for them. By following their own impulses under the guidance of their own judgment, they would find more happiness, and would confer more, than by obeying any moral principles or maxims whatever.'

Once again, Mill rounded this argument off by drawing in warrant from scripture: 'to the pure all things are pure' (Titus 1:15). Marriage laws are designed to constrict base creatures who are just pursuing sexual gratification, he observed. At this point, what he had learned from Comte came in handy, and Mill floats the possibility that traditional marriage laws were a force for good within their own stage of human development: 'There can, I think, be no doubt that for a long time the indissolubility of marriage acted powerfully to elevate the social position of women.' He then returns to the argument that there is the question of what is best for ordinary men and women and then there is the separate question of what is best for more elevated ones. Mill then more-or-less suggests that Harriet is so above average as to not be satisfied in a home that would make a more common woman happy. The way forward on the whole question must be based on the equality of the sexes: 'Determine whether marriage is to be a relation between two equal beings, or between a superior and an inferior, between a protector and a dependant; and all other doubts will easily be resolved.' Mill testifies to his own belief that women are not naturally inferior to men. Nevertheless, his thinking was still somewhat stereotypical: 'The great occupation of woman should be to *beautify* life.' He cautions that it would be unwise to create a situation in which a person lived through multiple failed marriages because this would undermine the 'sacredness' of the institution. Next he concedes that all of these questions become much more difficult once the union has produced a child. Such an outcome, he avers, should only be the result of the 'holiest' of affectionate partnerships. He lists reasons in which it would be right to dissolve a marriage, conveniently including explicitly Harriet's own precise situation: 'or in the case of a strong passion conceived by one of them for a third person'.

Harriet's treatise opened with the thought experiment of what she would do if she was God: 'If I could be Providence . . .' She argued that almost all men save for 'a few lofty minded' (that is, present company excepted) are motivated by a base desire for sexual intercourse whereas women, on the contrary, 'are quite exempt from this trait'. Women are raised with the one end of their becoming a wife in view, yet this is not a likely road to fulfilment: 'One observes very few marriages where there is any real sympathy or enjoyment of companionship between the parties.' Harriet too was thinking stadially—or at least progressively—and envisioned an enlightened future in which 'no one would marry'. She thought that the best plan would be no-fault divorce being freely available, but to put a check on remarriage: 'not *less* time than two years should elapse between suing for divorce and permission to contract again'. She also advocated for full gender equality. If women had equal rights and opportunities, then it would be their own responsibility to take care of any children the marriage had produced in the case of a divorce. As a kind of mirror image of Mill's treatise, Harriet's ends with a tribute to him, declaring her philosopher-friend to be the one person most worthy to be the 'apostle' of the loftiest virtue. There are also some loose scraps of paper upon which Harriet wrote more thoughts on this subject. One of these argues that it should not be assumed that the institution of marriage is currently working, quoting as a proof text for this claim 1 Thessalonians 5:21: 'Prove all things; hold fast that which is good.'[8]

Meanwhile, John Taylor declared that he wished for his wife to break off her relationship with Mill completely and cease and desist all communication with him. Though Mill had his anxieties about what the consequences would be in regard to his ambitions to become a well-respected, leading intellectual, the philosopher was ready to defy the world and live with Harriet. They flirted with the possibility of making a life for themselves together somewhere far, far away from the meddling crowd. In November 1833, Harriet went to Paris to make up her mind. Her close friends W. J. Fox and Eliza Flower were fully informed regarding this affair of the heart. Harriet wrote to them in the midst of her Parisian turmoil, piously musing that the relational muddle she and Mill were in might be providential: perhaps 'God had willed to show the type of the possible elevation of humanity'. She had a keen desire to keep up with the life of her congregation at South Place Chapel while she was away and begged them to take the time to write, however briefly, regarding 'what the next sermon is'.[9] (The volume of Fox's sermons published that year was titled, *Christian Morality: Sermons on the Principles of Morality inculcated in the Holy Scriptures.*)[10] That she would not concede to her husband's request was made readily apparent by the fact that Harriet invited Mill to join her in France. She would not give up meeting with Mill in person, let alone corresponding with him, that much was resolved promptly.

Moreover, Harriet had decided that they really were enduringly compatible and so she and Mill could live together for the rest of their lives harmoniously. Yet she also had unwavering affection for her husband and was not willing to reject him. A few years later Harriet explained her decision not to opt for an open and decisive break from John Taylor using the Utilitarian principle of the greatest happiness for the greatest number: 'I should spoil four lives & injure others.'[11] The compromise Harriet carved out was that she would not formally separate from her husband and she would continue, to a certain extent, to be a companion for him in life, though their sexual relationship was permanently over. As to the other man, she would continue to interact with Mill regularly, seeing him at least once a week in person, but this relationship too would not be a physical one. The evidence that this really was what happened is strong. Not only did Harriet and Mill assert it explicitly (as it were), they even trumpeted their relationship in the *Autobiography* as an inspiring tale which proved that chastity is possible. A man need not be 'a slave of his animal appetites'; they had decisively demonstrated that such 'impulses' could be set aside 'in regard for the feelings of others'. To conclude that they were brazenly lying about this would mean that one would also have to believe that they wrote private letters to each other referring to their twenty years of celibacy solely in order to mislead people who might read them after they were dead. The shocking truth is this: their relationship while John Taylor was still alive and before Mill became Harriet's second husband was 'entirely apart from sensuality'.[12]

Some find a romantic relationship that is chaste so improbable that they cannot help but be suspicious about such a claim. Others concede that it is what really happened, but lament such an unnatural way of life. The leading authority on Harriet Taylor Mill, the philosopher Jo Ellen Jacobs, confessed that Harriet's celibate life 'makes me sad'.[13] Multiple comments Harriet made over the years all indicate that she did not enjoy sexual intercourse. In her treatise on marriage and divorce, she asserted that men have 'all the pleasures such as there are' in the act, while for women sex is disagreeable. On another occasion, again writing as if declaring a universal truth, Harriet wrote that a woman entered marriage innocent of the facts of life and, when she did have sex, she discovered it to be an 'experience she abhorred'.[14] In other words, an arrangement where she was not having sex with either man in her life might have seemed a welcome and fortuitous one to Harriet. Mill, in his turn—as was repeatedly being observed already during the Victorian age—gave numerous clues across his life that his physical appetites were not very strong. He lived in his mind, not his body. It is highly likely that he took personal pride in having more self-control over his animal nature than his father had demonstrated and in exemplifying Malthusian values so admirably. Mill would set a good example for the lower orders. His gift to posterity would be not to have posterity.

And however unnatural or improbable it might strike people in the twenty-first century, Mill's relationship with Harriet was hardly unique in their time and milieu. Indeed, their closest friends as a couple, W. J. Fox and Eliza Flower, were living parallel lives. Fox did make the decision to leave his wife and set up house with Flower, but they nevertheless pursued a life of celibate cohabitation until death parted them fourteen years later.[15] Mill would later fail to be re-elected as a Member of Parliament partially because he donated money to the campaign of Charles Bradlaugh, Britain's leading atheist activist. Bradlaugh forged a similar relationship with Annie Besant, another prominent freethinking leader. Both Bradlaugh and Besant were separated from their spouses. They admitted that if they were both free, they would have married. Instead, they had a passionate but chaste relationship in which they did not live together but, like Mill and Harriet, saw each other frequently and went on holiday together.[16] One way that Mill defended his financial contribution to Bradlaugh's parliamentary candidacy was by pointedly observing that no accusations had been made against the atheist's 'moral character'.[17] The most striking parallel however is with Auguste Comte and Clotilde de Vaux. Comte worshipped her. Indeed, in his mind, she had a similar place—if not a larger one—in his own devotional life in his Religion of Humanity to that of the Virgin Mary in Roman Catholicism. In a letter to Mill, Comte described his relationship with Clotilde as a 'virtuous passion'.[18] As will be shown, like Comte with Clotilde, Mill also would venerate Harriet in a quasi-religious manner. Comte's principles prevented him from consummating his relationship with Clotilde. Indeed, passionate but chaste affairs seem to be everywhere one turns in Mill's world. His *Mütterlein*, Sarah Austin, had one with

Hermann von Pückler-Muskau. To the deep annoyance of his wife, Thomas Carlyle had an unconsummated but intense relationship with a woman from Mill's own past, Lady Harriet Baring. And even in the court of public opinion such relationships could be considered more admirable than blameworthy. Charles Dickens's *Hard Times* (1854) was an indictment of the kind of education Mill had received and the unfeeling, anti-sentiment attitude of men such as James Mill and Bentham. It also included a chaste but intense relationship between a married man, Stephen Blackpool, and a factory worker, Rachael. There is no doubt that Dickens intended readers to approve of this relationship and that, as a general rule, they did. Even for radicals and freethinkers during the Victorian age, long-term celibacy was not infrequently viewed as the best available way to live out the most passionate relationship in one's life.

Mill's entire education, training, and intellectual temperament were grounded in the need for precise definitions and classification. Bentham and his father both taught that failing to do this was how thinking went awry, and Mill heartily agreed. He recalled that his childhood studies 'had given me a strong relish for accurate classification'.[19] Mill's hobby was botany. It was satisfying to know that whatever one found in a forest or by the wayside had its own, proper name and could be arranged precisely in its Linnaean place. Reminding us today of *The Princess Bride*, Mill grumbled throughout his adult life that people were using the word 'inconceivable' wrongly. ('The use of the word inconceivable, being a complete perversion of it from its established meanings, I decline to recognise', he once fumed.)[20] An entry in Mill's diary was focused on pinning down the difference between an 'illusion' and a 'delusion'.[21] In *A System of Logic*, Mill taught that the first requisite of philosophical language is that 'every general name should have a meaning, steadily fixed, and precisely determined'.[22] Or, to start the other way around, to proceed logically one must use 'the operation of Naming'. In fact, creating a bit of unease that one might be going down the rabbit hole, Mill included an entire chapter in that tome in which he sought to define 'definition'.[23] The chapter, 'Of the Explanation of Laws of Nature', begins, of course, by defining 'explanation'.[24] Mill was concerned that people often used 'nomenclature' and 'terminology' as synonyms. He was delighted with his friend Alexander Bain's book on grammar: 'Nobody has so completely got to the bottom of Shall & Will.'[25] Harriet would sometimes fall in line with this habit. For example, writing to Mill in regard to her current condition: 'I mean by Happiness . . . a state of *satisfaction*, by satisfaction meaning . . .'[26] Yet, to his immense frustration, Mill found that the supreme relationship of his entire life could not be clearly defined, labelled, and classified. It therefore could not be referred to, and so it did not have a social existence. Celibacy is the love that dares not speak its name.

A System of Logic discussed the 'classes of nameable things', but his relationship with Harriet turned out to be in a class of unnameable things. Mill was repeatedly reduced to using vague circumlocutions: Harriet was 'a person to whom of all persons alive I am under the greatest obligations'; and their relationship was 'things as they are now'. The *Logic* taught: 'it is already obvious that whenever two things are said to be related, there is some fact, or series of facts, into which they both enter'.[27] But what was that fact or series of facts in this instance? Mill's default word for what he and Harriet were to each other became friendship. That was the term used in the *Autobiography* which included even in a chapter title the phrase: 'Commencement of the Most Valuable Friendship of My Life'. Mill's father directly accused him of being in love with another man's wife: 'He replied, he had no other feelings towards her, than he would have towards an equally able man.'[28] At the risk of labouring the all-too-obvious, such an anaemic explanation does not account for the possessive and proprietary language they used regarding each other—something one cannot imagine Mill doing with any male friend, however admirably capable. We have already seen that Mill wrote unequivocally that his entire life was devoted to her. As Harriet, however, had taken a vow to forsake all others for John Taylor these affirmations are particularly revealing when expressed by her. She would refer to Mill as 'my one sole interest & object' and 'my only & most precious'.[29] They both referred to each other as 'my own love'. Privately, they distinguished between the two paramount affectionate friendships with men in Harriet's life by qualifying that only her relationship with Mill included 'the stronger feeling' of 'passionate love'.[30] John Chapman, who was the editor of the *Westminster Review* at the time, heard Mill and Harriet's relationship described by onlookers as a 'violent friendship'.[31]

For the purpose of this volume, what is most interesting about Mill's relationship with Harriet Taylor is that it caused his sealed devotional sense dramatically and emphatically to burst forth and flow in torrents down this one tunnel of love. To begin in the shallow water, in his letters to Harriet, the philosopher habitually reached for religious language as the only words that could sufficiently express his heightened feelings: heaven, angel, blessed (all of these frequently recur and, indeed, they all can be found in the same paragraph). As if inspired by the extravagance of the pious language of the East, he could end a letter to her: 'With a thousand thousand blessings'.[32] And his praise for her was unstinting. Again, to begin at the shallow end, on one level he kept to the division of labour in a friendship of reciprocal superiority that he had constructed when Thomas Carlyle loomed so large in his life. Harriet was the Poet, the Artist, the intuitive Meaning-Maker, while he would play the humbler part of elucidating in argumentation and logic her insights. The whole point of this scheme was to explain why friends need each other, but Mill was sometimes uneasy with it in this one, supreme relationship because it tacitly implied that Harriet lacked something. So perhaps the scheme only worked one way. She certainly supplied what he lacked, but Harriet herself, as Mill enthused to her, was the ideal specimen, the archetype of 'Intellect—because you have all the faculties in equal perfection'.[33] As a widower, Mill was not ashamed to tell the French politician Louis Blanc: 'I do not speak from feeling but from long standing and sober conviction in saying that when she died this country lost the greatest mind it contained.'[34] Nor did Mill limit the pre-eminence of Harriet's intellect merely to the pool of those who were currently living. He told Harriet's son Algernon that his mother was: 'the profoundest thinker & most consummate reasoner I had ever known'.[35] This was a high compliment given whom Mill had known personally: Bentham, Coleridge, Wordsworth, Carlyle, and on and on. Mill was annoyed that he could not get the young man to consent to this sweeping claim: Algernon merely politely replied that he too was missing her while she was away. Harriet had a deep admiration for Shelley, whom she considered the greatest of modern poets, so Mill decided that Shelley, at least, was so high up as to serve as a point of reference for marking the vastness of the distance from all others occupied by his wife: 'in thought and intellect Shelley, so far as his powers were developed in his short life, was but a child to her. I have never known any intellect in man or woman which, taken for all in all, could be compared to her.'[36] We have not yet made it over to the deep end.

It is very common for sources on Mill to observe that he worshipped his wife. Mill's friend, the pastor of the Protestant church in Avignon, Louis Rey, observed that Harriet was 'his divinity'.[37] In the first collection of Mill's letters, published in 1910, the editor observed: 'The truth is, that he set her up as an idol and worshipped her.'[38] Leslie Stephen, in Mill's *Dictionary of National Biography* entry, likewise spoke of 'his idolatry of his wife'.[39] And so it goes on. To take a twenty-first century example, Richard Reeves refers to 'Mill's lifelong mission to deify Harriet'.[40] While the joy of revisionist history might make one long to try to overturn such a well-established assertion, the evidence that supports it would make that a Herculean task. For one, it was Mill's own analysis of the situation. Even for publication in his *Autobiography*, he wrote: 'Her memory is to me a religion.'[41] More empathetically, Mill wrote to his wife in March 1855, when he was away from her on a Continental tour: 'My darling will know that I am thinking all the time of her & that her existence & love are to me what the Deity is to a devout person.'[42]

One of the stranger expressions of this reverence was that Mill would often write to Harriet in the third person. This habit was prominent even when they were married so it was not the result of some kind of strategy of discretion in case their letters were intercepted. It runs across the decades, but one example will serve. Here is the first sentence of Mill's letter to his wife on 17 February 1857: 'What a pleasure it was to see her precious writing, but it was vexatious that she had such a bother the first day, how tired she must have been, no wonder her fingers were stiff.'[43] We have volumes of letters written by Mill to scores of different correspondents, but only with Harriet does he adopt this pious practice. Next, there was Mill's extreme submission to her judgement. He called her his 'philosopher', 'teacher', and 'guide'. Not only did he change his opinion whenever she expressed a differing one, but he himself boasted of this fact, claiming that he '*always*' came to 'think the same' as her.[44] That confession comes from a famous example in which he reversed a substantial argument at her prompting for a new edition of *Principles of Political Economy*. He observed: 'but that paragraph, p. 248, in the first edit, which you object to so strongly & totally, is what has always seemed to me the strongest part of the argument'. He is therefore waiting for further instructions: 'it is necessary to see whether the opinion has changed or not'. (Essentially he is asking in that statement: Did I change my mind without you informing me yet?) If you pity Mill for being in this submissive state, you are misunderstanding the situation. It was heavenly bliss. It is vital to grasp how delicious this experience was for Mill. Sterling had commended to Mill the theology of Friedrich Schleiermacher, the eminent German theologian, which Mill discussed with his friend. Schleiermacher famously defined religion as 'the feeling of absolute dependence'. Mill positively revelled in the feeling of being absolutely dependent upon Harriet. He habitually would not make the smallest decision in his personal life without appealing to her wisdom. Once again, a single instance will suffice to illustrate this chronic reality. In 1851, the state of South Carolina published a vanity volume of one of their favourite sons, John Caldwell Calhoun: *A Disquisition on Government; and, A Discourse on the Constitution of the United States*. Mill received one of the numerous complimentary copies that were sent to influential figures around the nation and beyond. It is hard to imagine how low-functioning someone who was a public name would have to be, not to know how to respond to such a gift: a short letter of thanks, ideally with some kind word about how interesting the topic of the book is, or how one hoped to find the time to read it, or how one had heard good things about the author, or the like. Mill, however, sends a whole series of letters to Harriet consulting her on the best way to reply. Eventually, he drafted a letter and she suggested a single word change, which he was delighted to believe made all the difference: 'Your "much" is a great improvement in the letter to the Americans. I thought it would have needed "much" more alteration. I will now send it.'[45] Keep in mind that Mill held a major leadership role in the colonial administration of the vast nation of India, a position equivalent to an Under-Secretary of State. He was fully capable of administrative efficiency, decisiveness, and executive action, but he craved the sensation of Harriet being his guide.

His devotional sense for her was so strong that his statements about her frequently are borrowed from traditional language for God. He could describe her in ways that an orthodox Christian would the Holy Spirit: 'the prompter of all my best thoughts, the guide of all my actions'.[46] Even for publication in the *Autobiography*, she is, like the breath of God in the third person of the Trinity, 'the inspirer of my best thoughts'.[47] Moreover, Mill extolled Harriet in ways that are often reminiscent of the devotional language for God in the Bible. He declared to her that she was the 'life of my life'.[48] ('The Lord is the strength of my life' Psalm 27:1.) His heart burst forth in praise to her: 'How truly you judge people, how true is what you always say.'[49] ('Lord God Almighty, true and righteous are thy judgments' Revelation 16:7; 'I know, O Lord, that thy judgments are right' Psalm 119:75—and many more such passages.) Most startling of all, he declares that Harriet is 'the only person living who is worthy to live'.[50] ('You alone, O Lord, are worthy!'—see Revelation 5.) It is hard to avoid the conclusion that when Mill reached for language with which to describe Harriet it was precisely the biblical or religious charge of words that made them seem fitting to express his convictions: 'One never repents of having followed your judgment.'[51] His reference to 'your blessed presence' perhaps succeeds at being even more pious than its biblical analogue.[52] ('In thy presence is fullness of joy' Psalm 16:11.)

Mill's honorific appellations for Harriet sometimes sounded like messianic titles. She is 'the most competent intellect'.[53] She is 'the blessed one' or the 'ever blessed one'. Or even the 'blessedest one'.[54] ('Blessedest' is sufficiently uncommon that it is not listed in the *Oxford English Dictionary*: one wonders if Mill was reaching for a construction that might carry the resonant freight of the Authorized Version of the Bible.) Mill was even determined to bestow upon Harriet those attributions which are often deemed to belong to God alone. He had a tendency to over-write his praise for her in ways that make the prose so tangled it is not easy to grasp, let alone excerpt. Let us make the attempt at a few of these instances before moving on to the crisp and unequivocal claims of the same ilk. Harriet was away from him on Valentine's Day 1854 and Mill's diary entry for that day refers to 'a soul and an intellectual like hers, such as the good principle perhaps never succeeded in creating before—one who seemed intended for an inhabitant of some remote heaven'.[55] Befitting her Unitarian background and their friends and connections from that denomination, this can be read as a kind of Arian Christology; she is the firstborn over all creation, the greatest of all the works of the Father. In January 1854, Mill wrote to his wife: 'This morning I watched the loveliest dawn & sunrise & felt that I was looking directly to where she is & that that sun came straight from her.'[56] Shades of thanking the deity for causing the sun to rise? Indeed, sometimes Mill's faith in Harriet could slide towards superstition: 'I feel as if no really dangerous illness could actually happen to me while I have her to care for me; and yet I feel as if by coming away from her I had parted with a kind of talisman, and was more open to the attacks of the enemy than while I was with her.'[57] The use of the spiritual warfare language associated with the work of the devil and demons—'attacks of the enemy'—is no less arresting than the talismanic fetishism. (And this surprising pronouncement from one of the most famous rationalists in British history was his very first effort in a New Year's resolution diary dedicated to recording 'one thought per day which is worth writing down'.) Or—hardest of all to associate with the well-known, public Mill—his faith could veer towards fanaticism: 'I am ready to kill myself for not being like her and worthy of her.'[58]

Mill's favourite adjective for Harriet was 'perfect'. For instance, he wrote to her in January 1854 (after they had been married for several years) and referred to 'your perfect judgment'.[59] He even toyed with the one attribute for a living being most reserved for God alone—infinite—as befitting Harriet. Mill would extol someone that he thought was unquestionably outstanding, before reverently adding that Harriet was incomparably greater. For example, he commended Sarah Austin to Comte as 'a truly superior woman', but then added the pious aside that Harriet surpasses her 'infinitely'.[60] This judgement too he was willing to put in print. After praising Carlyle in the *Autobiography*, Mill relativizes the sage's high worth by observing that Harriet's mind and nature included all that his did 'and infinitely more'.[61] Once again, Mill's whole training and special contribution to thought was marked by the central importance of using the correct word, making precise statements, and avoiding the vice (which his Utilitarian set particularly attributed to religious people) of making claims without being able to offer sufficient proof or warrant for them, of 'accepting insufficient evidence as sufficient'.[62] Yet what precisely does it mean to say that Harriet's mind contains 'infinitely more' than Carlyle's—and how would one go about substantiating such a proposition? What would count as sufficient evidence? Still, Mill is willing to make this assertion—not just as a flourish in a love letter—but as an assessment for publication. One final divine attribute: Mill also repeatedly credited Harriet with infallibility and inerrancy. Once again, he was willing to write this for publication in the *Autobiography*, observing that other geniuses he had met had proven themselves to be fallible, but in her he found truth without 'any mixture of error'.[63] More straightforwardly, he wrote that 'her intellect is supreme and her judgment infallible'.[64] In the same generation in which the First Vatican Council pronounced for papal infallibility, Mill was making the same declaration for Harriet.

What is one to make of all this? The most important thing to realize is that Mill was being utterly sincere in these statements. He really did believe that she had the greatest mind he had ever known. The thought really did strike him again and again in wonder and delight that her judgement was perfect, that she inspired all of his best thoughts, and so on. As with so much language arising from a devotional sense, it would be something of a category mistake to ask whether or not he meant these claims to be taken literally. If pressed by someone in this way, Mill no doubt would have immediately decided that they were being 'vulgar' (a frequent charge), and have sought to break off all relations with them (a frequent outcome when people took an approach to Harriet that he did not deem sufficiently honouring). The real point is this: if he ever had been, he was no longer completely tone deaf; he was no longer fully colour blind. He had heard something, and it was an exquisite sound. He had glimpsed something, and it was a captivating sight. He had a devotional sense. He had Harriet.

Notes

1. Harriet Taylor to John Taylor, 3 July [*c.*1828], Jo Ellen Jacobs (ed.), *The Complete Works of Harriet Taylor Mill*, Bloomington, IN: Indiana University Press, 1998, p. 440.
2. Bertrand Russell and Patricia Russell (eds), *The Amberley Papers: The Letters and Diaries of Lord and Lady Amberley*, 2 vols, London: Hogarth Press, 1937, I, p. 371.
3. Jacobs, *Complete Works*, p. 9.

4. John Stuart Mill, *Autobiography and Literary Essays* (Collected Works of John Stuart Mill I), ed. J. M. Robson, Indianapolis: Liberty Fund, 2006 (reprint of Toronto: University of Toronto Press, 1981), p. 193.
5. Sandra J. Peart (ed.), *Hayek on Mill: The Mill–Taylor Friendship and Related Writings* (The Collected Works of F. A. Hayek XVI), Chicago: University of Chicago Press, 2015, p. 36.
6. Richard Garnett with Edward Garnett, *The Life of W. J. Fox: Public Teacher and Social Reformer*, London: John Lane, 1909. (We are not told the surname of the first Eliza, who died young.)
7. Peart, *Hayek on Mill*, pp. 67–72 (both essays are printed here in full).
8. Jacobs, *Complete Works*, p. 19.
9. Jacobs, *Complete Works*, p. 328.
10. W. J. Fox, *Christian Morality: Sermons on the Principles of Morality inculcated in the Holy Scriptures*, Boston: Leonard C. Bowlers, 1833. This volume would give the reader a faithful indication of the nature of Fox's ministry at this time, but as the preface is dated July 1833 it cannot contain any of the sermons that Harriet missed while in Paris (though it might contain ones she heard earlier that year).
11. Jacobs, *Complete Works*, p. 332.
12. CWJSM I (*Autobiography and Literary Essays*), p. 236.
13. Jo Ellen Jacobs, *The Voice of Harriet Taylor Mill*, Bloomington, IN: University Press, 2002, p. xxvi.
14. Jacobs, *Complete Works*, p. 9.
15. People are naturally suspicious of this claim as well, yet there is also evidence and compelling arguments to support it, including in Mill's own private letters to Fox. See, also, Garnett, *W. J. Fox*.
16. Timothy Larsen, *A People of One Book: The Bible and the Victorians*, Oxford: Oxford University Press, 2011, p. 73; Hypatia Bradlaugh Bonner, *Charles Bradlaugh: His Life and Work*, 2 vols, London: T. Fisher Unwin, 1895.
17. Francis E. Mineka and Dwight N. Lindley (eds), *The Later Letters of John Stuart Mill, 1849–1873* (Collected Works of John Stuart Mill XVI), Toronto: University of Toronto Press, 1972, p. 1492.
18. Auguste Comte to John Stuart Mill, 6 May 1846: Oscar A. Haac (translator and editor), *The Correspondence of John Stuart Mill and Auguste Comte*, New Brunswick, NJ: Transaction Publishers, 1995. p. 369.
19. CWJSM I (*Autobiography and Literary Essays*), p. 69.
20. John Stuart Mill, *Essays on Ethics, Religion and Society* (Collected Works of John Stuart Mill X), ed. J. M. Robson, Indianapolis: Liberty Fund, 2006 (reprint of Toronto: University of Toronto Press, 1969), p. 76.
21. John M. Robson (ed.), *Journals and Debating Speeches* (Collected Works of John Stuart Mill XXVII), Toronto: University of Toronto Press, 1988, p. 642.

22. John Stuart Mill, *A System of Logic, Ratiocinative and Inductive, being a connected view of principles of evidence and the methods of scientific investigation* (Collected Works of John Stuart Mill VIII), ed. J. M. Robson, Indianapolis: Liberty Fund, 2006 (reprint of Toronto: University of Toronto Press, 1974), p. 668.
23. CWJSM VII (*A System of Logic*), pp. 132–54 (Book 1, chapter VIII: 'Of Definition').
24. CWJSM VII (*A System of Logic*), p. 464.
25. John Stuart Mill to Alexander Bain, 18 March 1864: CWJSM XV (*Later Letters*), p. 926.
26. Peart, *Hayek on Mill*, p. 86.
27. CWJSM VII (*A System of Logic*), p. 23.
28. Alexander Bain, *John Stuart Mill: A Criticism: with personal recollections*, London: Longmans, Green, and Co., 1882, p. 163.
29. Jacobs, *Complete Works*, pp. 32–3.
30. Francis E. Mineka (ed.), *The Earlier Letters of John Stuart Mill, 1812–1848* (Collected Works of John Stuart Mill XII), Toronto: University of Toronto Press, 1963, p. 187.
31. Peart, *Hayek on Mill*, p. 178.
32. CWJSM XIV (*Later Letters*), p. 154.
33. CWJSM XIV (*Later Letters*), pp. 42–3. (Mill used the word 'type'. I have deemed that the word archetype would better convey his meaning to readers today. If anyone should disagree, I trust this note has undone the damage.)
34. CWJSM XV (*Later Letters*), p. 601.
35. CWJSM XIV (*Later Letters*), p. 166.
36. CWJSM I (*Autobiography and Literary Essays*), p. 619.
37. Louis Rey, 'The Romance of John Stuart Mill', *Nineteenth Century*, Vol. LXXIV, No. 439 (September 1913), pp. 502–26.
38. Hugh S. R. Elliot (ed.), *The Letters of John Stuart Mill*, 2 vols, London: Longmans, Green, and Co., 1910, I, p. xxiv.
39. Leslie Stephen, 'Mill, John Stuart (1806–1873)', in *Dictionary of National Biography*, Vol. XIII, Sidney Lee (ed.), New York: Macmillan, 1909, pp. 390–9.
40. Richard Reeves, *John Stuart Mill: Victorian Firebrand*, London: Atlantic Books, 2007, pp. 206–7.
41. CWJSM I (*Autobiography and Literary Essays*), p. 251.
42. CWJSM XIV (*Later Letters*), p. 373.
43. CWJSM XV (*Later Letters*), p. 523.
44. CWJSM XIV (*Later Letters*), p. 9.
45. CWJSM XIV (*Later Letters*), pp. 175–6.
46. CWJSM XV (*Later Letters*), p. 574.

47. CWJSM I (*Autobiography and Literary Essays*), p. 264.
48. CWJSM XIV (*Later Letters*), p. 291.
49. CWJSM XIV (*Later Letters*), p. 175.
50. CWJSM XIV (*Later Letters*), p. 273.
51. CWJSM XIV (*Later Letters*), p. 156.
52. CWJSM XIV (*Later Letters*), p. 4.
53. John M. Robson (ed.), *Journals and Debating Speeches* (Collected Works of John Stuart Mill XXVII), Toronto: University of Toronto Press, 1988, p. 654.
54. CWJSM XIV (*Later Letters*), p. 290.
55. CWJSM XXVII (*Journals and Debating Speeches*), p. 654.
56. CWJSM XV (*Later Letters*), pp. 133–4.
57. CWJSM XXVII (*Journals and Debating Speeches*), p. 641.
58. CWJSM XXVII (*Journals and Debating Speeches*), p. 660.
59. CWJSM XIV (*Later Letters*), p. 126.
60. Haac, *Mill and Comte*, p. 221. (He does not mention Harriet by name, but it would be impossible for anyone who has studied Mill not to know what he means.)
61. CWJSM I (*Autobiography and Literary Essays*), p. 183.
62. CWJSM VII (*A System of Logic*), p. 197.
63. CWJSM I (*Autobiography and Literary Essays*), p. 253.
64. CWJSM I (*Autobiography and Literary Essays*), p. 620.

7
All This Have I Proved by Wisdom

'All this have I proved by wisdom.'

(Ecclesiastes 7:23)

His friend, disciple, and biographer, Alexander Bain, suspected that Mill's famed, precocious homeschooled education was less than it seemed. There was one area of study, however, in which Mill was truly a phenomenon, Bain conceded: 'doubtless his mind was cast for Logic from the first.... the one thing, in my judgment, where Mill was most markedly in advance of his years was, Logic.... he was able to chop Logic with his father in regard to the foundations and demonstrations of Geometry. I have never known a similar case of precocity.'[1] Mill himself sensed that this was his area of strength. He was a logician, not a poet. His contribution was to method, not meaning. He had learned that there was more to life than logic, but that was still where his aptitude lay. Carlyle had mischievously poked his philosopher friend by defining logic as 'the art of telling others what you believe'. In other words, the Scottish sage was dismissing it as simply a way of generating *ex post facto* rationalizations for things that one already thought and would continue to believe irrespective of whether or not a formal argument has told for or against it. Mill retorted crisply: 'I call it, the art, not certainly of knowing things, but of knowing whether you know them or not: not of finding out the truth, but of deciding whether it is the truth that you have found out.'[2] The real point, however, is that it is more a science than an art, and therefore John Stuart Mill had something to add to this subject in a way that Carlyle never could.

And there was room for a fresh effort. Mill had always been frustrated with the existing textbooks: logic was an important area of thought that had not yet been presented in a sufficiently satisfying way, he discerned. When Mill's student group of likeminded young men turned to the subject of logic in 1827, they were so 'disgusted' by the available textbook that they ended up having privately printed for their own use a work from two centuries earlier by the Jesuit Philippe Du Trieu, *Manuductio ad Logicam* (1662).[3] Also in 1827, Jeremy Bentham's nephew (and later his heir), George Bentham tried his hand: *Outline of a New System of Logic, with a critical examination of Dr Whatley's 'Elements of Logic'*. In the long run, this book has been hailed as the first to quantify the predicate, an achievement that was overlooked because the publisher promptly went bankrupt and most of the print run was destroyed, so George Bentham's effort remained little known. Mill was not impressed. He thought the clergyman (Whately would even be elevated to the Archbishopric of Dublin in a couple of years' time) had the better of the exchange: 'Mr George Bentham seems not to be aware, that Dr Whately is a far greater master of the science than *he* is . . . It would therefore have been wiser in him not to have assumed the tone of undisputed & indisputable superiority over Whately, which marks the greater part of his critique.'[4] Not that Mill thought that Richard Whately's *Elements of Logic* (1826) deserved to reign unchallenged either. There was work to be done. A couple years later, in 1830, Mill would take up the task himself in earnest. In a letter to Sterling in October 1830 in which he declared that his contribution was in the area of method and that his next task must be 'to complete my speculations on Logic' he also, in the same passage, derided 'Messrs. Drummond, M'Niel, Irving, & others, who possess the hidden key to the Interpretation of the Prophecies'.[5] Those named were apocalyptic, conservative Christian writers who were reading the Bible as predicting current or imminent events. Mill's point was that logic provided an open, transparent, rational method rather than a hermetic, mystical, irrational one. Yet, as he proceeded with the project, Mill hit problems that bedevilled him. He gnawed away at it for over a decade. The impetus he needed to bring his own work to fruition came in 1840 with the publication of the Reverend Dr William Whewell's *The Philosophy of the Inductive Sciences: from the earliest to the present time.* Now Mill had what he needed to energize him: a big, recent, important foil ('it gave me what I greatly desired, a full treatment of the subject by an antagonist').[6]

Throughout his life Mill was at war with a dominant philosophical school, the intuitionists (as he labelled them), who emphasized some ideas being known a priori, that is, that they are innate. The chief champion of this school in Britain that Mill would target was Sir William Hamilton, but behind him stood Immanuel Kant and the German Idealists. As would become clear later, Herbert Spencer—who otherwise would have been a natural ally for Mill—also advocated a version of the doctrine of innate ideas. Mill, on the other hand, stood for the belief that knowledge is derived from experience. This is a metaphysical question and so a textbook on logic is not the place where it could be addressed directly and decisively. Nevertheless, a main motivation for writing his *A System of Logic* for Mill was to have a current textbook on this subject available which stood for 'the opposite doctrine' from intuitionism.[7] In indirect service of that end, Mill argued for the primacy of induction. The major premise of a syllogism is itself a truth that has been derived from experience, which has been arrived at through induction: 'The true reason why we believe the Duke of Wellington will die, is that his fathers, and our fathers, and all other persons who were contemporary with them, have died.'[8] Mill was so keen to advance this view that he even took on its stronghold of mathematics, where a Platonic perspective was (and is) particularly apt to reign. Mill was not having it. Mathematical ideas too were derived from experience: 'All numbers must be numbers of something: there are no such things as numbers in the abstract.'[9] Thus the field was taken: 'From these considerations it would appear that Deductive or Demonstrative Sciences are all, without exception, Inductive Sciences.'[10] He was for a logic of induction and against an epistemology of intuition.

The first edition of Mill's *A System of Logic, Ratiocinative and Inductive, being a connected view of the principles of Evidence and the Methods of Scientific Investigation*, was published in 1843. It was a bulky tome: 1,204 pages in length (it would grow in subsequent editions, but the words-per-page were increased to keep the pagination down). It was divided into six books: Of Names and Propositions; Of Reasoning; Of Induction; Of Operations Subsidiary to Induction; On Fallacies; and On the Logic of the Moral Sciences. It is a technical text designed for the earnest, painstaking student of the subject matter. At the risk of alienating the reader, here is just one paragraph to help establish this point. It is from

Book III (Of Induction), chapter XXIII (Of Approximate Generalizations, and Probable Evidence):

> If, on the average, two of every three As are Bs, and three of every four Cs are Bs, the probability that something which is both an A and a C is a B, will be more than two in three, or than three in four. Of every twelve things which are As, all expect four are Bs by the supposition; and if the whole twelve, and consequently those four, have the characters of C likewise, three of these will be Bs on that ground. To state the argument in another way; a thing which is both an A and a C, but which is not a B, is found in only one of three sections of the class A, and in only one of the four sections of the class C; but this fourth of C being spread over the whole of A indiscriminately, only one-third part of it (or one-twelfth of the whole number) belongs to the third section of A; therefore a thing which is not a B occurs only once, among twelve things which are both As and Cs. The argument would in the language of the doctrine of chances, be thus expressed: the chance that an A is not a B is $1/3$, the chance that a C is not a B is $1/4$; hence if the thing be both an A and a C, the chance is $1/3$ of $1/4 = 1/12$.[11]

Despite Mill being her 'one sole interest & object', Harriet Taylor deemed *A System of Logic* to be 'so very dry a book'.[12] Mill promised his friend Caroline Fox a complimentary copy, but he told her that he would mark for her the most interesting sections as trying to work one's way through the whole thing would be far too tedious: 'It would be like my reading a book on mining because you live in Cornwall—it would be making Friendship a burden!'[13] The year before it was published Mill had confided to Gustave d'Eichthal that he felt that he must pursue this project even though 'I do not expect to find many readers for this book.'[14] And that was also the opinion of someone whose business it was to know: Mill first submitted the manuscript for publication to John Murray who, annoyingly sat on it for months, before getting cold feet and turning it down.

What one could never have predicted would be that inside this dry, technical, textbook on logic is the omnipresence, as it were, of God. This is not generally commented upon in discussions of Mill's *Logic*, yet it is certainly remarkable. It would seem quite natural, even likely, that one might write an entire book on logic, both ratiocinative and inductive, without ever mentioning the Deity. After all, there are even entire books of the Bible that never mention God. In *A System of Logic*, however, Mill uses the word 'God' close to fifty times! No telling how many times he refers to God with a pronoun, but he uses other nouns in order to discuss God around thirty additional times, giving us a grand total of about eighty direct, proper noun references. The other terms he uses include Jehovah, Father, Divine Intelligence, Holy Ghost, omnipotent Being, Divine Mind, Almighty, Deity, Infinite Being, Creator, Divine Nature, Maker, Ruler of the World, a divine mind, an all-governing Being, and supernatural being. 'Deity' appears at least a half a dozen times, and 'divine' more than twenty. In contrast to these eighty evocations of God, here are the counts for some other proper nouns: Plato is named twenty-five times; Aristotle, thirty-eight; Leibnitz, nineteen; Descartes, nineteen; Comte, twenty-seven; Locke, twenty-two; Hume, ten; Kant, four; Hamilton, thirty-four, and Whately, forty-one. (So much praise is heaped upon Whately throughout the book than one starts to wonder if the most logical mind that Mill had ever encountered was that of an archbishop.) Delightfully, Bentham and Coleridge are each mentioned eight times.

Some of these evocations of the divine are substantive discussions of theological questions. Mill is fighting the intuitionists in this volume and therefore it is natural that he would oppose belief in God as innate. He introduces the ontological argument, for example, in order to oppose it:

> The following is an argument of Descartes to prove, in his *á priori* manner, the being of a God. The conception, says he, of an infinite Being proves the real existence of such a being. For if there is not really any such being, *I* must have made the conception; but if I could make it, I can also unmake it; which evidently is not true; therefore there must be, externally to myself, an archetype, from which the conception was derived.[15]

The actual claim that knowledge of God is innate is once again a metaphysical one that is not within the proper purview of this book, but Mill reminds readers that it has been wielded by fanatics:

> it is hardly possible to mention any of the habitual judgments of mankind on subjects of a high degree of abstraction, from the being of a God and the immortality of the soul down to the multiplication table, which are not, or have not been, considered a matter of direct

> intuition. So strong is the tendency to ascribe an intuitive character to judgments which are mere inferences, and often false ones. No one can doubt that many a deluded visionary has actually believed that he was directly inspired from Heaven, and that the Almighty had conversed with him face to face; which yet was only, on his part, a conclusion drawn from appearances to his senses, or feelings in his internal consciousness, which afforded no warrant for any such belief. A caution, therefore, against this class of errors, is not only needful but indispensable; though to determine whether, on any of the great questions of metaphysics, such errors are actually committed, belongs not to this place, but as I have so often said, to a different science.[16]

And so, not being within his jurisdiction, intuitionist believers in God are let off with a warning.

Another major polemic is against what are now called god-of-the-gap theories. Whether or not God is the final cause is beyond the scope of what a textbook on logic can address, but Mill wanted his readers to think about how often the Deity has been brought in gratuitously to explain matters that should be understood to have more immediate causes. There is an origins-of-religion theory that he flirts with here. In the past, people explained matters such as thunder by evoking direct, divine action. As our knowledge has advanced, however, we know how to explain these matters naturalistically. Ergo, perhaps belief in God is in large part the product of a lack of understanding. At the very least, God recedes from more and more discussions: 'As the notion of fixed laws of succession among external phenomena gradually establishes itself, the propensity to refer all phenomena to voluntary agency slowly gives way before it.'[17] Those who rush to explain matters by evoking God make themselves ridiculous: 'The *deus ex machinâ* was ultimately called in to produce a spark on the occasion of a flint and steel coming together, or to break an egg on the occasion of its falling on the ground. All this, undoubtedly, shows that it is the disposition of mankind in general, not to be satisfied with knowing that one fact is invariably antecedent and another consequent, but to look out for something which may seem to be explaining their being so.'[18] In this discussion, therefore, God is being introduced in order to point out that God should not be introduced into so many discussions. Mill enthusiastically commends Comte's stadial scheme: the theological, then the metaphysical, culminating in the positivist. He concedes that Comte himself understood this to mean that theology has no place in our glorious, scientific age. Mill explicitly disagrees with the French thinker on this point. He argues instead that this stadial scheme only rules out the god-of-the-gaps; a theology based on a God who 'rules by universal laws' will still be valid in the positivist stage.[19]

Another substantive discussion is on miracles and Hume's critique of miracles. Here Mill argues that a belief in miracles is not a violation of the law of cause and effect that he has been advocating. A miracle is not an effect without a cause. It is a claim that another cause has been introduced into the situation, namely, the agency of God. As he would argue elsewhere, if God exists then a belief in miracles is not illogical. Nevertheless, while God can give warrant to miracles, miracles cannot give warrant to God. It is impossible for a miracle to prove that God exists because to identify something as a miracle is to presume the Deity's existence. In the manuscript version of the *Logic*, Mill capped this argument with a proof text: 'St. Paul expressly warned the churches, if any one came to them working miracles, to observe what he taught, and unless he preached "Christ, and him crucified," not to listen to the teaching'[20] (1 Corinthians 2:2; Galatians 1:8).

More difficult to discern is to what extent—if at all—Mill wanted to comment on the question of the existence of God in his recurring remarks about fictitious creatures. This is not clear because it is a matter that it was natural, perhaps even necessary, to address in a textbook on logic. A definition can be correct, for instance, but that does not thereby imply that what it refers to exists. It can be a definition of a nonentity: 'A dragon is a serpent breathing flame. This proposition, considered only as a definition, is indisputably correct. A dragon *is* a serpent breathing flame: the word *means* that.'[21] Variations on that point are made over and over again. All kinds of elusive creatures suddenly and unexpectedly bolt up as the chapters of the *Logic* unfold: centaurs, hobgoblins, unicorns. One suspects that Mill wanted the reader to draw the conclusion that just because one can discuss God—even name divine attributes—this should not lull one into assuming that God actually exists. This suspicion is strengthened by the fact that Mill sometimes finds ways to mix the Almighty up in his mythical menagerie: 'God is as much a general term to the Christian or Jew as to the Polytheist; and dragon, hippogriff, chimera, mermaid, ghost, are as much so as if real objects existed, corresponding to those names.'[22] Other passages may also be read or over-read in such ways. One wonders if this example was covertly in the service of Mill's Unitarian Christology: 'No men are gods, means that the attributes of man are never accompanied by the attributes, or at least never by all the attributes, signified by the word god.'[23] Likewise, it is possible that Mill sought subtly to make a theological point with the syllogism:

> Aristides was virtuous,
> Aristides was a pagan,
> therefore
> Some pagan was virtuous[24]

Speaking of syllogisms, Mill includes the one so popular for generations in introductory philosophy courses: 'All men are mortal, Socrates is a man, therefore Socrates is mortal.' So far, so clear. What is arresting, however, is how often religion appears in *A System of Logic* in the most gratuitous of ways. It would seem that Mill's brain must have been bursting with religious thoughts. A particularly pregnant case study for this is Book I, chapter IV, 'Of Propositions'. It is a short chapter—just five-and-a-half pages in the eighth edition. Yet the reader is given as a sentence to examine: 'Peter and James preached at Jerusalem and in Galilee.'[25] (The point is to discern that it contains four, separate propositions.) With only one paragraph in between we are then invited to consider: 'If the Koran comes from God, Mahomet is the prophet of God.' (The lesson of this example is that it is merely an assertion of what can be inferred: 'nothing is affirmed or denied either of the Koran or of Mahomet'.) In the following paragraph, we plunge into one of the more rarified discussions in Christian theology, the question of the *filioque* clause. I defy anyone to find a modern work on logic being used as a textbook in national universities today that includes a reference to the question of the double or single procession of the Holy Spirit in the Triune Godhead! Two paragraphs on one reads: '"The Founder of Christianity was crucified", is as much a singular proposition as "Christ was crucified".'[26] Thus in the space of two pages which have as their themes simple and complex propositions and singular propositions—none of which particularly invite the mind to contemplate matters spiritual—there are illustrations about the preaching ministry of two apostles of Christ; the prophetic ministry of Mohammad; the relationship of the Holy Spirit to the other persons of the Trinity; and the crucifixion of Jesus of Nazareth.

Moreover, religious illustrations recur across all four books. In Book III, chapter II, 'Of Inductions Improperly So Called', an early proposition for discussion is: 'All the Apostles were Jews'.[27] Here is a passage from Book IV, chapter V, 'On the Natural History of the Variations in the Meaning of Terms':

> The law of language which operates in these trivial instances, is the very same in conformity to which the terms θεός, Deus, and God, were adopted from Polytheism by Christianity, to express the single object of its own adoration. Almost all the terminology of the Christian Church is made up of words originally used in a much more general acceptation: *Ecclesia*, Assembly; *Bishop*, Episcopus, Overseer; *Priest*, Presbyter, Elder; *Deacon*, Diaconus; Administrator; *Sacrament*, a vow of allegiance; *Evangelium*, good tidings; and some words, as *Minister*, are still used both in the general and in the limited sense.[28]

In Book V, chapter III 'Fallacies of Simple Inspection; or a priori Fallacies', Mill makes the point that just because we cannot imagine something—or even because it is inconceivable to our minds—does not mean that it is actually impossible. He gives as an example the orthodox, Christian doctrine of *creatio ex nihilo*. Book VI, chapter II, 'Of Liberty and Necessity', given its subject matter, logically, as it were, raises the question of the doctrine of divine foreknowledge. This is merely an illustrative rather than an exhaustive list. Mill was persistently exploring the logical within the theological.

John Murray having turned it down, *A System of Logic* was published by John W. Parker, the official publisher of the Society for Promoting Christian Knowledge and a prominent printer of Bibles and prayer books. Mill wrote to Barclay Fox: 'Does it not amuse you to see how I stick to the high-church booksellers?'[29] One of the earliest and most important reviews of Mill's *Logic* appeared in the Tractarian *British Critic and Quarterly Theological Review*. It was written by the Reverend W. G. Ward, and was seventy-eight pages long. Most scholars just quote one line from it: 'if Mr. Mill's principles be adopted as a full statement of the truth, the whole fabric of Christian Theology must totter and fail'.[30] This makes it sound like Ward was condemning the

Logic, which he was not. He was condemning Mill's underlying philosophical convictions which could be spotted occasionally in the *Logic* and which Ward interpreted as ruling out the realm of the spirit. In the field of speculation, however, Ward lauded Mill as one who 'reigns absolutely without a rival'. Ward defended the Platonic view of mathematics. Indeed, he championed the intuitive school in general:

> Whatever else may be erased from the conscience, this original idea, that 'right' and 'wrong' are words with a meaning, and that a meaning wholly unconnected with consequences and results, this, if anything, is most certainly an innate idea of the human mind.[31]

This underlying discussion, as we have seen, is one that was very important to Mill and part of his motivation for the project. Nevertheless, this should not be confused with the formal rules of logic that Mill is explicitly expounding in this book. Theology need not be uneasy or embarrassed in the face of induction; Ward himself is clear on that:

> But it appears to us plainly God's will, that the inductive philosophy, shall be studied; and moreover, when it shall have been applied to those higher objects which Mr. Mill desires to include within its scope, it cannot but be a most valuable minister in the Church's service.[32]

Mill had no doubt that Ward had written a favourable review. He reported to Comte triumphantly: 'What will perhaps astonish you is that the Anglo-Catholic school... has seen fit to bestow a lofty approval on my work.'[33]

Precisely because it was essentially a textbook on logic—that it was primarily about method rather than meaning—whether or not *A System of Logic* was an assault on religion was often in the eye of the beholder. This variable reaction was even true for Mill himself. At various times, he claimed both that it was and that it was not an anti-theological work. Rather than wondering on which occasion he was saying what he really thought, it seems better to suppose that sometimes he was seeing matters through his Benthamite side and sometimes through his Coleridgian side. He was most keen to be a champion of religious scepticism in his correspondence with Comte. He was enthralled with Comte at that time and he was worried that the Frenchman would dislike *A System of Logic* for not being forthrightly anti-religious. Mill explained that an English reading public would not tolerate rank religious scepticism and therefore he had taken the prudent path of not antagonizing pious people, though those who have eyes to see could infer from the book that the author is not himself a believer. In Britain, the only way for radicals to deal with theology is to ignore it, he averred: 'We can only evade the issue by simply eliminating it from all social and philosophical discussion and by passing over all questions pertaining to it on our agenda.'[34] (If the contents of *A System of Logic* were Mill's idea of ignoring theology, it makes one stagger to try to imagine how much religious content there would have been in the book without this self-restraint!) Nevertheless, Mill went on, he hoped to set off a domino chain: the school of intuition is supported by the theological interests and they, in turn, support the old social order. Therefore, to bring about social reform one first needs to undermine belief in innate ideas, he had decided. After the third edition, the *North America Review* hailed *A System of Logic* as a 'standard' text which was willing to stand for 'the anti-innate principle & anti-natural-theology doctrines'.[35] Many religious sceptics were fervent admirers: George Henry Lewis was enraptured; George Grote claimed it was the best book in his library; Alexander Bain asserted that the section on induction was the best thing Mill ever wrote.

On the opposite side of the equation, Mill wrote to a correspondent in 1861: 'I am desirous to explain, that neither in the Logic nor in any other of my publications had I any purpose of undermining Theism; nor, I believe, have most readers of the Logic perceived any such tendency in it.'[36] Again, he was not being disingenuous. Mill hoped that *A System of Logic* would undermine pernicious religion—which, for him, was primarily religion which bolstered unjust social systems—but he did not see it as an attack upon religion per se. And he was right that neither did the Christian community generally. Mill's best male friend, the Reverend John Sterling, was even convinced that the effect of the *Logic* would be to awaken a more spiritual sensibility in crass sceptics: 'Sterling thinks that Mill's book will induce some to believe in the existence of certain elements in human nature, such as Reverence, to which they have nothing answering in their own consciousness.'[37] Mill himself would have been deeply gratified to discover that his first *magnum opus* really was a two-way bridge which assisted the religious in becoming more rational and the irreligious in becoming more reverent. Proving Murray quite wrong, the book was an immediate and enduring commercial success. A major reason for its staying power was that Anglican Oxford soon adopted it as a textbook. Anglican Cambridge followed suit. One of Mill's surviving letters is to his publisher, whom he asks to send a complimentary copy of *A System of Logic* to the Reverend A. J. Ashworth, a Baptist minister in Leeds.[38] Mill's friend, the Quaker Barclay Fox, lived in Cornwall, but he would come to see the philosopher when he was in town. Fox saw Mill at his office at India House in May 1843 and the report was good: 'His work on logic has had an extraordinary sale in the first month after publication.'[39] Almost exactly a year later he was back again and the *Logic* was such a phenomenon that the topic of conversation was still the same: 'I called on J. Mill for half an hour & talked over common friends & the success of his great work.'[40] It was Mill's first book and it had done very well indeed.

Book VI, chapter V of *A System of Logic* was 'Of Ethology, or the Science of the Formation of Character'. 'Ethology' was a word of Mill's own coining. He also hoped to achieve the much more difficult task of founding the science that it named. Ethology would uncover the scientific laws which would connect the circumstances of a people's life with their resulting character. Mill intended his next book to be his elucidation of this new science. Alas, although he had figured out that character is key, he could not figure out the key to character. Mill therefore abandoned this plan and turned to the other discipline beside logic that his father had most thoroughly trained him in, namely, political economy. Fourteen years earlier Mill had written a series of essays on this topic. He conceded that they were 'too abstract' to gain a popular readership. Given the commercial success of *A System of Logic*, however, his 'high-church bookseller' was willing to take the risk and so Mill's *Essays on Some Unsettled Questions of Political Economy* was published by J. W. Parker in 1844. Mill's more substantive goal was to write 'a systematic treatise on Political Economy, for none of the existing ones are at all up to the present state of speculation'.[41] This was fulfilled with the publication in 1848 of *Principles of Political Economy, with some of their applications to Social Philosophy*. Another massive achievement, it was issued in two volumes and was close to 1,200 pages in length. Substantial changes were made to the various editions which appeared across the rest of Mill's life. Harriet was fully involved in this project and he recorded in his own retrospective account of his publications that it should be viewed as 'a joint production with my wife'.[42] Harriet was responsible for radical changes in the views adopted in the third edition (1852), but already in 1849 Mill was telling her regarding the publication of the second edition: 'being wholly your work, as well as all the best of the book itself so that you have a redoubled title to your joint ownership of it'.[43] The discussion that follows will use the version in the *Collected Works of John Stuart Mill* which is based on the seventh edition from 1871—Mill's last effort.

Principles of Political Economy is comprised of five books: Production (thirteen chapters); Distribution (sixteen chapters); Exchange (twenty-six chapters); Influence of the Progress of Society on Production and Distribution (seven chapters); On the Influence of Government (eleven chapters). As with *A System of Logic*, it is important to keep in mind that this is a technical textbook for the dedicated student of the subject. Once again, one example to evoke this reality will more than suffice:

> let us now suppose the opposite and still more extreme case of a machine which lasts for ever, and requires no repairs. In this case, which is as well suited for the purpose of illustration as if it were a possible one, it will be unnecessary that the manufacturer should ever be repaid the 500*l.* which he gave for the machine, since he has always the machine itself, worth 500*l.*; but he must be paid, as before, a profit on it. The commodity B, therefore, which in the case previously supposed was sold for 1200*l.* of which sum 1000*l.* were to replace the capital and 200*l.* were profit, can now be sold for 700*l.*, being 500*l.* to replace wages, and 200*l.* profit on the entire capital. Profit, therefore enters into the value of B in the ratio of 200*l.* out of 700*l.*, being two-sevenths of the whole, or 28 4/7 per cent, while in the case of A, as before, it enters only in the ratio of one-sixth, or 16 2/3 per cent.[44]

The present volume on the spiritual life of J. S. Mill is not the place to make a proper presentation of what Mill argues in *Principles of Political Economy*, let alone assess it—we will merely highlight some features, especially ones that illuminate his biography or his relationship to religion.

Book I, chapter III is 'Of Unproductive Labour'. Mill was using 'productive' in a specific, technical sense to mean labour that produces useful outputs or enhancements fixed and embodied in material objects. To cultivate crops, to manufacture goods, to turn cloth into clothes, to craft a piece of wood into a musical instrument—these are the kind of activities that Mill means by productive labour. Such a definition means that everyone in the entertainment industry, for instance, is engaged in 'unproductive labour'. One can hear the protest of Mr Sleary, the circus owner in Charles Dickens's indictment of Benthamite political economy:

> 'People must be amuthed, Thquire, thomehow', continued Sleary, rendered more pursy than ever, by so much talking; 'they can't be alwayth a working, nor yet they can't be alwayth a learning. Making the betht of uth; not the wurth. I've got my living out of the horthe-riding all my life, I know; but I conthider that I lay down the philosophy of the thubject when I thay to you, Thquire, make the betht of uth; not the wortht!'[45]

And Mill's excluded activities included much more than actors and acrobats: physicians, teachers, lawyers, soldiers, servants, and much more will all be deemed 'unproductive'. Even full-time mothers are only providing 'unproductive services'. A hardhearted person might come away from *Principles of Political Economy* resenting his own grandmother for her unproductive existence. Mill was aware that some find such language judgemental or stigmatizing in tone, but he stuck with it. He was not arguing that production was 'the sole end of human existence'; he was only identifying clearly which activities created wealth for the economy as a whole rather than just the individuals concerned.[46] Nevertheless, it is difficult not to hear a pejorative note creeping in on occasion. Here, for instance, is a passage on religious activities:

> To a religious person the saving of a soul must appear a far more important service than the saving of a life; but he will not therefore call a missionary or a clergyman productive labourers, unless they teach, as the South Sea Missionaries have in some cases done, the arts of civilization in addition to the doctrines of their religion. It is, on the contrary, evident that the greater number of missionaries or clergymen a nation maintains, the less it has to expend on other things; while the more it expends judiciously in keeping agriculturists and manufacturers at work, the more it will have for every other purpose.[47]

Mill's very first example of an object 'devoted to unproductive use' is Westminster Abbey.[48] Moreover, Mill was a moralist at heart. It is often the case that one senses moral disapproval underneath the economic analysis, even shades of Mr Gradgrind's unnatural austerity:

> But consumption on pleasures or luxuries, whether by the idle or by the industrious, since production is neither its object nor is in any way advanced by it, must be reckoned unproductive: with a reservation perhaps of a certain quantum of enjoyment which may be classed among necessaries, since anything short of it would not be consistent with the greatest efficiency of labour . . . The annual consumption of gold lace, pine apples, or champagne, must be reckoned unproductive, since these things give no assistance to production, nor any support to life or strength, but what would equally be given by things much less costly.[49]

Mill recommends taxing conspicuous consumption. Moreover, this additional charge is not merely to raise revenue, but in the hopes that it will discourage such unseemly behaviour.

Book I, chapter XI ('Of the Law of the Increase of Capital') argues that capital is the result of 'abstinence from present consumption for the sake of a future good'.[50] Mill uses the word 'abstinence' over forty times in *Principles of Political Economy*. Not only does that way of constructing the discussion lend itself to moralizing, but Mill himself would use the word 'abstinence' in the way that it is most often used in conversations today, namely, in regard to celibacy: 'it is possible to delay marriage, and to live in abstinence while unmarried'.[51] Mill viewed sexual intercourse as an 'indulgence' that needed to be restricted for the good of society. Malthusian teaching dominates the book, recurring over and over again. Mill rages against unbridled breeding. What it means to be human beings is to not 'propagate like swine'; the human race is not 'a nest of ants or a colony of beavers'. 'Civilization' means 'a struggle against the animal instincts'.[52] Evoking his own harm principle which he famously articulated in *On Liberty*, Mill claimed that a goal of society ought to be 'to secure to all persons complete independence and freedom of action, subject to no restriction but that of not doing injury to others'.[53] The 'evils of over-population', however, meant that Mill believed that two consenting adults deciding to have a baby could very well inflict an injury on others. A labourer should look upon his neighbour having a large family 'as doing him a wrong—as filling up the place which he was entitled to share'.[54] Nor is this just a problem if it happens among the lower orders. Mill and Harriet singled out for condemnation the peerage and the clergy for their pernicious habit of creating 'enormous families'. Likewise, they repeatedly condemn the Catholic priesthood for allowing married couples so much sexual free licence. Martial overindulgence ought to be seen as the equivalent of 'a man who is intemperate in drink'.[55] At times Mill could sound like some medieval saint advocating for the ideal of celibate marriages. Some parts of Mill's corpus might be useful for advancing a libertarian point of view, but on sexual relations he is decidedly willing to recommend coercion. He approves of governments forbidding people to marry who are not in a 'comfortable' financial position. Once married, the government should be able 'to repress, by penalties of some description' excessive breeding.[56] One could have certainly quoted Mill's *Principles of Political Economy* to give warrant to China's one-child policy. To evoke Thomas Hardy, *Done because we are too menny*.

Matters spiritual or theological do not keep leaping out in persistent and surprising ways in *Principles of Political Economy* as they do in *A System of Logic*. Nevertheless, as has already been shown, religion does recur in Mill's second great work as well. He commends monastic orders for establishing communities that do not foster wealth inequality or extravagant consumption. The Jesuits in Paraguay created a society of communitarian living that Mill believed could serve as a model for others. He fumes against the Holy Inquisition and—presumably with Richard Carlile in mind—observed that these dark days are not yet long gone: 'Within the last fifteen or twenty years several individuals have suffered imprisonment, for the public profession, sometimes in a very temperate manner, of disbelief in religion.'[57] Mill had kind things to say about clergymen authors, including the Reverend Thomas Chalmers and the Reverend Richard Jones. And, as with almost all Victorians, Mill's language is leavened with biblical quotations and idioms.[58] To take just one instance, he used the biblical phrase for someone condemned to do only menial work, 'a hewer of wood and a drawer of water' (Joshua 9:21).[59] Symbolically illustrating that religion was always close to hand in the nineteenth century, when Mill looked at his library for a book to service as a model for the right size for how he desired *Principles of Political Economy* to be printed, he lit upon George Eliot's translation of D. F. Strauss's *The Life of Jesus Critically Examined*, which had just been published two years earlier.[60] Religion is not a preoccupation of *Principles of Political Economy*, but it is still much more prominent than one would imagine finding in a textbook on economic theory today.

At the risk of committing the sin of presentism, one cannot help but notice that many of Mill's judgements have saliency in late twentieth-century and current debates. At the very least, this list will help to indicate the wide and ambitious range of issues that Mill tackled in *Principles of Political Economy*. Already in his Preliminary Remarks we read of the way a societal pattern can be set in which the rich get richer and the poor poorer: 'When inequality of wealth once commences, in a community not constantly engaged in repairing by industry the injuries of fortune, its advances are gigantic; the great masses of wealth swallow up the smaller.'[61] Mill therefore was in favour of policies that serve the goal of the redistribution of wealth. On gender, Mill explored the issue of why women generally receive lower wages than men. He argued that one of the benefits of women's liberation would be to lower the birth rate. Clichés being older than one might think, already in the mid-nineteenth century we find him making the assertion that women are better at multi-tasking than men. Mill was sceptical of schemes for reparations to redress historic wrongs. He believed that government has the right to confiscate private land in the national interest. He was in favour of high inheritance, estate, or so-called 'death' taxes: it is no exception if these are so severe that they leave an heir without enough money with which to support his wife and children as anyone who has a family ought to support it by 'his own exertions'. Mill was in favour of international free trade and against trade barriers or tariffs. His teaching lends itself to supporting the idea of a minimum wage. He advocated for both government services and simultaneously permitting private competition, citing the delivery of mail as an example. Space programmes can take comfort in the fact that Mill believed that it was fitting for governments to fund 'a voyage of geographical or scientific exploration'.[62] He observed that turning people into the owners of where they live would lead to the improvement of the properties. Defenders of the euro can quote Mill's claim that insisting upon having a national currency is 'barbarism'.[63] And authors cannot pretend they were not warned: 'scarcely any writer can hope to gain a living by books, and to do so by magazines and reviews becomes daily more difficult'.[64] Mill's *Principles of Political Economy* is a still-flowing fount of arguments regarding how societies ought to be organized: he being dead yet speaketh.

If it is unrealistic to imagine that one will make a living by writing books, it is highly fortuitous to have a salaried position which makes it congenial to spend a significant amount of one's time writing books. Mill typically spent a six-hour workday at the India Office, but he dispatched with the official dispatches in half that time, leaving him several hours to work on his own projects. Both *A System of Logic* and *Principles of Political Economy* were largely written at his office during business hours.

Mill's second large, ambitious book was also a tremendous success. It too would reign as a key textbook in its field for a biblical generation. These two works together established John Stuart Mill as one of the most prominent and important intellectuals in Britain. His youthful ambition to make a name for himself was now fulfilled. Mill would enter the 1850s with his place in the pantheon of eminent Victorians forever secure.

Notes

1. Alexander Bain, *John Stuart Mill: A Criticism: with personal recollections*, London: Longmans, Green, and Co., 1882, p. 139.
2. John Stuart Mill to Thomas Carlyle, 8 August 1837: Francis E. Mineka (ed.), *The Earlier Letters of John Stuart Mill, 1812–1848* (Collected Works of John Stuart Mill XII), Toronto: University of Toronto Press, 1963, p. 347.
3. John Stuart Mill, *Autobiography and Literary Essays* (Collected Works of John Stuart Mill I), ed. J. M. Robson, Indianapolis: Liberty Fund, 2006 (reprint of Toronto: University of Toronto Press, 1981), p. 125.
4. John Stuart Mill to John Bowring, 10 March 1828: CWJSM XII (*Earlier Letters*), p. 23.
5. CWJSM XII (*Earlier Letters*), p. 79.
6. CWJSM I (*Autobiography and Literary Essays*), p. 231.
7. CWJSM I (*Autobiography and Literary Essays*), p. 233.
8. John Stuart Mill, *A System of Logic, Ratiocinative and Inductive, being a connected view of principles of evidence and the methods of scientific investigation* (Collected Works of John Stuart Mill VII), ed. J. M. Robson, Indianapolis: Liberty Fund, 2006 (reprint of Toronto: University of Toronto Press, 1974), p. 195. (The discussion of *A System of Logic* throughout this chapter will not make distinctions between editions. The tabulations of his use of various words given in this chapter apply to the eighth edition.)

9. CWJSM VII (*A System of Logic*), p. 254. For a twenty-first-century presentation of the Platonic view by an astrophysicist, see Mario Livio, *Is God a Mathematician?*, New York: Simon & Schuster, 2009.
10. CWJSM VII (*A System of Logic*), p. 253.
11. CWJSM VII (*A System of Logic*), pp. 598–9.
12. Harriet Taylor to Arthur Hardy, 7 September 1856: Jo Ellen Jacobs (ed.), *The Complete Works of Harriet Taylor Mill*, Bloomington, IN: Indiana University Press, 1998, p. 423. (Arthur was her favourite sibling.)
13. Horace N. Pym (ed.), *Memories of Old Friends: being extracts from the Journals and Letters of Caroline Fox of Penjerrick, Cornwall*, London: Smith, Elder, and Co., 1882, p. 166.
14. John Stuart Mill to Gustave d'Eichthal, 10 January 1842: CWJSM XII (*Earlier Letters*), p. 496.
15. CWJSM VIII (*A System of Logic*), p. 813.
16. CWJSM VIII (*A System of Logic*), p. 784.
17. CWJSM VII (*A System of Logic*), p. 358.
18. CWJSM VII (*A System of Logic*), p. 361.
19. CWJSM VIII (*A System of Logic*), pp. 928–9.
20. CWJSM VII (*A System of Logic*), pp. 625–6.
21. CWJSM VII (*A System of Logic*), p. 146.
22. CWJSM VII (*A System of Logic*), p. 118.
23. CWJSM VII (*A System of Logic*), p. 117.
24. CWJSM VII (*A System of Logic*), p. 169.
25. CWJSM VII (*A System of Logic*), p. 82.
26. CWJSM VII (*A System of Logic*), p. 84.
27. CWJSM VII (*A System of Logic*), p. 288.
28. CWJSM VIII (*A System of Logic*), pp. 694–5.
29. John Stuart Mill to Barclay Fox, 5 April 1842: CWJSM XIII (*Earlier Letters*), p. 513.
30. [W. G. Ward], 'Mill's *Logic*', *British Critic and Quarterly Theological Review*, XXXIV, LXVIII (October 1843), pp. 349–427 (here 356). (The reader should note that there were serious printer's errors with the pagination for this article. I see no alternative to just giving the number at the top of the page, but there are a whole series of numbers that recur later in the article affixed to different text, so one might need to hunt out a page's doppelgänger in order to find a quotation.)
31. Ward, 'Mill's *Logic*', p. 400.
32. Ward, 'Mill's *Logic*', p. 413.
33. John Stuart Mill to Auguste Comte, 8 December 1843: Oscar A. Haac (translator and editor), *The Correspondence of John Stuart Mill and Auguste Comte*, New Brunswick, NJ: Transaction Publishers, 1995, p. 214.

34. John Stuart Mill to Auguste Comte, 3 April 1844: Haac, *Mill and Comte*, p. 227. (This is Mill continuing to expound on the same thought after the publication of *A System of Logic*.)
35. Francis E. Mineka and Dwight N. Lindley (eds), *The Later Letters of John Stuart Mill, 1849–1873* (Collected Works of John Stuart Mill XIV), Toronto: University of Toronto Press, 1972, p. 149.
36. CWJSM XV (*Later Letters*), p. 754.
37. Pym, *Memories*, p. 179.
38. CWJSM XV (*Later Letters*), p. 1819. Mineka and Lindley were defeated in their attempt to place Ashworth ('Not otherwise identified'), but he was the Baptist minister at Zion Chapel, Bramley: C. E. Shipley (ed.), *The Baptists of Yorkshire*, Bradford: Wm. Byles & Sons, 1912, p. 144.
39. R. L. Brett (ed.), *Barclay Fox's Journal*, Fowey: Cornwall Editions, 2008, p. 341.
40. Brett, *Barclay Fox's Journal*, pp. 385–6.
41. John Stuart Mill to John Sterling, 29 May 1844: CWJSM XIII (*Earlier Letters*), p. 630.
42. Ney MacMinn, J. R. Hainds, and James McNab McCrimmon (eds), *Bibliography of the Published Writings of John Stuart Mill, edited from his Manuscript with Corrections and Notes*, Bristol: Thoemmes, 1990 (originally 1945), p. 69.
43. John Stuart Mill to Harriet Taylor, 17 March 1849: CWJSM XIV (*Later Letters*), p. 17.
44. John Stuart Mill, *Principles of Political Economy with some of their applications to social philosophy* (Collected Works of John Stuart Mill III), ed. J. M. Robson, Indianapolis: Liberty Fund, 2006 (reprint of Toronto: University of Toronto Press, 1965), pp. 483–4.
45. Charles Dickens, *Hard Times. For These Days*, London: Bradbury & Evans, 1854, p. 49.
46. CWJSM II (*Principles of Political Economy*), p. 43.
47. CWJSM II (*Principles of Political Economy*), p. 50.
48. CWJSM II (*Principles of Political Economy*), p. 74.
49. CWJSM II (*Principles of Political Economy*), pp. 52–3.
50. CWJSM II (*Principles of Political Economy*), p. 160.
51. CWJSM II (*Principles of Political Economy*), p. 369.
52. CWJSM II (*Principles of Political Economy*), pp. 367–8.
53. CWJSM II (*Principles of Political Economy*), pp. 208–9.
54. CWJSM II (*Principles of Political Economy*), p. 371.
55. CWJSM II (*Principles of Political Economy*), p. 368.
56. CWJSM II (*Principles of Political Economy*), p. 206.
57. CWJSM III (*Principles of Political Economy*), p. 935.

58. For the wider context, see Timothy Larsen, *A People of One Book: The Bible and the Victorians*, Oxford: Oxford University Press, 2011.
59. CWJSM II (*Principles of Political Economy*), p. 108.
60. CWJSM XVII (*Later Letters*), p. 2007.
61. CWJSM III (*Principles of Political Economy*), p. 16.
62. CWJSM III (*Principles of Political Economy*), p. 968.
63. CWJSM III (*Principles of Political Economy*), p. 626.
64. CWJSM II (*Principles of Political Economy*), p. 392.

8
And They Shall be One Flesh

'Therefore shall a man leave his father and mother, and shall cleave unto his wife: and they shall be one flesh.'

(Genesis 2:24)

When you have secured the love of someone so extraordinary as to possess the greatest mind in the entire country, nothing is more natural than to want to show off your good fortune. Mill was inordinately proud of Harriet and his relationship with her. As has already been discussed, however, the true nature of this relationship was indefinable, unclassifiable, and unrecognizable in terms of any existing categories in society. Mill and Harriet had given up the dream of running away together. They were committed to celibacy. She had not abandoned her position in the wider world as Mrs John Taylor. What could Mill and Harriet have as a social life together? In the beginning, he would dine at least once a week at her house, often with John Taylor obligingly spending the evening at his club. A few months before their define-the-relationship talk in Paris, the Reverend W. J. Fox wrote to Mill saying that he had been at the Taylors' house on Wednesday and was sorry to have missed him as he had hoped—perhaps even expected—the philosopher would have been there as well. Mill replied that he regretted not seeing Fox but, in his own case, 'it cannot be right in present circumstances to be there *every* evening'.[1] A few months into the post-Paris settlement, Mill managed to have some time together with Harriet, Fox, Eliza Flower, and Sarah Flower. It was a tremendous joy for Mill to have something other than a quiet, *sub rosa* evening with the love of his life. He wrote to Fox about it on St Valentine's Day: 'I hope we shall meet oftener—we four or rather five—as we did on Tuesday—I do not see half enough of you—and I do not, half enough, see *anybody* along with her—*that*

I think is chiefly what is wanting now—that, and other things like it.'[2] After over a year of this want being largely left unfulfilled, the couple decided to take the risk and see if they could move around a bit in society together. J. A. Roebuck, who had once been Mill's best friend—and who had been at the dinner party where the couple first met—witnessed the attempt, which probably occurred on 15 June 1835:

> This intimacy went on, I seeing and knowing nothing of it, till on the occasion of an evening party at Mrs. Charles Buller's, I saw Mill enter the room with Mrs. Taylor hanging upon his arm.
>
> The manner of the lady, the evident devotion of the gentleman, soon attracted universal attention, and a suppressed titter went round the room. My affection for Mill was so warm and so sincere that I was hurt by anything which brought ridicule upon him. I saw, or thought I saw, how mischievous might be this affair, and as we had become in all things like brothers, I determined, most unwisely, to speak to him on the subject.[3]

Roebuck was stunned when Mill, in retaliation for what he deemed to be this impertinent meddling—dropped him cold from that moment onwards: their friendship came to an abrupt and permanent end. Having shot the messenger, Mill nevertheless got the message: his relationship with Harriet could not have a public, social existence.

Mill and Harriet spent twenty years during which their bond together—the most important relationship in their lives—was not publicly acknowledged. Mill's surviving letters are littered with cryptic comments saying that he is not able to meet people on certain days—or even make definite plans. Mill had made a provisional agreement to visit Carlyle in Scotland in 1833, but as that became the crisis year for his relationship with Harriet he had to put him off with vague disclaimers about other obligations being in a state of uncertainty. Eventually, however, Carlyle became one of the very few people who was officially in on the secret. Indeed, the sage took a prurient interest in the exact nature of the relationship. Like many people today, of all the varieties of unruly relationships, he seemed to have discovered to his own surprise that he found celibacy to be one of the more outrageous. Flummoxed by his certainty that their relationship really was chaste, he took to referring to Harriet behind her back with the derisive nickname, 'Platonica'. Disapproving of Fox's relationship with Eliza Flower, Carlyle poured forth his scorn for Utilitarians:

> Most of these people are very indignant at marriage and the like; and frequently indeed are obliged to divorce their own wives, or be divorced; for tho' the *world* is already blooming (or is one day to do it) in everlasting 'happiness of the greatest number', these people's own *houses* (I always find) are little Hells of improvidence, discord, and unreason.[4]

Nevertheless, a few months later, the Scotsman was ready to give Mill and Harriet his benediction: 'Thanks to Mrs. Taylor for her kind sympathies. May God guide, and bless you both! That is my true prayer.'[5]

Carlyle and Fox were rare souls who were both privy to the existence of this passion from Mill's own lips and pen—and whose friendship Mill did not forsake. Harriet and Mill became obsessed with the thought that people were gossiping about them. Even when Harriet was a widow and someone merely enquired after her health—intimating that he had heard she was not well (which was indeed the case)—Mill railed against the 'gossiping creature' who might have dared to presume to mention Harriet's state of health.[6] But what would it mean to be someone's genuine friend and yet to take no interest at all in the most important relationship in his life? The circle could not be squared, so it had to be broken. The result was that, as had happened with Roebuck, Mill began to purge his life of those who had hitherto been closest to him. John and Sarah Austin and George and Harriet Grote all stood condemned for committing the sin of gossip and were excommunicated. George Henry Lewes wrote to Comte in March 1848: 'Of John Mill, I have seen nothing; all his old friends seen dropping off one by one.'[7] Indeed, seven years earlier Mill had already turned down an invitation from Lewes with the explanation: 'I never go to evening parties in the *flesh*.'[8] To a large extent, Mill simply withdrew from social life altogether. As he wrote in an early draft of his *Autobiography*, 'But from the time when I could really call her my friend I wished for no other.'[9] Harriet Taylor was all the society he needed.

The other friends that Mill continued to have either did not know about his relationship with Harriet (if there truly were any in this category) or pretended they did not (or at least colluded with Mill's desire never to break the spell of silence and secrecy). Alexander Bain reported that when he came to London in 1842 the affair was common knowledge. Nevertheless, one never became so close to Mill for him to make the most passionate relationship in his life a recognized fact: 'The upshot was that everyone of Mill's friends abstained from all allusions to Mrs. Taylor.'[10] This was true even of Mill's best friend beside Harriet—John Sterling. Maybe it was even because this was true that Sterling was and remained his best friend besides Harriet. The furthest Mill was willing to go was not to reveal his secret to Sterling, but to concede that he did have a secret that he was not revealing: 'And even now I am very far from appearing to you as I am—for though there is nothing that I do not desire to shew, there is much that I never do shew, & much that I think you cannot even guess.'[11] For a few years, Mill was glad for the friendship of Barclay Fox and his sister Caroline. They also knew Sterling, creating another little circle Mill could enjoy to give some variety to his sequestered existence. Moreover, the Foxes were safely ensconced in Cornwall and only came to London a few times a year, making it easier for Mill to keep his worlds apart. The philosopher explained to Caroline that his life in London was very different: 'Mill says that he scarcely ever goes into society, for he gets no good there, and does more by staying away.'[12] After a few years of continuing to reside in the family home with her husband, John and Harriet Taylor worked out an arrangement where she would have a place of her own in the country. For a while this was in Kent, but then she found a house at Walton-on-Thames in Surrey. When Harriet's presence there was officially acknowledged, it would be claimed that she sometimes went away to the countryside for her health. It was often not acknowledged, however. Harriet went to great lengths not to let her own parents understand the real state of her marriage. Her letters would be forwarded back and forth to give them the illusion that she was writing from the family home in Regent's Park, London. When she was away on a continental trip (with Mill) in the summer of 1844, the plan was hatched back at home that her oldest son, Herbert, might pay a visit to his grandparents (her parents). Harriet was annoyed by this and tried to put a stop to it on the grounds that 'there would be no end to questionings & wonderments at every thing I do'.[13] Harriet liked her younger brother, Arthur, who lived in Australia. Nevertheless, when he made a visit to England in 1848, Harriet became highly anxious about the situation, not being able to imagine how she could host him without his figuring out the real state of things in her life. Finding the home-front problem insoluble, she took off for continental Europe on the grounds of ill health.

As a matter of established routine in their lives, every Saturday Mill would go to Walton-on-Thames to spend what we now call the weekend with Harriet. Her youngest child and only girl, Helen, lived with Harriet. Helen Taylor was unwittingly turned into her mother's chaperon and character reference. She resented the fact that she was not allowed to attend school. Instead, ostensibly because of her mother's delicate health, Helen was meant to be constantly nearby to attend to her. They even slept together in the same bed.[14] When Barclay Fox came to London for the Yearly Meeting of the Society of Friends in May 1840, Mill was keen to meet his friend and join him in his desired tour of the museum at his India House offices. He told Fox that he would not want to go on a Saturday as it would be too crowded, before candidly admitting that he had an ulterior motive: 'besides which I have a secret reason which I do not mean to tell you, viz. that Saturday week is the only possible day on which I could not be there to welcome you, as I am inexorably bound to pass that Saturday and Sunday more than thirty miles from town.... the case is such that there is no help for it'.[15] This exclusion from his weekly calendar became a standard refrain. For instance, when the Irish politician Charles Gavan Duffy desired to meet him, Mill suggested they meet on Friday at India House, but if not, he was flexible: 'any other day except Saturday or Sunday will suit me equally well'.[16] In 1842, Mill was intoxicated with Comte's thought and very keen that they should meet. Nevertheless, he regretfully explained that he could not make even a very short trip to France because of 'the particular circumstances of my life'. And again the following year: 'I have always been close to certain that the circumstances of my most intimate personal relations would keep me in London this winter.'[17] Beside these weekly meetings, Mill and Harriet schemed over the years to arrange to be in continental Europe at the same time so that they could surreptitiously holiday together. It was vital that no one learn where either of them had gone so that there was no chance that anyone could figure out that they were in the same place at the same time. Mill continued to live with his mother and sisters in the family home, yet he would not even tell them where he was going. For a trip to Italy in 1839, Mill went so far as to mislead people into believing that he would be in Malta. Mill and Harriet had been indiscreet before they learnt to be discreet. For a trip in the summer of 1836, Harriet brought her children along and Mill brought two of his younger brothers, George and Henry. George Mill and Algernon Taylor became enduring friends. The couple even left the children with a nurse and did a side trip to Italy on their own. George's letters home were sufficiently detailed to make the situation apparent. It was on account of this escapade that James Mill felt it was his duty to confront his son about his relationship with Mrs Taylor.[18] After that second indiscretion leading once again to a confrontation, Mill and Harriet seem to have maintained vigilantly ever after the plan to have a chaperon forever on watch. When Mill and Harriet came to write the *Autobiography*, they knew that this is what was needed to be explained if people were to understand that their relationship really was chaste: 'so as to preclude other and different versions of our lives at Kesn and Waln—our summer excursions &c.'[19] (Kesn and Waln refer to his weekly visits to her at her country homes—Kenton Heath and then Walton-on-Thames. 'Summer excursions' primarily means the continental trips.)

If being together in society was not possible, perhaps there was another way in which they could show off what they had found in each other. Harriet had collaborated closely with Mill on *Principles of Political Economy* and they hit upon the idea of him dedicating it to her. Comte had already shown the way with his Clotilde, writing to Mill in 1846: 'In her admirable modesty, she had finally accepted the public dedication of a work in which her sweet influence played such a great involuntary role.'[20] Harriet wrote to her husband, proposing the plan and soliciting his advice. John Taylor wrote back, confessing that it was never pleasant to disagree with her, but nonetheless insisting that the idea showed 'a want of taste & tact which I could not have believed possible': 'The dedication will revive recollections now forgotten & will create observations and talk that cannot but be extremely unpleasant to me.'[21] Once the idea had occurred to them, however, Mill and Harriet could not let it go: finally there was a suitable way to celebrate openly what they meant to each other. They decided that a fitting compromise would be not to have the dedication in the general print run, but to create gift copies which did include it. Harriet had reassured her husband in the initial appeal that any such dedication would be 'short & judicious', but Mill was ever and always prolix and unmeasured when he spoke of Harriet. Given later efforts, no doubt it seemed to him a marvel of restraint and concision that it was confined to a single sentence: 'To Mrs. John Taylor as the most eminently qualified of all persons known to the author either to originate or to appreciate speculations on social improvement, this attempt to explain and diffuse ideas many of which were first learned from herself, is with the highest respect and regard dedicated.'[22] It is hard to know what there is to say about the Victorian tragicomedy that is the necessity that he address her as 'Mrs. John Taylor'. This dedication was the third and final indiscretion. In his *Autobiography*, Mill lied about how the compromise came about: 'A few dedicatory lines, acknowledging what the book owed to her, were prefixed to some of the presentation copies of the *Political Economy* on its first publication. Her dislike of publicity alone prevented their insertion in the other copies of the work.'[23] The year after the publication of *Principles of Political Economy* Harriet complained to Mill that 'the public' now knew about 'our intimacy' and she seemed to blame her brother Arthur because he had received one of the gift copies.[24] Once again, one feels the doublemindedness inherent in all this—they somehow wanted public recognition without public discussion, even public awareness.

Mill and Harriet were very much looking forward to one of their continental escapes which they had arranged to begin in late December 1848. John Taylor did not realize that Mill had been able to obtain sick leave and that the philosopher was planning to meet his wife on her excursion. Taylor naively volunteered himself to be her companion, but Harriet brushed him off by saying that his own health was too poor to travel and that she was quite capable of travelling without 'an escort'. Taylor was not at ease. He did not want her to go. Harriet retorted that all his fussing was giving her a headache: 'Your saying that you are sorry I am going has given me ever since I read your note so <u>intense</u> a head-ache, that I can scarcely see to write. However it is only one of the vexations I have to bear & perhaps every body has.'[25] But John Taylor had terminal cancer. In March, he wrote to his wife, telling her that his health had deteriorated and asking her to return home. But that would have spoiled everything. Mill had not even arrived yet and, once he did, they had planned three long-anticipated weeks together. Harriet was forced to be explicit. She told her husband the full plan that she had arranged, explaining that Mill really was in poor health and therefore she must be by his side: 'I feel it a duty to do all in my power for his health.'[26] When she arrived back in London in mid-May, Harriet saw at once that her husband was dying. So much of what she did and said in these weeks after her return indicates that she was overcome with guilt. She threw herself into nursing Taylor unceasingly, day and night. She sensed keenly that her actions had made his life more difficult: 'the only feeling to set against extreme sadness & the constant acute sense of being in an utterly false position—It is now that I feel in this most serious affair of his life the terrible consequences of the different milieu.'[27] She even momentarily wavered in the reason that she and Mill had given—and would again give—in order to justify what they had done: that Taylor was not a fitting companion for her because he was not her equal. At this moment, she claimed he was a greater man than most of the famous and beloved intellectuals, writing to Mill:

> alas I feel as if he besides you is the only life I value in this wretched world. He is so thoroughly true direct honest strong & with all the realities of nice feelings, as I constantly see now. What a contrast is such a man to the vapid sentimental egotists Stirling, Carlyle, &c. who let inflated conceit of their own assumed superiority run away with all true strength & humility.[28]

Her husband was 'one of the most upright generous true and good men that ever lived'. If one is surprised to see her attack the late John Sterling, Mill's best male friend, in truth, she was lashing out all around. Mill himself is bitterly scolded for not showing enough feeling during this situation. His bad behaviour on one Sunday in June: 'I can never forget as long as I live'. Harriet ordered him to not visit, and eventually not even to write. She also lashed out at Providence:

> but why shd he have these torments to endure! what good to any body is all this—He never hurt or harmed a creature on earth. If they want the life why cant they take it—what useless torture is all this![29]

Such an outburst does not make sense, of course, unless there is a divine 'they' to call to account. Another possibility was one that Mill himself often found attractive, the Manichean theology of God being limited in power but at war with the forces of evil. Harriet tried that possibility as well: 'Thank God (the good one who must abhor this wicked work of the demons as much as I do).'[30] Reaching for the most sacred meaning of suffering, Harriet decided that Taylor was a Christ-figure, a man of sorrows, and acquainted with grief:

> From that time till Mid day yesterday his suffering has been more such as one hears of the tortures inflicted by demons than anything else. Often I have thought, what would crucifixion be compared to this—mercy—his patience firmness & courage are & have been infinite. He has never uttered a complaint of the slightest kind. Three days & most of the nights he lay with the mouth wide open & eyes turned up or rolling round as if asking for some mercy & all that time paroxysms, as he said, 'the tortures of the damned' coming on about each two hours.[31]

Those four sentences are thick with christological allusions: the change that happened at noon (Mark 15:33); the demonic assault; the pain of crucifixion; his 'infinite' qualities; his not complaining ('He was oppressed, and he was afflicted, yet he opened not his mouth: he is brought as a lamb to the slaughter, and as a sheep before her shearers is dumb, so he openeth not his mouth' Isaiah 53:7); and the three days and three nights of the descent into hell. John Taylor died on 18 July 1849. Harriet asked Mill's advice on finding a suitable Anglican clergyman for the funeral. She could not decide which would be more likely to arouse unwelcome comment: if Mill attended the funeral or if he stayed away. She thought perhaps a funeral for the family only would be the best solution as then no friends—however close—would be present.

Having worked so hard to maintain a fragile position of propriety, Mill and Harriet were not about to throw it away now. After all three figures in that old love triangle were dead, Harriet's son Algernon was still faithfully keeping to the official story: 'John Stuart Mill, the fast friend for many years of my father and mother, and equally esteemed by both. After the latter had been two years a widow he married her, and thus became my stepfather.'[32] In her bold essay on marriage early in their relationship in which Harriet had recommended universal no-fault divorce, she nevertheless put a surprising brake on remarriage: 'not *less* time than two years should elapse between suing for divorce and permission to contract again'.[33] Harriet was a widow, not a divorcée, yet despite having waited for each other for twenty years, she and Mill allotted almost two years as a respectable period for mourning and the awakening of new love. Jacob working for seven years for his Rachel has nothing on John Stuart Mill and his two decades of passionate waiting. As an engaged man, he wrote to Harriet of his longing for their coming nuptial: 'The time that seems long, the time that I am often impatient of the length of, is the time till spring—the time till we have a home, till we are together in our life instead of this unsatisfactory this depressing coming and going.'[34] Only Harriet's two younger children, Algernon and Helen, were invited to the wedding. It was a secular ceremony. John Stuart Mill and Harriet Hardy Taylor were married at the registry office, Melcombe Regis, Dorset, on 21 April (Easter Monday) 1851.

Having finally entered the married state for the first time at the age of forty-five, Mill soon adopted a remarkably Christian view of his marriage. When Mill's brother George heard of the wedding, he wrote to his friend Algernon (Harriet's son) a jaunty letter, expressing surprise on the grounds that he thought that Harriet was opposed to marriage on principle. Mill was livid. He cut George off forever, not even renewing contact when he knew that he was dying slowly and in tremendous pain. Mill's position was that George did not know what principles Harriet held and he had no right to presume, let alone judge. George was on to something however. Harriet had written in her private essay for Mill that in the future no one would marry, so at that time in her life she was certainly not in favour of marriage in principle (though perhaps accepted it as sometimes a prudent expediency given current cultural realities). Mill the botanist, Mill the logician, nevertheless, finally had a word that served fully to elucidate the fact that Harriet was the most important person in his life: she was his *wife*. How he loved that word! It instantly became the habitual way that he referred to Harriet. He wrote a five-sentence letter to his sister Clara in which he used the phrase 'my wife' four times.[35] Harriet, by contrast, always referred to her second husband as 'Mr. Mill' in her letters. Mill would write to his mother and mention 'my wife'; Harriet would write to her mother and refer to 'Mr. Mill'. And this was how he now addressed Harriet herself, opening his letters with the greeting: 'My dearest wife'. On the outside, the envelope was addressed to 'Mrs. J. S. Mill' or, when she was in France, 'Madame J. S. Mill'.

In his *Autobiography*, Mill reflects that beside Harriet's death, their marriage was the most important event in his private life. He wailed at his loss: 'For seven and a half years that blessing was mine; for seven and a half only!'[36] Those are curious statements. Surely the most important event was when he had secured her love. Surely they had had over a quarter of a century together in love, companionship, and intellectual collaboration. Why start the clock of his blessedness only after their trip to the Melcombe Regis registry office? Did Mill see something sacramental in the married state that sets it apart? If that sounds far-fetched, so do some of his own comments. He wrote to 'my dearest wife' in July 1852: 'I do beg you to let us even now be married again, and this time at church.'[37] Mill wanted to be as married to Harriet as he possibly could be and, at least in a weak moment, he suspected that people who had been married with the proper, religious ceremony in a consecrated church building were somehow more married than those who had not. Most startling of all is a denunciation Mill wrote to his sister Clara after she had allegedly slighted Harriet: 'You are certainly mistaken if you suppose that I said you had been uncivil to my wife. I said you had been wanting in all good feeling and even common civility to us. My wife and I are one.'[38] Mill is evoking Christian teaching based in Genesis 2:24, and reaffirmed by Christ himself: 'Wherefore they are no more twain, but one flesh. What therefore God hath joined together, let not man put asunder' (Matthew 19:6). As feminists, Mill and Harriet spent their lives at war with the theologically grounded, legally enforced assumption that husband and wife are one. Yet here is Mill making the claim himself! Mill's marriage was sacred. In 1870, a woman wrote to him, explaining that she had very different thoughts and feelings from her husband and asking if therefore it would be justifiable for her to divorce him. Mill was by then so far away from Harriet's early commitment to no-fault divorce that he told this woman that she did not have a good moral case for divorce, and he recommended instead that she continue to live with her husband in the reasonable hope that the two of them would grow together, learning to feel and think more alike.[39]

As had already been true with *Principles of Political Economy* when her first husband was still alive, during the years of his marriage Mill credited Harriet with the 'joint production' of his books. Increasingly, he asked her to choose the theme of whatever he was to write next.

In one sense, this was merely an expression of the division of labour he had worked out when interacting with Carlyle: he would find the logical exposition of the meaning that someone else of worth had discerned. Mill had written to Comte in March 1843: 'I should like to use your friendly advice to good advantage, asking where I should direct my intellectual efforts, especially when you will be in a better position to judge my kind of talent.'[40] Now Mill had someone with perfect judgement who knew him intimately to direct him. In 1832, he had gone on a walking tour in Cornwall. He visited St Michael's Chair, where legend had it that 'whoever sits in the chair ensures the prerogative of rule during the married state'.[41] Fortunately for Mill, he did not risk it: he found being ruled by Harriet a delight; he was not submitting to it, he was fostering it. It was a splendid sensation. He had now found the perfect relationship of reciprocal superiority for his work: 'I should like everyone to know that I am the Dumont & you are the originating mind, the Bentham.'[42] Harriet was the St Francis who could have a mystical vision of a winged Seraph in the form of the Crucified; Mill was the St Bonaventure who could give it a rational exposition in *The Soul's Journey into God*. Mill maintained that his literary career would be at an end without her: 'What would be the use of my outliving you! I could write nothing worth keeping alive for except with your prompting.'[43] As a good Malthusian, one wonders if the books became a kind of substitute for having children with Harriet: he insisted that they were conceived together with her, and they both played their full parts in raising them.

In the autumn of 1858, because Harriet's health was deteriorating, they went on a continental trip together in order to give her the benefit of a better climate. They were intending just to pass through Avignon, but she died there from a haemorrhage of the lung on 3 November 1858. Is that all there is? Mill could not help but start to hope for there to be a life beyond this one: 'She is buried in the cemetery of the town of Avignon & with her all our earthly happiness.'[44] He had left himself room to hope for heavenly happiness yet to come. As to this life, Mill became determined to sanctify it by ever living to do her will: 'The only consolation possible is the determination to live always as in her sight'; 'the sole motive that remains strong enough to give any interest to life is the desire to do what she would have wished'.[45]

Avignon had meant nothing to him, but now it became Mill's new home. He spent lavish amounts of money on an ornate, marble tomb for Harriet. He bought a house close by where he could see her grave from his window. He lived for much of each year there for the last fifteen years of his life. He visited her grave daily. All this too is rather surprising if one only knows Mill the rationalist. For instance, Mill had dismissed the Christian practice of worshipping on Sunday as 'superstition': 'The devotion which is not felt equally at all times does not deserve the name.'[46] Surely by the same logic the devotion that is not felt equally in all places does not deserve the name. Christians hallow Sunday because on that day their Saviour rose from the dead. Mill hallowed Avignon because in that place his beloved wife had died. The woman he loved was not to be found at the place where her mortal remains had been interred. If visiting her grave daily is therefore superstitious, then so be it. Once again, we see Mill coming to understand the ways of a devotional sense—the logic of devotion—through his relationship with his beloved Harriet.

After her death, Mill redoubled his campaign to announce Harriet's greatness to the world. In the case of his father, James Mill, he had been convinced that the dignified thing to do was to just put his name and life dates on his gravestone. For Harriet, Mill strained to explain all that she was that the world had now lost:

> To the beloved memory of Harriet Mill, the dearly beloved and deeply regretted wife of John Stuart Mill / Her great and loving heart, her noble soul, her clear powerful original and comprehensive intellect, made her the guide and support, the instructor in wisdom and the example in goodness. As she was the sole earthly delight of those who had the happiness to belong to her, as earnest for the public good as she was generous and devoted to all who surrounded her, her influence has been felt in many of the greatest improvements of the age and will be in those still to come / Were there but a few hearts and intellects like hers, the earth would already become the hoped-for heaven. She died to the irreparable loss of those who survive her at Avignon, Nov. 3 1858.[47]

The line about the earth becoming the hoped-for heaven is a reference to the Lord's Prayer: 'Thy kingdom come. Thy will be done in earth, as it is in heaven' (Matthew 6:10). Essentially, Mill is saying that Harriet was helping to bring in the millennial age of the divine kingdom of peace, justice, and righteousness.

Another dense syntax of exaltation came in the dedication of *On Liberty* (1859):

> To the beloved and deplored memory of her who was the inspirer, and in part the author, of all that is best in my writings—the friend and wife whose exalted sense of truth and right was my strongest incitement, and whose approbation was my chief reward—I dedicate this volume. Like all that I have written for many years, it belongs as much to her as to me; but the work as it stands has had, in a very insufficient degree, the inestimable advantage of her revision; some of the most important portions having been reserved for a more careful re-examination, which they are now never destined to receive. Were I but capable of interpreting to the world one half the great thoughts and noble feelings which are buried in her grave, I should be the medium of a greater benefit to it, than is ever likely to arise from anything that I can write, unprompted and unassisted by her all but unrivalled wisdom.[48]

Then there was what he said about her in the *Autobiography*.

Mill's latent frustration, which was being manifested in all these over-written tributes, was that he could not point to an objective achievement of Harriet's which he could invite people to assess directly for themselves. Save for a few early, minor pieces in the *Monthly Repository* and her contributions to the books that were published under his name, Harriet's only publication was *Enfranchisement of Women*, which originally had appeared anonymously in 1851 in the *Westminster Review*. Packe asserted, 'Both of them [Mill and Harriet] were well aware that it was not a very striking paper', but I do not know what evidence led him to that claim.[49] In his own effort at the same theme, *The Subjection of Women* (1869), Mill had carefully praised Madame de Staël as: 'The greatest woman who has left writings behind her sufficient to give her an eminent rank in the literature of her country.'[50] Harriet was in the category of a great woman who had left behind insufficient writings to allow her to be given an eminent rank. The philosopher Jo Ellen Jacobs rebukes those who reject Mill's statements about Harriet: 'I believe him. He is to be commended for his honesty, and other scholars should stop calling his statements "extravagant".'[51] Nevertheless, Jacobs wrote that in a book in which she dealt with her own frustration that Harriet had left insufficient writings to reveal her genius by recovering her voice through composing a fictional Harriet Taylor Mill diary.

Harriet's *Enfranchisement of Women* became a best-selling classic amongst women's rights advocates in the United States. One of them, Paulina Wright Davis, agreed with Mill that Harriet was a truly extraordinary person and therefore proposed that a biography of her needed to be written, as that is typically a tribute that is paid to the greatest people of their time and place. In believing Mill's glowing report about Harriet, Davis unintentionally once again threw the philosopher back onto the depressing realization that the only evidence to substantiate his claims was his own testimony as an eyewitness. He feared that any attempt to chronicle Harriet's greatness would be an embarrassment:

> Were it possible in a memoir to have the formation and growth of a mind like hers portrayed, to do so would be as valuable a benefit to mankind as was ever conferred by a biography.
>
> But such a psychological history is seldom possible, and in her case the materials for it do not exist. All that could be furnished is her birth-place, parentage, and a few dates! and it seems to me that her memory is more honored by the absence of any attempt at a biographical notice, than by the presence of a most meagre one.[52]

Victorian biographers of Mill who were themselves rationalists and sceptics and who admired him, found this discrepancy between what he claimed and what he could prove regrettable. Bain wrote of Mill's statements about Harriet: 'Unfortunately for both, he outraged all reasonable credibility in describing her matchless genius, without being able to supply any corroborating testimony.'[53] Equally revolted and unsympathetic, Leslie Stephen pronounced that Mill's 'vehement hyperboles, however, seem to betray a sense that he could give no tangible proof of their accuracy'.[54] But, to adopt one of his own observations, Mill had merely rediscovered what was already known the world over, that what it means for something to be held on faith is that one cannot offer irrefutable proofs; that one must be content to bear witness to what one has seen and heard. Who hath believed our report? And to whom is the arm of the Lord revealed? A crucial feature of *A System of Logic* was that the author put all of the weight on proof; yet John Stuart Mill discovered that one of the most important things which he wanted to convince the world of was something that he could not prove.

Notes

1. John Stuart Mill to W. J. Fox, 18 May 1833: Francis E. Mineka (ed.), *The Earlier Letters of John Stuart Mill, 1812–1848* (Collected Works of John Stuart Mill XII), Toronto: University of Toronto Press, 1963, p. 158.
2. John Stuart Mill to W. J. Fox, 14 February 1834: CWJSM XII (*Earlier Letters*), pp. 213–14. (The date is not on the letter, but the editors have plausibly reconstructed it.)
3. Robert Eadon Leader, *Life and Letters of John Roebuck*, London: Edward Arnold, 1897, pp. 38–9. F. A. Hayek figured out the probable date of this party: Sandra J. Peart (ed.), *Hayek on Mill: The Mill–Taylor Friendship and Related Writings* (The Collected Works of F. A. Hayek XVI), Chicago: University of Chicago Press, 2015, p. 73.
4. Peart, *Hayek on Mill*, p. 76.
5. Michael St John Packe, *The Life of John Stuart Mill*, London: Secker and Warburg, 1954, p. 187.
6. Francis E. Mineka and Dwight N. Lindley (eds), *The Later Letters of John Stuart Mill, 1849–1873* (Collected Works of John Stuart Mill XIV), Toronto: University of Toronto Press, 1972, p. 168.
7. Mary Pickering, *Auguste Comte: Volume II: An Intellectual Biography*, Cambridge: Cambridge University Press, 2009, p. 97.
8. John Stuart Mill to George Henry Lewes, 1 March 1841: CWJSM XIII (*Earlier Letters*), p. 467.
9. John Stuart Mill, *Autobiography and Literary Essays* (Collected Works of John Stuart Mill I), ed. J. M. Robson, Indianapolis, IN: Liberty Fund, 2006 (reprint of Toronto: University of Toronto Press, 1981), p. 619.
10. Alexander Bain, *John Stuart Mill: A Criticism: with personal recollections*, London: Longmans, Green, and Co., 1882, p. 164.
11. John Stuart Mill to John Sterling, 22 April 1840: CWJSM XIII (*Earlier Letters*), p. 429.
12. Horace N. Pym (ed.), *Memories of Old Friends: being extracts from the Journals and Letters of Caroline Fox of Penjerrick, Cornwall*, London: Smith, Elder, and Co., 1882, p. 206. (Entry for 29 May 1846.)
13. Jo Ellen Jacobs (ed.), *The Complete Works of Harriet Taylor Mill*, Bloomington, IN: Indiana University Press, 1998, p. 459.
14. Mary Taylor, 'Some Notes on the Private Life of John Stuart Mill', Hugh S. R. Elliot (ed.), *The Letters of John Stuart Mill*, 2 vols, London: Longmans, Green, and Co., 1910, I, p. xlii. (This is an account by Helen's niece who had her aunt live with her in her declining years.)
15. John Stuart Mill to Barclay Fox, 22 May 1840: CWJSM XIII (*Earlier Letters*), p. 435.

16. CWJSM XIV (*Later Letters*), p. 57.
17. Oscar A. Haac (translator and editor), *The Correspondence of John Stuart Mill and Auguste Comte*, New Brunswick, NJ: Transaction Publishers, 1995, pp. 69, 130.
18. Bertrand Russell and Patricia Russell (eds), *The Amberley Papers: The Letters and Diaries of Lord and Lady Amberley*, 2 vols, London: Hogarth Press, 1937, I, p. 371.
19. Jacobs, *Complete Works*, p. 375.
20. Haac, *Mill and Comte*, p. 370.
21. Jacobs, *Complete Works*, p. 472.
22. Peart, *Hayek on Mill*, p. xxxiv.
23. CWJSM I (*Autobiography and Literary Essays*), p. 257.
24. Jacobs, *Complete Works*, p. 371.
25. Harriet Taylor to John Taylor, 19 December 1848: Jacobs, *Complete Works*, p. 489.
26. Jacobs, *Complete Works*, p. 501.
27. Jacobs, *Complete Works*, p. 355.
28. Jacobs, *Complete Works*, p. 359.
29. Jacobs, *Complete Works*, p. 358.
30. Jacobs, *Complete Works*, p. 366. (John Taylor was often remarking 'Thank God' and Harriet is provided a theological gloss to ensure the correctness of that sentiment.)
31. Jacobs, *Complete Works*, p. 366.
32. Algernon Taylor, *Memories of a Student, 1838–1888*, privately printed, n.d. [1892], pp. 10–11.
33. Peart, *Hayek on Mill*, p. 71.
34. CWJSM XIV (*Later Letters*), pp. 49–50.
35. CWJSM XIV (*Later Letters*), p. 82.
36. CWJSM I (*Autobiography and Literary Essays*), p. 247.
37. John Stuart Mill to Harriet Mill, 13 July 1852: CWJSM XIV (*Later Letters*), p. 97.
38. John Stuart Mill to Clara Mill, 5 March 1852: CWJSM XIV (*Later Letters*), p. 82. (It is possible that Mill decided upon further reflection not to send this letter.)
39. CWJSM XVII (*Later Letters*), p. 1715.
40. Haac, *Mill and Comte*, p. 139.
41. John M. Robson (ed.), *Journals and Debating Speeches* (Collected Works of John Stuart Mill XXVII), Toronto: University of Toronto Press, 1988, p. 634.
42. CWJSM XIV (*Later Letters*), p. 112.
43. CWJSM XIV (*Later Letters*), p. 165.

44. CWJSM XV (*Later Letters*), p. 582.
45. CWJSM XV (*Later Letters*), pp. 574, 577–8.
46. CWJSM XV (*Later Letters*), p. 513.
47. Peart, *Hayek on Mill*, p. 257. (It is laid out in lines like a poem. I have therefore added some punctuation for clarity.)
48. John Stuart Mill, *Essays on Politics and Society*, ed. J. M. Robson (Collected Works of John Stuart Mill XVIII), New York: Routledge, 1977, p. 216.
49. Packe, *Mill*, p. 347.
50. John Stuart Mill, *Essays on Equality, Law, and Education*, ed. John M. Robinson and Stefani Collini (Collected Works of John Stuart Mill XXI), Toronto: University of Toronto Press, 1984, p. 279.
51. Jo Ellen Jacobs, *The Voice of Harriet Taylor Mill*, Bloomington, IN: Indiana University Press, 2002, p. 252.
52. John Stuart Mill to Paulina Wright Davis, 22 July 1870: CWJSM XVII (*Later Letters*), p. 1748.
53. Bain, *John Stuart Mill*, p. 171.
54. Leslie Stephen, 'Mill, John Stuart (1806–1873)', in *Dictionary of National Biography*, Vol. XIII, Sidney Lee (ed.), New York: Macmillan, 1909, pp. 390–9 (here 394).

9
Called Unto Liberty

'Ye have been called unto liberty.'
(Galatians 5:13)

Mill's *On Liberty* is one of the great texts of western literature. It is a heady blend of lucid argumentation and passionate indignant. In his *Autobiography*, Mill created an origins myth for his most popular work, one befitting the illustrious place it holds in the canon: 'I had first planned and written it as a short essay, in 1854. It was in mounting the steps of the Capitol, in January 1855, that the thought first arose of converting it into a volume.'[1] As it happened, however, Mill wrote to Harriet every evening on that trip, chronicling all he had seen and done throughout each day. We therefore know that it was actually a day at the Vatican when Mill was thus inspired. To be precise, it was 15 January 1855:

> Today is bright... the Piazza of St Peter's with its soldiers exercising was bright... I went to the Vatican & began seeing the statues... On Thursday I believe there will be fine music at St Peter's which I will certainly hear... On my way here [the inn] cogitating thereon I came back to an idea we have talked about & thought that the best thing to write & publish at present would be a volume on Liberty.[2]

On the following day, Mill wrote: 'I have had Lucas sitting with me a part of this evening talking about all manner of things—I talking infidelity as freely as he Catholicism.' Frederick Lucas was British, an adult convert to Roman Catholicism, and the founder of the Catholic journal, the *Tablet*. Mill was representing the side of free thought or unbelief in their private conversations about religion. Two days later, Mill attended Mass at St Peter's Basilica. The day after that, 19 January, he went to the Sistine Chapel. The next day Mill reported: 'At present it feels as if any place would be very flat which does not contain St Peter's.' On the following day, he attended Mass at the basilica of St Agnes. It was only the day after that—22 January—that Mill first went to the Capitol. Mill's propitious birth legend for *On Liberty* might have been inspired by the final words of the religious sceptic Edward Gibbon's celebrated *The Decline and Fall of the Roman Empire*: 'It was among the ruins of the Capitol that I first conceived the idea of a work which has amused and exercised near twenty years of my life, and which, however inadequate to my own wishes, I finally deliver to the curiosity of the public.'[3] The true, Vatican origins, however, are even more apposite, as much of *On Liberty* is a protest against restrictions and limitations arising from the influence of Christian orthodoxy.

Joseph Hamburger argued that Mill's 'prime target' in *On Liberty* was organized Christianity.[4] A month after Mill first conceived of the idea, in his daily letter to his wife Harriet he wrote that he believed that his proposed book on liberty would be 'a sensation'.[5] Mill's books had continued to appear with the 'high-church' (actually more and more Broad Church) Christian publisher and printer of Bibles and Prayer Books, John W. Parker. Mill therefore offered him *On Liberty* as well, but he warned Parker to examine its contents before making a decision 'as there are some things in it which may give offence to prejudices'.[6] As with Christian readers in general, Parker was more sympathetic to the main thrusts of *On Liberty* than Mill assumed would be the case.

In terms of lucid argumentation, the most significant feature of *On Liberty* is its articulation of the harm principle:

> The object of this Essay is to assert one very simple principle . . . That principle is, that the sole end for which mankind are warranted, individually or collectively, in interfering with the liberty of action of any of their number, is self-protection. That the only purpose for which power can be rightfully exercised over any member of a civilized community, against his will, is to prevent harm to others. His own good, either physical or moral, is not a sufficient warrant. He cannot rightfully be compelled to do or forbear because it will be better for him to do so, because it will make him happier, because, in the opinions of others, to do so would be wise, or even right. . . . the conduct from which it is desired to deter him, must be calculated to produce evil to

> some one else. The only part of the conduct of any one, for which he is amenable to society, is that which concerns others. In the part which merely concerns himself, his independence is, of right, absolute. Over himself, over his own body and mind, the individual is sovereign.[7]

This is a resonant, powerful argument. It has won the day in his home country and many places beside, and Mill deserves a substantial portion of the credit for this. Indeed, *On Liberty* has so thoroughly and permanently taken the field in this regard that, ironically, the harm principle itself seems to fall under strictures given elsewhere in Mill's treatise: do so many people now find it so self-evident—take it so for granted—that it is, for them, 'a dead dogma, not a living truth'?[8] As Mill recommends in such cases, do they need to try to create imaginary opponents of the harm principle in their minds because they do not know any real ones in their lives? This possibility is a high tribute to its crisp cogency.

Mill underestimated—or at least set aside for another day—how difficult it is to decide what constitutes harm to others and how much this would itself be a site of disagreement between different political, religious, ideological, philosophical, and cultural groups.[9] As has been shown, Mill was convinced, for instance, that having a large family constituted harm to others. He reasserted this very example in *On Liberty*:

> And in a country either over-peopled, or threatened with being so, to produce children, beyond a very small number, with the effect of reducing the reward of labour by their competition, is a serious offence against all who live by the remuneration of their labour. The laws which, in many countries on the Continent, forbid marriage unless the parties can show that they have the means of supporting a family, do not exceed the legitimate of the State.... Such laws are interferences of the State to prohibit a mischievous act—an act injurious to others, which ought to be a subject of reprobation, and social stigma, even when it is not deemed expedient to superadd legal punishment.[10]

Many people, however, would not accept Mill's reasons for why a couple deciding together to have another child constitutes harm to others. On the contrary, they would see the right to choose to have a baby with a willing partner as one of the most basic exercises of their individual liberty. Not a few would even argue that increasing the birth rate might be in the interests of the nation and the economy.

In other words, the criterion of harm, though agreed upon by all parties, does not necessarily result in an end to a fundamental dispute between them. Nevertheless, even if it is not always an easy principle to implement in an uncontested way, the harm principle itself is both clear and compelling.

Much of *On Liberty* carries the tone of an exasperated person who is not going to put up with it anymore. This is precisely what makes it so popular. Christians and atheists, orthodox and freethinkers, Tories and Radicals, English and Irish, Britons and Indians, women and men, young and old, one and all, everyone, everyone wants decisively to throw off those who are trying to hinder their liberty, to suppress their opinions, to silence their voices. Mill is Everyman, every person. Christians feel this way too and were by-and-large also glad to have someone give vent so effectively to their feelings. These very qualities of the piece, however, make it not always easy to discern what is principle and what is protest. Does Mill truly believe that it is vital for society that the opposite side on every issue be represented? That if an opinion has become universal, then we must ourselves generate 'the strongest arguments which the most skilful devil's advocate can conjure up'?[11] His examples of beliefs that need to be challenged are all ones with which he does not agree. If it is a principle, however, then it must be equally applicable to his own most sacred convictions. It is not as obvious as one would assume that he truly thinks so.

In fact, at the risk of seeming mischievous, Mill's own devotion—Harriet—(by this time deceased), was unwittingly attacked in the very same year (1859) that *On Liberty* was published. Elizabeth Gaskell wrote *The Life of Charlotte Brontë* and included in it a letter by the author of *Jane Eyre* which contained this passage:

> Of all the articles respecting which you question me, I have seen none, except that notable one in the *Westminster* on the Emancipation of Women. But why are you and I to think (perhaps I should rather say to *feel*) so exactly alike on some points that there can be no discussion between us? Your words on this paper express my thoughts. Well argued it is—clear, logical—but vast is the hiatus of omission; harsh the consequent jar on every finer chord of the soul. What is this hiatus? I think I know; and knowing, I will venture to say. I think the writer forgets there is such a thing as self-sacrificing love and disinterested devotion. When I first read the paper, I thought it was the work of a

> powerful-minded, clear-headed woman, who had a hard, jealous heart, muscles of iron, and nerves of bend leather; a woman who longed for power, and had never felt affection. To many women affection is sweet, and power conquered indifferent—though we all like influence won. I believe J. S. Mill would make a hard, dry, dismal world of it; and yet he speaks admirable sense through a great portion of his article—especially when he says, that if there be a natural unfitness in women for men's employment, there is no need to make laws on the subject...[12]

As was the general report, Brontë believed that Mill was the author of 'The Emancipation of Women'. The true author, however, had been Harriet Taylor. Thus Brontë's comment that she initially thought that the author was a woman was correct, and therefore all of her disparaging remarks about the kind of woman who would write in this way were about the Perfect One to whom Mill had devoted his life, whose memory was to him 'a religion'. Mill was outraged. He wrote two indignant letters to Gaskell, maintaining in both of them that an author should not include material 'that might be offensive to the feelings of individuals'.[13] Now the entire burden of *On Liberty* is that opinions need to be expressed freely without being suppressed because some people will find them offensive. Mill very much wanted to convince the world that Harriet was a superior being and therefore someone putting the contrary view should be—on the reckoning of his treatise—essential to making his case a living truth: if Brontë's dismissive remarks did not exist, he would have to invent them. It might be countered that this is personal rather than ideological, but the very thing Mill is trying to overturn in *On Liberty* is the fact that Christians are intimately devoted to their Father in heaven and therefore take attacks upon God personally. The *British Quarterly Review*, which agreed with Mill's call for liberty, nevertheless cautioned (somewhat over-heatedly): 'Be it recollected that a sincere theist would sooner hear his dearest friend calumniated, his father's or his mother's honour assailed, than the existence of that Infinitely Good Being in whom he believes, called in question.'[14] If it is argued that God does not actually exist, so disparaging remarks regarding the deity cannot be a true, personal attack, then one could no less argue that Harriet did not exist on account of her being dead by this time. *On Liberty* is so satisfying precisely because it naturally causes readers to imagine the joy of heroically resisting someone else trying to limit their freedom rather than stoically enduring while what they cherish the most is being vilified.

Mill himself is more explicit about another tension in his presentation, namely, the one regarding social disapproval. Before it was published, Mill summarized the theme of *On Liberty* in one sentence: 'Its subject is moral, social, & intellectual liberty, asserted against the despotism of society whether exercised by governments or by public opinion.'[15] Mill understood, however, that legal restrictions in Britain against liberty of opinion and expression were rapidly falling away and would continue to do so whether he wrote or not. As it was inconvenient for his case against organized Christianity, Mill ignored the extent to which it was Dissenting evangelical Christians who were the engines for this move towards civil and religious equality before the law.[16] In its review of *On Liberty*, the evangelical Nonconformist *British Quarterly Review*—which banged on unceasingly about full equality for all irrespective of their beliefs—dryly remarked: 'It may surprise some of our readers to learn that the subject of liberty, "civil or social", has been "seldom stated and hardly discussed in general terms".'[17] Civil liberty did not need a champion—it was already conquering.

That leaves Mill's second concern, the 'despotism' of 'public opinion'. He objects to the reality and the effects of social disapprobation. If people will be affronted and shun you because they find your views offensive, then that is bad for society: 'Protection, therefore, against the tyranny of the magistrate is not enough: there needs protection also against the tyranny of the prevailing opinion and feeling.'[18] A good society is one in which people feel free—socially as well as legally—to say what they think. Mill saw Victorian culture as socially oppressive: 'That so few now dare to be eccentric, marks the chief danger of the time.'[19] It is even less clear in this case to what extent there is a general principle being advanced here, or if it is primarily a protest against specific features of the current state of things. Mill himself recognizes a right to shun disagreeable people: that is simply personal liberty being exercised by the shunner. More than that, Mill even recommends that social disapproval be used for social control. In the quote above from *On Liberty* itself in which he is advocating Malthusianism, he maintains that 'social stigma' is a good way to advance the cause. In *Principles of Political Economy*—in his hopes that a socialist utopia might be possible—Mill explained approvingly what could make it work:

> every member of the association would be amenable to the most universal, and one of the strongest, of personal motives, that of public opinion. The force of this motive in deterring from any act or omission positively reproved by the community, no one is likely to deny...[20]

In his *Autobiography*, Mill advised motivating people to do good through 'the fear of shame'.[21] And John Mill spent his entire career helping to administer Britain's colonial rule over India. One would think the right of Indians to the liberty to not be forcibly governed by a nation from half way around the world would be an easy application of *On Liberty*'s message, but the man who had risen to Chief Examiner in the East India Company was ready with his answer: 'Despotism is a legitimate mode of government in dealing with barbarians.' The warrant for this, he asserted, is because the 'early difficulties in the way of spontaneous progress are so great'.[22] That rationale, however, is based in the argument that force may be applied for the person's own good, something which his articulation of the scope of the harm principle explicitly ruled out. Put simply, Mill does not seem to mind coercion so much when it is being used to implement a view that he is convinced is right and true. Joseph Hamburger argued that Mill wanted liberty to clear away the bad influence of organized Christianity, but then control would emerge to enforce the beliefs he approved of which would replace orthodoxy.[23]

And so we come to Mill's critique of Christianity in *On Liberty*. He had always been ambitious to be an intellectual leader in society as a whole. Mill was well aware, nevertheless, that to depart too blatantly from the religious convictions of his countrymen and women could well result in his forfeiting his influence over them. As he wrote to Comte in 1841:

> You are doubtless aware that here an author who should openly admit to antireligious or even antichristian opinions, would compromise not only his social position, which I feel myself capable of sacrificing to a sufficiently high objective, but also, and this would be more serious, his chance of being read.[24]

This is the particular despotism of public opinion with which Mill was fed up. To always be concealing and dissembling makes one start to feel like a coward or a hypocrite, but to speak out boldly was to alienate your audience. Something has to give. What Mill wanted to give way was the social disapproval of religious scepticism and unbelief. Religion is a persistent concern in *On Liberty*. When Mill offers concrete examples, again and again they are about religious beliefs and practices. There is a sense in which Mill was frustrated by the sheer force of religious belief, by how tenaciously believers hold to their beliefs. He speaks, for instance, of 'religion, the most powerful of the elements which have entered in the formation of moral feelings'. He observes: 'the *odium theologicum*, in a sincere bigot, is one of the most unequivocal cases of moral feeling'.[25] Mill longed for orthodox Christians to hold their convictions more loosely, more provisionally, less exclusively. He tries to help this along with various thought experiments: Socrates was condemned for atheism, but we now think of him as virtuous; perhaps, Victorian Christians, the atheists you revile today are also virtuous; Marcus Aurelius was virtuous, yet he had a blind spot in his assumption that Christianity was bad for humanity; dear Christians, maybe the freethinkers you assume are bad for humanity are actually good for it as well; Jesus himself was executed for blasphemy; who is the good man that you might be attacking on the mistaken assumption that he is a blasphemer? Those who tried to reform the Church—heroes now honoured by devout Protestants such as Jan Hus—were persecuted as heretics: who are you shunning as a heretic who might, in truth, be a noble reformer? In *On Liberty*, Mill was appealing to dogmatic Christians, calling them to become more liberal.

One of the longer sections of *On Liberty* is a sustained critique of Christian morality. At first glance, it can appear not to relate very closely to the general themes being expounded in this tract. Mill argues that Christianity does not offer a self-contained, sufficient system of morality. The Hebrew scriptures provide a model 'intended only for a barbarous people'. As to the New Testament: 'The Gospel always refers to a pre-existing morality... often impossible to be interpreted literally, and possessing rather the impressiveness of poetry or eloquence than the precision of legislation.'[26] The morality which the early church formulated was a reaction against paganism and it is therefore 'incomplete and one-sided'. Christian morality is negative rather than positive; it is focused upon avoiding vice rather than cultivating virtue. This passage can read like Mill is trying to criticize Christianity in any way he possibly can—that he is simply venting against the established faith of his land—but the real point is not that Christianity is wrong, but that it is incomplete. Mill is not trying to get Christians to abandon their morality, but to put an end to their assumption that no one else has anything to add to it, that everyone else is wrong. It is his old denunciation of sectarianism, of one-sidedness: 'on every subject on which difference of opinion is possible, the truth depends on a balance to be struck between two sets of conflicting reasons'.[27] In some ways, Mill was anticipating Matthew Arnold's argument in *Culture and Anarchy* (1869). Mill too wanted Victorian Christians to balance their Hebraism with some more Hellenism:

> 'Pagan self-assertion' is one of the elements of human worth, as well as 'Christian self-denial'. There is a Greek ideal of self-development, which the Platonic and Christian ideal of self-government blends with, but does not supersede.[28]

On Liberty is a tract for all times, but it was also a tract for the times—a revolt against the degree to which a self-satisfied, dominant, dogmatic Christianity did not allow for other voices to flourish in nineteenth-century Britain.

As with *A System of Logic*, Mill was once again surprised to discover that Christians liked *On Liberty*. In line with his own sense of his strengths, however, both books were more about method than meaning and the opposing team usually thinks that they too can win while playing by the same rules. Freethinkers might assume that orthodox Christians are not very logical and not very liberal, but religious believers generally do not imagine that logic or liberty are somehow the rightful possessions of their opponents. The faithful believe themselves to be no less logical, no less liberal, than their critics. Mill braced himself for the onslaught. He wrote to the Secularist leader and editor of the *Reasoner*, George Jacob Holyoake, appealing to him not to run an early review of *On Liberty* so that it would not immediately get labelled anti-Christian, although, he mused: 'It is likely enough to be called an infidel book in any case.'[29] Mill waited for the reaction. High-profile Christians did not waste any time getting in their praise. Mill assumed that F. D. Maurice would think it was his duty to oppose the book, but the clergyman was pleased to laud it. The Reverend

Charles Kingsley, who was appointed a chaplain to Her Majesty the Queen that same year, became engrossed as soon as he found a copy of *On Liberty* in a bookshop. He stayed standing there, reading it with delight. Kingsley claimed it made him 'a clearer headed & braver minded man upon the spot', and specifically praised the section on Christian morality.[30] William Gladstone, that great defender of the faith, liked it. Mill soon learned that 'many sincere Christians' agreed with him about liberty.[31] Eventually, he became so accustomed to *On Liberty* being compatible with traditional, organized Christianity that he wrote a long, fascinating explanation regarding how one passage could be harmonized with the doctrine of divine providence. One could not imagine Bentham, Bradlaugh, Holyoake—or any such thoroughgoing opponent of religion—writing this theological reflection of Mill's:

> The difficulty which you feel I understand to be this: how is the opinion that Christianity might have been extinguished by persecution, compatible with the belief that God intended & preordained that Christianity should subsist? I conceive there is no inconsistency between the two opinions. If Xtianity would have perished had it been persecuted in a certain manner, if God had preordained that it shd not perish, the reasonable inference is that God preordained that it should not be persecuted in that manner. The preservation of Xtianity thus brought about would be no 'accident' but part of the divine plan.
>
> The relation between means & ends is quite compatible with a providential government of human affairs. It is only necessary to suppose that God, when he willed the end, willed the means necessary to its accomplishment. If the Maker of all things intended that a certain thing should come to pass, it is reasonable to suppose that provision was made in the general arrangements of the universe for its coming to pass consistently with these arrangements.[32]

In fact, it was prominent fellow freethinkers rather than prominent orthodox Christians who expressed unease with *On Liberty*. Carlyle loathed the book. The agnostic and Benthamite James Fitzjames Stephen would eventually make an all-out assault on it.[33] Even Alexander Bain did not have a favourable first reading of this treatise. The point is not, of course, that most freethinkers did not like it. The point is that dislike of the book did not fall neatly along religious lines. The real headline is that almost everyone liked the book. Mill became more popular than ever.

The last time Caroline Fox mentioned Mill in her journal it was in reference to *On Liberty*, so this is a convenient point at which to loop back in time and present Mill's relationship with Barclay Fox and his diarist sister, Caroline. In his largely isolated life in the early 1840s, Mill developed a rare and deep intimacy with the Fox family. He freely and frequently bestowed upon both Barclay and Caroline the often-withheld status of being his friends. Barclay over and over again commented upon Mill's remarkable warm-heartedness toward him. For instance, here is an entry from Barclay's journal for 14 May 1840: 'Returned to City and called on John Mill at the India House, most cordial affectionate & in short J. Millish.'[34] The Fox family were prominent members of the Society of Friends. Barclay and Caroline's mother, Maria, was a recorded Quaker minister who would go on itinerant preaching tours, even as far as Ireland and France. Their cousin was the eminent Quaker prisoner reformer and minister, Elizabeth Fry. Barclay and Caroline were both devout. His journal, for example, records that he would attend two worship services on a typical Sunday. Caroline's journal, however, is far fuller, so her life and thoughts will predominate in this discussion. Barclay and Caroline's father, Robert Were Fox, was also a pious Quaker who served as an elder at their quarterly meeting for a half a century and was a supporter of the Bible Society. R. W. Fox was also a Fellow of the Royal Society and a noted geologist who theorized that the inside of the earth was hot and whose study of magnetic fields led to the invention of a better compass which was then used on polar expeditions. As religion will be emphasized here, it is important to keep in mind by way of perspective that many of Caroline's entries are scientific in nature—sometimes strikingly spiritual and strikingly scientific entries appear side by side. In 1852, she attended the annual meetings of the British Association for the Advancement of Science in Dublin. Here is Caroline's report: 'Owen's bone theory, Stoke's revelation of the invisible outside ray of the spectrum through the action of sulphate of quinine, Dr. Robinson and Lord Rosse on the nebulæ and telescope, and Colonel Chesney on the Euphrates Expedition, were amongst the most memorable incidents of the week.'[35] Caroline's intense, lifelong piety, however, is of particular interest given the theme of this volume. Many of these incidents in her journal are supernatural testimonies. These are often stories of the Holy Spirit prompting someone to go somewhere or do something that seemed random or irrational but that led to dramatic, favourable consequences such as saving a life. Caroline records an account she clearly believes to be true of a modern case of demonic possession. She writes of her evangelistic efforts as she attempted to share the Gospel with a working-class woman. She does her daily, private devotions with the aid of Catherine Long, *Heavenly Thoughts for Morning Hours* (1855). Her birthday and New Year's Day will both repeatedly prompt her to resolve to live to do God's will. As she lay ill in 1866 on what proved to be her deathbed, Caroline wrote her final entry: 'Surely I know more than ever of the reality of that declaration, "This is Life Eternal, that they might know Thee the only true God and Jesus Christ whom Thou hast sent." [John 17:3] . . . I had before been craving for a little more spiritual life on any terms, and how mercifully this has been granted!'[36] Her 'Bible cases of conversion' was published posthumously in the *Friends' Quarterly Examiner*.

There were multiple reasons why these relationships would become usually close ones for John Stuart Mill. His favourite sibling, Henry, who had tuberculosis, had been brought to Cornwall for his health, and the Foxes became close to him and were at the heart of the sacred drama of his deathbed and passing. John Sterling was there as well, and thus Mill's best male friend was part of the same, intimate circle. Eventually, Sterling would propose marriage to Caroline (who, though she was truly fond of him, proved to be too much of a Quaker to accept an Anglican clergyman). Moreover, the Society of Friends was a form of Christianity that Mill was predisposed to admire. Even his father, James Mill, had taught him that the Society of Friends was a worthy faith. Quakers aligned well with the social commitments of James and John Mill. They too were anti-aristocratic and anti-clerical. They were at the vanguard of the anti-slavery movement. For John—what was even more important and much rarer in Victorian society—Friends were in favour of gender equality, including opening all church offices and ministries to women. Quakers stood for the simple faith of Christ and the Gospels as opposed to ecclesiastical establishments and church tradition. They took Christ's words literally, even passing triumphantly Bentham's 'swear not at all' standard of faithfulness. Not that Mill was entirely uncritical: as was also his complaint in regard to Benthamites and, indeed, most groups, he told Caroline that the Quakers would do more good if they were less sectarian in spirit.

In Caroline's journal one can gain a rare glimpse of a Mill set free. The Cornish Mill is a long way from the reputation he sometimes had of being a 'cold, stern, and dry' sort of person: the Utilitarian philosopher who always wore black and never relished his food.[37] Mill playfully observes to Caroline that his Christian name provides him with the protection of eminent patrons, 'St. John the Evangelist, and the Baptist, and many others', but he muses that their popularity could make his case harder to prioritize and therefore it might be a better strategy to cultivate the favour of some more obscure saints. Mill was so exhilarated walking with the Foxes in the country that he began to enthuse about how high-hearted nature made him 'and illustrated it, with an apology, by jumping'.[38] On another occasion, they visited a cavern: 'J. S. Mill proposed leaving the lighted candles there as an offering to the gnomes.'[39] If asked to speculate upon what Mill might do if he found himself in a cave, one would probably lean toward answers along the lines of attempting to identify geological epochs or collecting samples of the varieties of moss. If in a didactic frame of mind, perhaps he might discourse on Plato. If one were prompted to imagine him in a Romantic mood, then perhaps one would suggest that he might declaim a poem by Wordsworth. One would randomly and without any foreknowledge guess the name Rumpelstiltskin, however, before generating the answer that, if he found himself in a cave, John Stuart Mill would leave an oblation for a mythical race of subterranean dwarfs. Most delightful of all, perhaps from his own collection of botanical specimens, Mill created for Caroline a 'Calendar of Odours' so that at any time she could inhale the fragrances of the specific month that took her fancy. Both Mill and Caroline were born in May, and for their birth month he included: 'Lilac, night-flowering stocks and rockets, laburnum, hawthorn, seringa, sweet-briar.'[40] Perhaps what happened in Cornwall was doomed to stay in Cornwall. Mill was embarrassed by his own expansiveness: 'I really do not think I talked so much about myself in the whole year previous as I have done in the few weeks of my intercourse with your family.'[41]

The Fox family knew exactly who Mill was and where to place him on various ideological spectrums. The first time Barclay met

Mill, he immediately identified him as 'the exquisite writer in the *London & Westminster*'.[42] Sterling explained to them about Mill's anti-religious upbringing. With the Foxes, however, Mill was surprisingly spiritual, theological, Christian, even Quaker. This is not an optical illusion arising from Caroline and Barclay recording what Mill said in their own religious vernacular, as their reports incidentally contain specific linguistic tics of his. Nor is it merely a matter of Mill being a chameleon. It is unquestionably true that Mill often fell in line to a degree with the person with whom he was interacting, sounding more like his interlocutor or correspondent than he would elsewhere in his life. He did this out of a sympathetic instinct. Nevertheless, it is truer to say that different people brought out of Mill different things that were inside him—whether religiously sceptical or spiritually infused thoughts, just to stay with the topic at hand—rather than that he was feigning agreement. Barclay was struck by Mill's 'sincerity'—that he was 'candid', 'genuine', and 'earnest'—and the Friend was reading the philosopher aright.[43]

Yet how religiously inflected is the Mill of the Cornish coast! He was reading the Quaker mystic John Woolman and praising 'spiritual religion'.[44] His life advice to Barclay was: 'For the aim of your strivings, consult the inward guide which will infallibly point out your own peculiar legitimate end and province.... Never relax nor give way to self indulgence or desultory habits, and your reward will be ample according to your self denial. There is work to be done by every man.'[45] The last line Mill would reiterate across the decades, but the first one, with its 'consult the inward guide', is classic Quaker spirituality. (If one wonders if Barclay imported the phrase, Caroline records the philosopher as saying something very similar a month later: 'Every one has an infallible guide in the sanctuary of his own heart if he will but wait and listen.')[46] Mill could sound like he believed in divine providence: 'John Mill speaks thankfully of the tissue of circumstances which has located them here.'[47] He could wax eloquent upon how the Authorized Version of the Bible had introduced into 'the soul' of the English language 'such grand ideas expressed with such sublime simplicity'. He could, at the very least, not strike a sceptical note in discussions about the need for Christian missions to heathen lands. Some of Mill's pronouncements were specifically Christian. Here he is on being a social reformer: 'No one should attempt anything intended to benefit his age, without at first making a stern resolution to take up his cross and to bear it [Matthew 16:24]. If he does not begin by counting the cost [Luke 14:28], all his schemes must end in disappointment.'[48] When dealing with our own bad motives, it is startling to hear Mill sermonize, 'the only certain mode of overcoming this and all other egotisms is to implore the grace of God'.[49] And here is Mill expounding orthodox, biblical theology in a specifically Augustinian key: 'What there is in us that appears evil is, if thoroughly examined, either disproportioned or misdirected good, for our Maker has stamped His own image on everything that lives.'[50] This Mill is no more and no less the 'real' Mill than the anti-religious-dogma Mill revealed in his correspondence with Auguste Comte. Christ seemed closer in Cornwall.

Barclay Fox died in 1855. Caroline wrote to Mill a Christian letter of spiritual testimony, using Barclay's triumphant faith to the very end as her evidence for the truthfulness of the Gospel. By that time, Mill was married and no longer living two lives, but just one. They naturally lost touch. The Mill of *On Liberty* was not the J. S. Mill that Caroline Fox remembered:

> I am reading that terrible book of John Mill's on Liberty, so clear, and calm, and cold: he lays it on one as a tremendous duty to get oneself well contradicted, and admit always a devil's advocate into the presence of your dearest, most sacred Truths, as they are apt to grow windy and worthless without such tests, if indeed they can stand the shock of argument at all. He looks you through like a basilisk, relentless as Fate. We knew him well at one time, and owe him very much; I fear his remorseless logic has led him far since then. This book is dedicated to his wife's memory in a few most touching words. He is in many senses isolated, and must sometimes shiver with the cold.[51]

A month later, she was still not over the shock: 'Mill makes me shiver, his blade is so keen and so unhesitating.'[52] Mill the logician and Mill the Romantic were both still alive and well but, for Caroline Fox, the candles in the cavern had gone out. One wonders if the calendar still held its wild scents.

Notes

1. John Stuart Mill, *Autobiography and Literary Essays* (Collected Works of John Stuart Mill I), ed. J. M. Robson, Indianapolis: Liberty Fund, 2006 (reprint of Toronto: University of Toronto Press, 1981), p. 249.
2. John Stuart Mill to Harriet Mill, 15 January 1855: Francis E. Mineka and Dwight N. Lindley (eds), *The Later Letters of John Stuart Mill, 1849–1873* (Collected Works of John Stuart Mill XIV), Toronto: University of Toronto Press, 1972, p. 295. I was delighted to realize this only to be deflated when I then discovered that I was not the first: Richard Reeves, *John Stuart Mill: Victorian Firebrand*, London: Atlantic Books, 2007, p. 251.
3. Edward Gibbon, *The Decline and Fall of the Roman Empire*, with notes by the Revd H. H. Milman, 5 vols, New York: The Kelmscott Society, n.d. (the final part was originally published in 1789), vol. 5, p. 565.
4. Joseph Hamburger, 'Religion and *On Liberty*', in Michael Laine (ed.), *A Cultivated Mind: Essays on J. S. Mill presented to John M. Robson*, Toronto: University of Toronto Press, 1991, pp. 139–81 (here 157).
5. John Stuart Mill to Harriet Mill, 17 February 1855: CWJSM XIV (*Later Letters*), p. 332.
6. John Stuart Mill to John W. Parker, 30 November 1858: CWJSM XV (*Later Letters*), p. 579.
7. John Stuart Mill, *Essays on Politics and Society*, ed. J. M. Robson (Collected Works of John Stuart Mill XIX), New York: Routledge, 1977, p. 224.
8. CWJSM XIX (*Essays on Politics and Society*), p. 243.
9. Alan Ryan, 'Mill in a liberal landscape', in John Skorupski (ed.), *The Cambridge Companion to Mill*, Cambridge: Cambridge University Press, 1998, pp. 497–543.
10. CWJSM XIX (*Essays on Politics and Society*), p. 304.
11. CWJSM XIX (*Essays on Politics and Society*), p. 245.
12. E. C. Gaskell, *The Life of Charlotte Brontë*, New York: D. Appleton, 1862, p. 189.
13. John Stuart Mill to Elizabeth Gaskell, [July 1859]: CWJSM XV (*Later Letters*), pp. 629–30.
14. Andrew Pyle, *Liberty: Contemporary Responses to John Stuart Mill*, South Bend, IN: St. Augustine's Press, 1994, pp. 198–9. (This collection reprints fifteen reviews of *On Liberty* from the nineteenth century.)
15. John Stuart Mill to Theodore Gomperz, 4 December 1858: CWJSM XV (*Later Letters*), p. 581.
16. Timothy Larsen, *Friends of Religious Equality: Nonconformist Politics in Mid-Victorian England*, Woodbridge: Boydell, 1999; Timothy Larsen, 'Charles Bradlaugh, Militant Unbelief, and the Civil Rights of Atheists', in Caroline Litzenberger and Eileen Groth Lyon (eds), *The Human Tradition in Modern Britain*, Lanham: Rowman & Littlefield, 2006, pp. 127–38.

17. Pyle, *Liberty*, p. 184.
18. CWJSM XIX (*Essays on Politics and Society*), p. 220.
19. CWJSM XIX (*Essays on Politics and Society*), p. 269.
20. John Stuart Mill, *Principles of Political Economy with some of their applications to social philosophy* (Collected Works of John Stuart Mill 2), ed. J. M. Robson, Indianapolis: Liberty Fund, 2006 (reprint of Toronto: University of Toronto Press, 1965), p. 205.
21. CWJSM I (*Autobiography and Literary Essays*), p. 241.
22. CWJSM XIX (*Essays on Politics and Society*), p. 224.
23. Hamburger, 'Religion and *On Liberty*', pp. 139–81 (here 168).
24. Oscar A. Haac (translator and editor), *The Correspondence of John Stuart Mill and Auguste Comte*, New Brunswick, NJ: Transaction Publishers, 1995, p. 42.
25. CWJSM XIX (*Essays on Politics and Society*), pp. 222, 226.
26. CWJSM XIX (*Essays on Politics and Society*), p. 254.
27. CWJSM XIX (*Essays on Politics and Society*), p. 244.
28. CWJSM XIX (*Essays on Politics and Society*), p. 266. On this theme, see Robert Devigne, *Reforming Liberalism: J. S. Mill's Use of Ancient, Religious, Liberal, and Romantic Moralities*, New Haven: Yale University Press, 2006; Robert Devigne, 'Mill on Liberty and Religion: An Unfinished Dialectic', in Eldon J. Eisenach, *Mill and the Moral Character of Liberalism*, University Park, PA: Pennsylvania State University Press, 1998, pp. 231–56. (Arnold himself, however, thought that Mill was part of the problem.)
29. John Stuart Mill to George Jacob Holyoake, [February 1859]: CWJSM XV (*Later Letters*), p. 593.
30. John Stuart Mill to Harriet Mill, 15 January 1855: CWJSM XV (*Later Letters*), pp. 631–2.
31. CWJSM XV (*Later Letters*), p. 631.
32. John Stuart Mill to Henry Franks, 21 July 1865: CWJSM XVI (*Later Letters*), p. 1080.
33. James Fitzjames Stephen, *Liberty, Equality, Fraternity*, London: Smith, Elder, & Co., 1873.
34. R. L. Brett (ed.), *Barclay Fox's Journal*, Fowey, Cornwall: Cornwall Editions, 2008, p. 192.
35. Horace N. Pym (ed.), *Memories of Old Friends: being extracts from the Journals and Letters of Caroline Fox of Penjerrick, Cornwall*, London: Smith, Elder, and Co., 1882, p. 280.
36. Pym, *Memories*, p. 337.
37. Herbert Spencer et al, *John Stuart Mill: His Life and Work*, Boston: James R. Osgood, 1873, p. 35. (From a sketch by W. T. Thornton who is evoking this caricature in order to challenge it.)
38. Pym, *Memories*, p. 79.

39. Pym, *Memories*, p. 71.
40. Pym, *Memories*, p. 87.
41. John Stuart Mill to Caroline Fox ('My dear friend'), 16 April 1840: Pym, *Memories*, p. 94.
42. Brett, *Barclay Fox's Journal*, p. 182.
43. Brett, *Barclay Fox's Journal*, pp. 183–4.
44. Pym, *Memories*, p. 82.
45. Brett, *Barclay Fox's Journal*, pp. 183–4.
46. Pym, *Memories*, p. 86.
47. Pym, *Memories*, p. 71.
48. Pym, *Memories*, p. 72.
49. Pym, *Memories*, p. 81.
50. Pym, *Memories*, p. 74.
51. Pym, *Memories*, p. 322.
52. Pym, *Memories*, p. 322.

10
Love Thy Neighbour as Thyself

'Thou shalt love thy neighbour as thyself.'
(Matthew 22:39)

As Mill had explained to Carlyle in 1834, although he was no longer a Benthamite sectarian—one of the people called Utilitarians—he was still a freelance Utilitarian and was likely to remain so. When his father died in 1836, Mill was candid that this loss was also an opportunity. In particular, he would be able to take the *London and Westminster Review* in a broader direction. He could 'soften the harder & sterner features' of its Utilitarianism.[1] Mill made good on this goal with his 'Bentham' article in the August 1838 issue; and held on to the review despite the tremendous financial loss it was inflicting on him personally so he could finish presenting his more expansive vision with 'Coleridge' in the March 1840 issue. Taken together, Mill had declared in these two articles that Bentham's views were too narrow and that the intellectual's task was to see an opposite school of thought as also possessing part of the truth which needed to be grasped as well. Still, Mill did not attempt to set out his own, constructive version of Utilitarianism in the *London and Westminster Review*—a version that would not be so hard and stern and which would be more conducive to Coleridgian insights. He began working on such a project in the 1850s. It was published in the last three issues of *Fraser's Magazine* for 1861, and then as a single volume early in 1863. It was titled simply *Utilitarianism*.

Mill's Utilitarianism had the twin goals of affirming the principle of utility—the greatest happiness principle—in the face of its critics and to save this principle from the embarrassments and limitations in which, in his view, Bentham had placed it. Mill was with Bentham on the main assertion: 'The utilitarian doctrine is, that happiness is desirable, and the only thing desirable, as an end; all other things being only desirable as means to that end.'[2] Mill observed that precisely because this was taken as foundational it could not be demonstrated: 'to be incapable of proof by reasoning is common to all first principles; to the first premises of our knowledge, as well as to those of our conduct.... No reason can be given why the general happiness is desirable, except that each person, so far as he believes it to be attainable, desires his own happiness.'[3] Mill had put his cards on the table without equivocation: he was a Utilitarian, the greatest happiness principle was his principle. As with so many of his works, he also objected to an intuitive view of morals (singling out Kant by name), and insisted upon an inductive one. The principles of morality are not known a priori, Mill insisted; they are derived from 'observation and experience'.[4]

For our purposes, Mill's theological rationale for Utilitarianism is of particular interest:

> If it be a true belief that God desires, above all things, the happiness of his creatures, and that this was his purpose in their creation, utility is not only not a godless doctrine, but more profoundly religious than any other. If it be meant that utilitarianism does not recognise the revealed will of God as the supreme law of morals, I answer, that an utilitarian who believes in the perfect goodness and wisdom of God, necessarily believes that whatever God has thought fit to reveal on the subject of morals, must fulfil the requirements of utility in a supreme degree.[5]

Utilitarianism is completely compatible, Mill observes, with 'the Christian revelation', as it does not deny that revelation but merely provides a way 'to *interpret* to us the will of God'.[6] It is easy today for people to imagine that such statements must be a mere fig leaf to cover over what is, in truth, an anti-Christian view, but in Mill's day people had a memory of the principle of utility being championed by clergymen before Bentham ever entered the field. Indeed, what would come to be called Utilitarianism (according to Mill, through his own use of that term), was most associated with the one person who was also known as the greatest apologist for orthodox Christianity, the Reverend William Paley.[7] Paley's defences of the Christian faith were standard texts, not least at the University of Oxford: *Horae Paulinae, or the Truth of the Scripture History of St Paul* (1790), *Views of the Evidences of*

Christianity (1794), and *Natural Theology: or, Evidences of the Existence and Attributes of the Deity* (1802). Yet this was the same person whose name had been most connected to the principle of utility. Even as late as 1839—by which time Bentham had been dead for seven years and it had been seventeen years since Mill had founded the Utilitarian Society—a book was published advocating for Utilitarianism with the title, *A Discourse on Ethics of the School of Paley*. Moreover, in 1842 Mill declared that book on the School of Paley to be 'one of the best extant defences of utilitarianism'.[8] The author was the barrister William Smith. In his *Discourse*, Smith described the principle of utility as a 'system of Christian ethics'.[9] Yet one can clearly see how the book would have pleased Mill. It argues, for instance, against intuitionism and in favour of the principle of associationism. It excels at careful definitions and classification. It is lucid on the greatest happiness principle—to promote virtue and to promote happiness are not two separate things but part of the same thing: 'The general welfare is, according to it, the acknowledged test whereby to determine the propriety with which our moral feelings are attached to instances of human conduct.'[10] Smith refutes the charge that Utilitarianism 'allows of no more elevated motive than a shifting, subservient, calculating prudence'.[11] He explains how punishment for immoral behaviour does not necessitate a doctrine of free will. Throughout the *Discourse*, Smith articulates how all that he is teaching is the perfect way for divine providence to have arranged matters. Moreover, 'The only immutable morality is this, that the happiness of all be protected and cultivated.'[12] God has made matters this way precisely in order to allow civilization to advance: if morality were fixed, then humanity would be forever trapped in a primitive state. Explicitly Christian warrants are woven throughout the *Discourse*, but the entire last chapter is given over to theological reflection. The final paragraph invites readers to return to the 'study of practical ethics in the works of Paley' with renewed confidence in its truthfulness.[13] Mill himself wrote a review in which he critiqued an attack on Utilitarianism that had Paley as its foil.[14] It is also worth mentioning in passing that Malthusianism was named after an Anglican clergyman whom Mill referred to as 'the Rev. T. R. Malthus'.[15] In its entry on Malthus, the *Oxford Dictionary of National Biography* reports that the author of *An Essay on the Principle of Population* was 'imbued with the spirit of the gospel and with the doctrines of Christianity; and that in the performance of his clerical duties he was conscientious, devout, and pious'.[16] No, Mill was not obfuscating or dissembling when he claimed that Utilitarianism is compatible with religion. In November 1859, he told the religious sceptic Alexander Bain the same thing in a private communication: 'I do not think of publishing my Utilitarianism till next winter at the earliest, though it is now finished...I have not written it in any hostile spirit towards Xtianity.'[17]

A second striking feature of *Utilitarianism* is its enlisting of the founder of Christianity in the cause: 'In the golden rule of Jesus of Nazareth, we read the complete spirit of the ethics of utility. To do as one would be done by, and to love one's neighbour as oneself, constitute the ideal perfection of utilitarian morality.'[18] Mill is referencing Matthew 7:12 and texts such as Mark 12:31. Once again, this is often read as mere rhetoric with which to try to dupe or seduce Christian readers. In other words, it is assumed that it is not telling us something important about what Mill himself believes, but only about what he believes many of his readers believe. There is no reason, however, to suspect that Mill is any less sincere in this case than in his recruiting of figures such as Socrates and Epicurus to the cause of utility. In fact, Mill was particularly fond of seeing Socrates and Jesus as the two great figures of the ancient world and of seeking to align them both with his causes. Mill used the same scriptural quotation as one that expressed the principle of utility when corresponding with the religious sceptic George Grote:

> I do not see that the opinions you express in your letter on practical ethics constitute any difference between us. I agree in them entirely, and I consider them to follow conclusively from the conception of our own happiness as a unit, neither more nor less valuable than that of another, or, in Christian language, the doctrine of loving one's neighbour as oneself...[19]

To underline the obvious, Mill is not alluding to Matthew 22:39 in that letter because he thinks this would be a rhetorically effective way to appeal to Grote. Mill would even evoke Christ's Golden Rule when defending his actions to Harriet (emphatically not an audience for whom he would be condescending to use the Bible as mere sugarcoating): 'You see darling I tell you everything at the risk of making you uncomfortable but you will have the more confidence in what I tell you, & it is doing as I would be done by, for it is what I wish you to do to me.'[20]

Moreover, Mill continually expressed his reverence for Christ—in public and in private, in correspondence with both Christians and sceptics—throughout his adult life. Far from being a piece of pandering, Mill's tribute to Christ in *Utilitarianism* is at one with his unwavering witness across the decades to the nobility, greatness, and truthfulness of Jesus of Nazareth and his teachings.

When it comes to correcting Bentham, Mill introduces a new factor into the Utilitarian calculus: quality. Some have judged that this destroys hedonism and with it any viable system of utility, but Wendy Donner has argued that Mill does offer a coherent Utilitarianism: qualitative hedonism in contrast to Bentham's quantitative hedonism.[21] Here is Mill expounding on the point:

> Human beings have faculties more elevated than the animal appetites . . . It is quite compatible with the principle of utility to recognise the fact, that some *kinds* of pleasure are more desirable and more valuable than others. It would be absurd that while, in estimating all other things, quality is considered as well as quantity, the estimation of pleasures should be supposed to depend on quantity alone. . . . Few human creatures would consent to be changed into any of the lower animals, for a promise of the fullest allowance of a beast's pleasures; no intelligent human being would consent to be a fool, no instructed person would be an ignoramus, no person of feeling and conscience would be selfish and base, even though they should be persuaded that the fool, the dunce, or the rascal is better satisfied with his lot than they are with theirs. . . . It is better to be a human being dissatisfied than a pig satisfied; better to be Socrates dissatisfied than a fool satisfied.[22]

For what the opinion of a historian is worth, that is a pleasant and persuasive thought.

It is what happens next in the argument that is particularly interesting for our purposes. Mill has to concede the quotidian fact that people all the time, after knowing the delights of both, actually do opt for the low rather than the high road: they give up on poetry and content themselves with pornography. 'It may be questioned whether any one who has remained equally susceptible to both classes of pleasures, ever knowingly and calmly preferred the lower', is Mill's unfalsifiable reply.[23] That is the rarer case, however. What is more common is that people prefer crasser pleasures because they have never experienced the more elevated ones: they have never felt the deep joys of reading, so they assume vandalism holds greater delights. Mill continues:

> From this verdict of the only competent judges, I apprehend there can be no appeal. On a question which is the best worth having of two pleasures, or which of two modes of existence is the most grateful to the feelings, apart from its moral attributes and from its consequences, the judgment of those who are qualified by knowledge of both, or if they differ, that of the majority among them, must be admitted as final.[24]

Mill's goal here was to separate his version of Utilitarianism from Bentham's philistine insistence that push-pin (a simple child's game) was, in terms of utility, as good as poetry if it gave as much pleasure. The price Mill paid for this worthy triumph, however, was to move his Utilitarian scheme further away from the open and objective standards of logic and the natural sciences and closer to the realm of the devotional sense. Mill's argument is that if you have tried poetry, but not experienced its true joys, then you are not qualified to judge. People who have experienced the delights of both poetry and push-pin testify that the former is a higher kind of pleasure, and we should accept their witness as true. This is a classic devotional sense case for religion. Let's run it again with religion replacing poetry: if you have tried religion, but not experienced its true joys, then you are not qualified to judge. People who have experienced the delights of both worshipping God and of playing push-pin testify that the former is a higher kind of pleasure, and we should accept their witness as true. Mill's Utilitarianism has built into it a need to trust the myriads who tell us they have experienced something nobler, more elevated, more worthy, even when we have not shared that experience. Mill also rated the authority of testimony surprisingly highly.

It is time to return to Mill's private life. It is time to speak of Helen Taylor.[25] Mill's stepdaughter experienced the higher pleasures of Christian worship in abundance, so it is worth listening to her testimony. Harriet's youngest child and only daughter became the most important person in Mill's life after his wife's death. She was his closest companion and confidante in the last fifteen years of his life, and the editor of his posthumously published books, including the celebrated *Autobiography*. In 1868, Mill insisted that all that he produced of late was also Helen's: 'It must be remembered that I am not alone to do my work, and that it is the work of not one but of two persons.'[26] Ann P. Robson observed regarding Helen's influence of Mill: 'Her voice became as important or nearly so, as her mother's had been.'[27] Delighting to praise her, Mill even claimed that Helen's intellect was more 'considerable' and 'original' than his own. She was his 'advisor' and 'instructor'.[28] As he referred to her simply as 'my daughter', correspondents would sometimes mistakenly address her as 'Miss Mill'.[29] As we have seen, Harriet and Mill had fallen in love when Helen was a baby. Helen grew up living with her mother separate from her father and with Mill as a strong presence in their lives. Mill habitually spent at least one day a week with them and they would go on holiday together. As their lives were so entwined, to build up a fuller picture of religion in the life of John Stuart Mill it is valuable to come to understand Helen Taylor and religion.

Helen kept a diary from 1 January 1842 (when she was ten and a-half years old) until she was fifteen and a-half (the last entry is 18 January 1847). Although scholars have quoted snippets from it when discussing the lives of her mother and stepfather, it has never been published and it has never been the subject of a sustained analysis.[30] It would not be inaccurate to say that it is in large measure a spiritual or devotional diary. Its contents are truly startling when it comes to religion. Before presenting that material, however, it is worth highlighting a few other features. One surprise is that Mill is never mentioned. Helen typically recorded any visitor, including even her brother Algernon—who was just a year older than her—but had been sent away to be educated by a tutor with whom he was a boarder. Never referring to Mill would mean either that he was considered so much a part of the household as not to be worth mentioning or, more likely, that she had been instructed not to put anything about him in writing. Harriet and Mill were obsessed with their own privacy. In his letters to his few confidants, Mill would refrain from mentioning Harriet by name and would merely comment abruptly on how 'she' was doing.[31] The one possible direct reference to Mill comes in April 1845: 'Grandpapa here yesterday, he Mamma and I had a short discussion about him.' Nevertheless, the philosopher's presence—including on two continental holidays recorded in this diary—is not only known from other sources, but can even be inferred from what is here. For example, in April 1842: 'Mr Carlyle came. I like him very much.' Thomas Carlyle, of course, was not calling on Harriet at her retreat home in Surrey alone; he was there with Mill. In September 1846 we are even informed that John's younger brother had paid a visit: 'George Mill came here yesterday.' (Algernon was also there and the two boys had become friends when they had joined Harriet and Mill on a holiday trip.) Another clue comes in November 1846: 'The only remark I have ever seen about the Greeks which seemed to me really true was one in that article on Grote's Greece that their merit consisted not in carrying things to perfection but on inventing them.' This is a reference to an article in the current (October 1846) issue of the *Edinburgh Review*, written by Mill, but published anonymously, as was the journal's practice.[32] Mill's article would have been a topic of discussion among them and thus Helen's decision to read it.

Having finally worn down her mother's resistance, at the age of twenty-five Helen made a concerted, but ultimately abandoned, attempt to become a professional actor. This interest is on display in the diary, with Helen reading plays, performing them for the family ('we have been acting on the little theatre'), and industriously memorizing parts, including the whole of Lady Macbeth. In November 1846, Helen calculated that she had learned 1,500 lines that year. The entry for 1 March 1845 has a hilarious rant against *Romeo and Juliet*, culminating in the indictment: 'I do not believe that people do fall in love with one another after this fashion.' A year later, however, it was on her list of Shakespeare plays that she thought were good: perhaps its depiction of love made more sense once she was nearing fifteen. There is also evidence that Helen was already committed to women's rights. At the age of thirteen she was reading Mary Wollstonecraft, whom she praises for bravely proclaiming what she thought. Most of all, there is Helen's negative assessment of a recently published novel by Geraldine Jewsbury. Helen condemns it both for being anti-feminist and for being anti-Catholic:

> I was reading all day a story called Zoe, which is full of reflections about Religion, especially Catholic Religion. On the whole I do not like it. She declares women inferior to men. That is enough to 'do for her' with

> me.... Either she must be speaking falsely when she says so, or what right has she to place herself in the position of a man, and thrust herself forward as an author... what right has she to dispute the religion which many of the greatest men & certainly all of the best have declared to be true?

Which leads on to religion, the main preoccupation of the diary. Quite simply, if all one knew about Helen Taylor came from this manuscript, one would assume that she was a pious Roman Catholic. One would even assume she was being raised in a Catholic family: there is no hint that her faith is in any way distinctive in her life, family, and milieu—let alone contested. How can this be? There were apparently no Catholics even in the extended family: they were all Anglican, Methodist, or Unitarian. Helen's parents, John and Harriet Taylor, as has been shown, were Unitarians who—at the time of Helen's birth—were worshipping at W. J. Fox's South Place Chapel, a congregation so progressive even by Unitarian standards that it was sliding into freethought.[33] After the de facto separation from her husband, Harriet was not involved in organized religion. Jo Ellen Jacobs, the leading authority on Harriet Taylor Mill, has pronounced unequivocally that she had become an atheist.[34] (My own reading of the evidence Jacobs bases this assumption on is that it cannot be pushed further than to say that it reveals Harriet to have been a critic of orthodox theological assumptions and a freethinker.) There are only two traces of Helen's Unitarian birthright in the diary. One is mentioning reading *Self-Culture* (1838) by William Ellery Channing (1780–1842), a prominent American Unitarian minister. The other is the 10 February 1846 entry: 'London. I went on Sunday evening to hear a lecture of Mr. Fox's. It was on Theory and Practice, not so good as most of his are, but still very good.' Nor is the secret influence, Mill, the Saint of Rationalism, a likely source for this child's life of orthodox Christian worship.

So when and how did this ten-year-old girl throw in her lot with Roman Catholicism? Ironically, the one thing which betrays that she was not a conventional Catholic is her eccentric, ad hoc efforts to practise her faith. In the very first entry of her diary we are informed that Helen went to visit her grandmother. This is what she wrote on the following day, 2 January 1842: 'Staid at home. performed Mass. We made Nicholas a priest. He behaved extremely well but brother

Matthew behaved badly.' Then 4 January: 'Staid at home. Father Andrew performed Mass twice. Once with Father Thomas.' 5 January: 'Went to Mrs. Underwood, did not perform Mass.' 6 January: 'Brothers came home in the evening. Performed Mass twice.'[35] Such entries occur less frequently as time goes on—it would seem because she had won the right to walk to the nearest Catholic church and therefore could attend Mass—but throughout the diary Helen never abandoned this practice. Just a few weeks before the very last entry, aged fifteen, she wrote for Christmas Day 1846: 'I performed a Mass at Midnight the altar decorated with green, and sang "Adeste Fideles".' There is obviously a prominent component of the imaginative play of children involved here, and one that accords well with Helen's theatrical enthusiasms, but—as will become apparent—this practice is also clearly one part of a life of earnest piety, devotional exercises, and religious reflection.

The first mention of her attending Mass comes on Easter Day 1842, when Helen worshipped at the Spanish Ambassador's chapel—as she did again that Christmas. In the summer of 1844, Helen went to Rouen, France, with her mother (and Mill) and she spent her entire holiday trying to get to as many Catholic church services as possible, literally every day and often more than one in a day, even on her birthday. Her greatest disappointment was being thwarted in this desire. 26 July: 'I have been out again to the Cathedral, but just missed the service, at this instant the bells are ringing in a most tempting way. I have been out to see if they were ringing for Mass, but they are not.' Even a rare account of a different attraction, the Museum of Antiquities, is focused on the Christian objects: 'There was a stone crucifix which appeared to me the best thing in the collection.' On the trip back home, Helen writes of how she spent her last day in Rouen: 'I went this morning before we started for this place to St Ouen, the Cathedral, and St Maclou. They were all open and service was being performed at each. So I said an Ave Maria and Pater Noster in them all.' Her French idyll over, but not yet home, she was in Southampton on Sunday 12 August 1844, and her devotional life carried on: 'We went today to Mass to a little chapel which there is here.' Year after year, wherever she was and however brief the visit—Arundel, Ryde, Newport—she sought out the local Roman Catholic church in order to attend Mass. ('There is a Catholic chapel here where I mean to go to Mass tomorrow but I could not get into it today.')

By March 1845, Helen could attend Mass much more frequently because she no longer needed a chaperon: she had gained permission to walk by herself the four miles from her home at Walton-on-Thames, Surrey, to the Catholic Church at Weybridge. Helen calls it 'the little chapel', and a solitary thirteen-year-old girl from a non-Catholic family must have been conspicuous. *Historical Notes on English Catholic Missions* observes: 'The place was so small that not more than a dozen persons could be accommodated in it at one time!'[36] On Palm Sunday 1845: 'I received a branch of blessed Palm and kissed the hand of the Priest.' On Good Friday: 'I went to Weybridge again to day. The Altar was quite plain, no ornaments upon it, all black, and the Priest with Black & Silver robes. I kissed the cross going up to the Altar to it.' Algernon joined her for Mass on Easter Sunday and they heard 'a joyful sermon on the resurrection'. Helen would even sometimes go to Compline on a weekday. Mass now accessible, her ad hoc devotional efforts became focused on other services: 'Last night I have Vespers again to night I shall have them, and shall preach on the subject of the crucifixion.' When she was in London staying at the official family residence in Regent's Park where her father lived, Helen attended Mass at the Spanish Ambassador's chapel, the French Ambassador's chapel or, increasingly, the chapel to Our Lady at St John's Wood.

When she encountered Protestantism, Helen was critical. A visit to Westminster Abbey in January 1845 prompted her to claim that it would be much better in Roman Catholic hands, who would have the sense to include statues and crucifixes: 'Protestantism does not suit churches.' The few times she attended Anglican worship her comments were scathing: 'The sermon was dreadfully full of fine words and smooth expressions.' Or on another occasion: 'The sermon long, unmeaning and excessively pompous.' In contrast, she almost invariably reported that a Roman Catholic sermon was good. This was, if anything, even truer when they contained anti-Protestant polemics or Catholic apologetics. In May 1845, a sermon was 'extremely good'. It argued that persecution was a mark of the true Church and then tellingly expounded on the ongoing persecution of Catholics by Protestants in Britain. She also liked the sermon for Corpus Christi, which sought to prove that 'the Catholic Eucharist was truly Corpus Christi' and that this was the teaching of the church fathers: 'Then he enjoined everyone there to take the Sacrament describing its effects, and the spirit with which it should be received.' Even that statement, alas, does not lead Helen to reflect upon the presumed fact that she could not receive the sacrament herself. On another holiday, she went to Vespers at a Roman Catholic Church in Frankfurt but was disappointed by the ways she thought true Catholic worship had been diluted by the influence of the surrounding Lutheranism. Helen was disgusted by a performance she attended of Haydn's *Creation* at Exeter Hall during which the creation of light (the 'And God said, Let there be light' of Genesis 1:3) was accompanied by the tacky trick of turning on the gas lights.

Particularly fascinating is an entry in April 1845 on her reading of *The Ideal of a Christian Church* by the Tractarian the Reverend W. G. Ward:

> I think it very good he seems a splendid controversialist, and I think it would be difficult to refute his attacks on protestantism, which it seems to me can only be the religion of extremely unthinking or intensely cowardly people. It seems to me that Ward ought to profess himself Catholic, as I am sure he is in his heart. His reason for remaining in the English Church seems to be that he is afraid and not sure what he would do, he therefore thinks it safest to remain in the church in which God has placed him.[37]

As Ward would be received into the Roman Catholic Church later that same year, it would seem that this thirteen-year-old girl was not only a careful reader of advanced theological treatises but a prescient one.

Helen's diary is imbued with piety in other ways. It is highly attentive to the church year. On one occasion she even wrote 'Christmass' as if to emphasize that, however the festival might be observed by others, for her it was a day to go to Mass. The most seemingly inconspicuous of weekdays could prompt her to announce that it was St Thomas's Day, St Michael's Day, and so on. One of the last entries is 5 January 1847: 'I have been reading the life of St Simeon Stylites whose festival is to day.' Her devotional reading is another recurring theme, including Thomas à Kempis ('It is very pleasant when one reads of feelings which oneself has had'), and the lives of saints—St Bernard and St Hildegard being favourites. Saints are 'the best and the most courageous people of whom one reads'. Or on another occasion: 'I always admire Martyrs'—she was particularly pleased by one who literally turned the other cheek when struck by a soldier. Helen was memorizing parts in plays, but longed to find one where she could approve of what the character was saying: 'I am inclined to Schiller's Joan of Arc.' And Helen would also write for spiritual edification. From the entry for 2 April 1842: 'Wrote the first sermon I ever wrote.' She would copy out sermons written by others, and had her own altar at home which she would decorate for church festivals. She awoke on Easter Sunday 1846 from 'a pleasant dream' in which she was 'the chief singer of a splendid cathedral', but found herself unable to fulfil this duty until she was empowered by a gracious look from the bishop.

It is not clear how long these religious interests persisted in Helen's life. A letter from Mill to Harriet on 11 March 1854 (by which time Helen was twenty-two years old) discussed their plans for a trip to France. He observes that they will need to leave early as Easter, for Helen, 'begins with Palm Sunday'.[38] When Helen was staying in Newcastle in 1856—aged twenty-five—she was attending Mass there.[39] In other words, we have clear evidence that her early commitment to the Catholic Mass lasted for—at the bare minimum—fifteen years. Likewise when Algernon was aged twenty-five, he wanted to spend the 1856 Christmas holidays in the house, but Harriet was annoyed by this because they would all be away. Nevertheless, in a letter to Helen, their mother revealed that she thought she understood her son's motivation: 'I suppose he wants to return to pass Christmas week near the church.'[40] Indeed, there was speculation that Algernon would become a Catholic—or even a monk.[41] He did spend years visiting Catholic religious houses and eventually wrote *Convent Life in Italy* (1862) and *Scenes in French Monasteries* (1866).[42] In his *Memories of a Student, 1838–1888* there is an entire chapter called, 'High Mass', followed by another titled, 'Zelus domus tuæ comedit me', in which he recalled: 'something approaching to a passion for church-going early manifested itself to me'.[43] It is even possible that it was his enthusiasm for Catholicism that had rubbed off on Helen. Algernon recounted the first of his own innumerable attendances at Mass: 'At eleven years old I begged a Spanish school-companion,

Don Lucas Odêro, to take me with him to the French ambassador's chapel on Good Friday and again on Easter day.'[44] He recollects attending Mass with Helen, their mother, and with Mill. Algernon's *Memories* are filled with his own pious expressions and accounts of his avid, lifelong reading of devotional literature. His particular 'weakness' was for 'the Christian Fathers', but he was a deeply ecumenical Christian in terms of both his worship experiences and his reading, even including an exuberant endorsement of *Natural Law and the Spiritual World* (1883) by Henry Drummond, a Free Church of Scotland evangelist who worked closely with the American evangelical D. L. Moody. In May 1851, Mill was arranging for the publication of an article, 'Gregory of Nazianzum', in the *Westminster Review*. He said it was by 'a young friend' and the editor of *The Collected Works of John Stuart Mill* has its author as 'unidentified'.[45] It was actually by Algernon Taylor.[46] The article was not in keeping with the typical contents of the journal, which was known to be a voice for freethought. The book under review maintained scholarly objectivity by never referring to Gregory as a saint, but Algernon, after noticing this, pointedly speaks himself of 'St. Gregory' throughout. He criticizes the author for not offering a full defence of monastic asceticism and makes an appeal to his readers who are 'earnestly believing Christians'. Mill had just married the young author's mother the month before and was in his first weeks of living in the same house with Algernon. It would appear that the philosopher was looking for some way to relate to his religiously preoccupied stepson and the best he could think of was commissioning him to write about a church father for the *Westminster Review*! Algernon's own only son, Cyprian (named after a church father), was eventually committed to an asylum because he suffered from 'religious mania'.[47] Moreover, even Harriet's other child, Herbert, who had much less contact with her and the other children, spent several months 'as a member of the choir at High Mass in St. George's Cathedral, Southwark'.[48] If Harriet's children, like Mill would claim had been his own case, were being raised without religion, they all found it without the need of maternal guidance.

After Harriet's death, Helen helped Mill with his work, composing answers to many letters he received on his behalf and in his name. This is abundantly apparent because when a correspondent praised something he had said, he was eager to give Helen credit for actually having written it. Mill, for instance, made this acknowledgement in a letter to Mary Carpenter dated 3 February 1868 in which he went on to reflect on the arrangement:

> Without this help it would be impossible for me to carry on so very voluminous a correspondence as I am at present able to do: and we are so completely one in our opinions and feelings, that it makes hardly any difference which of us puts them into words. It is often with regret that I see attributed to myself work which I think good and which is chiefly hers.[49]

In a letter ostensibly from J. S. Mill written in that same year, one reads, 'The true humiliation is when honorable men become in the words of the Psalm, "emulous of evil doers".' The editors of the *Collected Works of John Stuart Mill* comment that this is 'an inaccurate quotation from *Ps.* 37:1'.[50] It is not, however, a misquotation from the Authorized Version but rather an accurate quotation from the Roman Catholic Douai–Rheims translation (Psalm 36:1 in the Catholic way of numbering the psalms): this is yet another trace of Helen's deep immersion in Catholic devotional resources. In 1865 the freethinking Lady Amberley (the mother of Bertrand Russell, who would go on to become one of Britain's most vocal religious sceptics) had written in her journal that Helen had once been 'much inclined to R. Catholicism' and that Thomas à Kempis's *Imitation of Christ* 'is still her favorite book'.[51] In a letter written in 1869 to Lady Amberley, Helen was emphatically critical of Catholicism as a pernicious influence in the sphere of politics, but nevertheless reflected tellingly (as will be seen below): 'There is so much that is exquisitely beautiful and touching in Catholicism that I never think any one quite safe from becoming a Catholic.'[52]

Mill's posthumously published essay, 'Theism', dismayed some of his most loyal followers because of the extent to which it seemed to them to depart from a lifetime of rejecting traditional religious claims. It has been standard to observe that a likely reason for this surprising openness to the existence of God and even the unique, divine mission of Jesus Christ was that Mill wrote this essay after his wife had died and therefore the absence of her strong influence must be the decisive reason.[53] That does seem to be a genuine factor as far as it goes. It is also well known, however, that Helen took Harriet's place in Mill's life as the intellect with which he was most seeking to work in harmony and service. He would carry on with his scheme of a relationship based on reciprocal superiority with Helen now supplying the better half that made his work whole. Mill went so far as to make the startling assertion that, when it came to his later writings, Helen's mind was more to be credited for their ideas than his own.[54] Charles Eliot Norton reported, 'Her words have an oracular value to him.'[55] Leslie Stephen likewise spoke of 'Mill's obedience to her'.[56] Jeff Lipkes wrote an entire monograph on why Mill's views on economics and religion changed in the last twelve years of his life, but explicitly ruled out any contribution from Helen Taylor—it would seem because he assumed that Helen so entirely concurred with Mill's earlier views that she could not have been an agent in his changing them.[57] Lipkes argues that, when it comes to Mill's more favourable view of religion late in life, the decisive influence was that of his friend, William Thomas Thornton, who was a Theist. Again, Thornton's contribution seems another genuine factor as far as it goes, but it was a mistake for Lipkes to set aside Helen's influence. Richard Reeves suggests that perhaps it was the influence of Mill's best friend in his life in Avignon, Louis Rey, the pastor of the Protestant church there.[58] Once again, by Mill's own account, Helen was a much more important influence. Moreover, we now know what Lipkes did not, that Helen's attitude to religion was certainly not a mere replica of the largely sceptical stance her stepfather maintained in the middle course of his life. In other words, we can now also offer an additional reason for the less sceptical approach advanced in 'Theism': Mill well knew how much the Christian faith meant to Helen and he was influenced accordingly to offer a more favourable and hopeful assessment of its validity. And to highlight one specific detail in that essay, working in continual collaboration with his beloved 'daughter' whose favourite book was *The Imitation of Christ*, Mill proclaimed fervently that 'the most valuable part' of the influence of Christianity upon society is its offering of Jesus Christ as 'a model for imitation'.[59]

At the end of her life, Helen Taylor lived in Torquay with Algernon's daughter Mary Taylor, who was her caregiver once Helen could no longer look after herself. We know that Mary worshipped at St John's, an Anglican church there.[60] Helen's own funeral was conducted by an Anglican clergyman, the Reverend James J. Large.[61] Nevertheless, there were reports that Helen had become a Roman Catholic sometime during her years of retirement from public life. She had served with Ernest Belford Bax on the executive committee of the radical political organization, the Social Democratic Federation. Bax wrote snide comments about Helen in his *Reminiscences*—depicting her as haughty and aloof—and also included the information that she had died 'in the bosom of the Catholic Church'.[62] Florence Fenwick Miller worked closely with Helen on the London School Board and, in direct contrast to Bax, was a friend and admirer who liked her heartily. In her unpublished memoir, Miller reflected on how puzzled she had been that Helen refused to support efforts to promote birth control. Helen was even a main financial supporter and animating spirit of the defence of marriage, traditionalist Moral Reform Union. This uncharacteristic stance for a political radical in their common milieu, Miller mused, could be explained 'probably from the fact that she had already secretly joined the Roman Catholic Church, as at the end of her life it became known she was a convert to that Church.' Indeed, 'when Miss Taylor's conversion was at last revealed', Miller felt that it made sense of 'many things that I had heard her say that had much surprised me at the time'.[63] It is hard to think of how or why these claims would have come to be made if they did not have some foundation in truth.[64] In short, it seems reasonably probable that Helen really did become a Catholic, and that Mary Taylor arranged for an Anglican burial out of her own preference or for the sake of convenience.[65] If Helen was not actually received into the Roman Catholic Church then, at the very least, it seems highly likely that people had assumed this was the case because they had become aware that, in her later years, she was a fellow traveller who was attending Mass and otherwise engaging in Catholic devotional practices and expressing Catholic preferences and convictions.

The *Oxford Dictionary of National Biography* entry on Helen Taylor makes no mention of religion. The index of *The Complete Works of Harriet Taylor Mill* has sub-entries under 'Taylor, Helen' on her career, clothing, friends, health, holidays, independence, money, and her mother's affection for, anger at, and letters to, but not on her religion. I have no quarrel with these secondary sources on this account, but Helen's diary serves to remind us how wrong scholars are who ignore or underestimate just how shaped by religion and how closely impinged upon by religiosity were even 'secular' figures in the nineteenth and early twentieth centuries. Mill's religious scepticism was experienced in a nineteenth-century world in which religion was highly likely to come close to home in specific and substantial ways. We do not seem to have sufficient surviving evidence to help us determine to what degree Helen Taylor did or did not continue to foster some kind of Christian piety and pursue religious practices during the years when she and Mill collaborated together after her mother's death and in her years of being active in radical politics after Mill's own death. However, even if one assumes that the middle-aged Helen Taylor was not an especially devout or religiously active person by the standards of traditional, organized Christianity, that approach to life, nevertheless, meant something different for someone of the Victorian era when one realizes just how much religiosity they often experienced before taking on such an identity and how often lives of spiritual devotion marked those closest to them. Despite what he said in his *Autobiography*, Christianity for Mill was not, and never had been, as remote as the worship of Zeus in the ancient world. The Christian faith was close to home.

Notes

1. John Stuart Mill to Edward Lytton Bulwer, 23 November 1836: Francis E. Mineka (ed.), *The Earlier Letters of John Stuart Mill, 1812–1848* (Collected Works of John Stuart Mill XII), Toronto: University of Toronto Press, 1963, p. 312.
2. John Stuart Mill, *Essays on Ethics, Religion and Society* (Collected Works of John Stuart Mill X), ed. J. M. Robson, Indianapolis: Liberty Fund, 2006 (reprint of Toronto: University of Toronto Press, 1969), p. 233. (As is generally the case throughout this book, I am using the text printed in the CWJSM and not attending to questions of differences between editions, as fascinating as such issues are. The Collected Works text is from the fourth edition, published in 1871.)
3. CWJSM X (*Essays on Ethics, Religion and Society*), p. 233.
4. CWJSM X (*Essays on Ethics, Religion and Society*), p. 206.
5. CWJSM X (*Essays on Ethics, Religion and Society*), p. 222.
6. CWJSM X (*Essays on Ethics, Religion and Society*), p. 222.

7. For this background, see James E. Crimmins, *Secular Utilitarianism: Social Science and the Critique of Religion in the Thought of Jeremy Bentham*, Oxford: Clarendon Press, 1990.
8. CWJSM XIII (*Earlier Letters*), p. 511.
9. William Smith, *A Discourse on Ethics of the School of Paley*, London: William Pickering, 1839, p. [v].
10. Smith, *Discourse*, p. 10.
11. Smith, *Discourse*, p. 24.
12. Smith, *Discourse*, p. 56.
13. Smith, *Discourse*, p. 86.
14. John Stuart Mill, *Autobiography and Literary Essays* (Collected Works of John Stuart Mill I), ed. J. M. Robson, Indianapolis: Liberty Fund, 2006 (reprint of Toronto: University of Toronto Press, 1981), p. 209.
15. Marion Filipiuk, Michael Laine, and John M. Robson (eds), *Additional Letters of John Stuart Mill* (Collected Works of John Stuart Mill XXXII), Toronto: University of Toronto Press, 1991, p. 6.
16. J. M. Pullen, 'Malthus, (Thomas) Robert (1766–1834)', in *Oxford Dictionary of National Biography*, accessed at oxforddnb.com
17. John Stuart Mill to Alexander Bain, 14 November 1859: Francis E. Mineka and Dwight N. Lindley (eds), *The Later Letters of John Stuart Mill, 1849–1873* (Collected Works of John Stuart Mill XV), Toronto: University of Toronto Press, 1972, pp. 645–56. (He goes on to say that he must teach what is true, and Christians must decide if they will accept it or not: 'By that course, in so far as we have any success, we are at least sure of doing something to improve Christianity.')
18. CWJSM X (*Essays on Ethics, Religion and Society*), p. 218.
19. John Stuart Mill to George Grote, 10 January 1862: CWJSM XV (*Later Letters*), p. 762.
20. CWJSM XIV (*Later Letters*), p. 283.
21. Wendy Donner, 'Mill's utilitarianism', in John Skorupski (ed.), *The Cambridge Companion to Mill*, Cambridge: Cambridge University Press, 1998, pp. 255–92.
22. CWJSM X (*Essays on Ethics, Religion and Society*), pp. 210–12.
23. CWJSM X (*Essays on Ethics, Religion and Society*), p. 213.
24. CWJSM X (*Essays on Ethics, Religion and Society*), p. 213.
25. This section draws upon Timothy Larsen, 'The Catholic Faith of John Stuart Mill's Stepdaughter: A Note on the Diary and Devotional Life of the Feminist Activist Helen Taylor (1831–1907)', *Catholic Historical Review*, 103, 3 (Summer 2017), pp. 465–81.
26. CWJSM XVI (*Later Letters*), p. 1506.

27. Bruce L. Kinzer, Ann P. Robson, and John M. Robson, *A Moralist In and Out of Parliament: John Stuart Mill at Westminster, 1865–1868*, Toronto: University of Toronto Press, 1992, p. 118. (All three authors took full responsibility for every statement in this book so, although Ann P. Robson drafted this chapter, this assessment can also be attributed to Kinzer and John M. Robson.)
28. CWJSM I (*Autobiography and Literary Essays*), p. 265.
29. CWJSM XVI (*Later Letters*), p. 1233. Mill had written to Arnold Ruge on 7 February 1867, referring to 'my daughter' and her editorial work on the posthumous writings of Henry Thomas Buckle. Ruge therefore wrote to 'Miss Mill' herself on 11 February 1867. Helen would likewise refer to Mill as simply 'my father'.
30. London, London School of Economics Archives, Mill–Taylor Collection, Volume 44, 'Diaries of Helen Taylor, 1842–1847'. The scholar who draws upon it the most is Jo Ellen Jacobs, *The Voice of Harriet Taylor Mill*, Bloomington: Indiana University Press, 2002. The best source on Helen Taylor is Janet Smith, 'The Feminism and Political Radicalism of Helen Taylor in Victorian Britain and Ireland', unpublished PhD thesis, London Metropolitan University, 2014. The theme of this thesis is Taylor's political activities from the 1870s onwards, but it also includes a brief presentation of the contents of the diary.
31. See, for example, J. S. Mill to W. J. Fox [27 January 1837]: CWJSM XII (*Earlier Letters*), p. 320.
32. [John Stuart Mill], 'Grote's History of Greece', *Edinburgh Review*, LXXXIV (October 1846), pp. 343–77.
33. Moncure D. Conway, *Centenary History of the South Place Society*, London: Williams and Norgate, 1894; S. K. Ratcliffe, *The Story of South Place*, London: Watts & Co., 1955. (Watts & Co. was a leading freethinking publisher.)
34. Jacobs, *Voice*, p. 150.
35. I do not know who Nicholas, Matthew, and Thomas were. Matthew is being called a brother in the general sense of Christian fellowship or (in the role play) the more specific one of a religious vocation. The 6 January entry, on the other hand, refers to her biological brothers: it means that Algernon and their older brother Herbert have paid a visit.
36. Bernard W. Kelly, *Historical Notes on English Catholic Missions*, London: Kegan Paul, Trench, Trübner & Co., 1907, p. 428.
37. W. G. Ward, *The Ideal of a Christian Church*, London: James Toovey, 1844.
38. John Stuart Mill to Harriet Taylor Mill, 11 March 1854: CWJSM XIV (*Later Letters*), p. 181.

39. Helen Taylor to Harriet Taylor Mill, 23 November [1856]. The original of this letter is in the Mill–Taylor Collection at the London School of Economics Archives, London, but I have only seen a transcript of it which was kindly provided to me by Dr Jo Ellen Jacobs. Helen was in Newcastle because this was the phase of her life when she was pursuing a career in acting. Therefore, it would be wrong to imagine that her commitment to the Mass was merely an expression of her commitment to the theatre and that, when she was able to pursue the latter, it replaced the former.
40. Harriet Taylor Mill to Helen Taylor, postmarked 13 December 1856: Jo Ellen Jacobs (ed.), *The Complete Works of Harriet Taylor Mill*, Bloomington: Indiana University Press, 1998, p. 530.
41. John Stuart Mill to Frederick Sinnett, 22 October 1857: CWJSM XV (*Later Letters*), p. 541.
42. Algernon Taylor, *Convent Life in Italy*, London: Charles J. Skeet, 1862; Algernon Taylor, *Scenes in French Monasteries*, London: Charles J. Skeet, 1864.
43. Algernon Taylor, *Memories of a Student, 1838–1888*, privately printed, n.d. [1892], p. 38.
44. Taylor, *Memories*, p. 39.
45. John Stuart Mill to William E. Hickson [May 1851]: CWJSM XIV (*Later Letters*), p. 66.
46. [Algernon Taylor], 'Gregory of Nazianzum', *Westminster Review*, LVI, CX (October 1851), pp. 53–65. The authorship of this article can be deduced from Taylor, *Memories*, p. 164. I am grateful to my post-graduate research assistant David Monahan for identifying this article and helping to make the connection to its author.
47. Jacobs, *Complete Works*, p. [589].
48. Taylor, *Memories*, p. 38.
49. John Stuart Mill to Mary Carpenter, 3 February 1868: CWJSM XVI (*Later Letters*), p. 1359.
50. John Stuart Mill to Thomas Beggs, 11 December 1868: CWJSM XVI (*Later Letters*), p. 1519.
51. Journal of Lady Amberley, entry for 20 February 1865: Bertrand Russell and Patricia Russell (eds), *The Amberley Papers: The Letters and Diaries of Lord and Lady Amberley*, 2 vols, London: Hogarth Press, 1937, I, p. 372. John Stuart Mill and Helen Taylor were Bertrand Russell's godparents. Also illustrating a theme of this book that religion is often closer to home than one might think in this time period and beyond—and had a way of reappearing—even in the case of prominent unbelievers who were raised by religious sceptics, Bertrand Russell's own daughter, Katharine,

converted to Christianity: Katharine Tait, *My Father Bertrand Russell*, New York: Harcourt Brace Jovanovich, 1975, chapter 9, 'Conversion' (pp. 174–89).

52. Helen Taylor to Lady Amberley, 11 September 1869: Russell, *Amberley Papers*, II, pp. 311–13 (here 313).
53. For example, Alan P. F. Sell, *Mill on God: The Pervasiveness and Elusiveness of Mill's Religious Thought*, Aldershot: Ashgate, 2004, p. 1; Linda C. Raeder, *John Stuart Mill and the Religion of Humanity*, Columbia, MO; University of Missouri Press, 2002, p. 364.
54. CWJSM I (*Autobiography and Literary Essays*), p. 265.
55. Charles Eliot Norton to Chauncey Wright, 18 September 1870: Sara Norton and M. A. De Wolfe Howe (eds), *The Letters of Charles Eliot Norton*, 2 vols, Boston: Houghton Mifflin, 1913, I, p. 400.
56. Leslie Stephen to Charles Eliot Norton, 25 December 1874: John W. Bicknell (ed.), *Selected Letters of Leslie Stephen: Volume 1: 1864–1882*, London: Macmillan, 1996, p. 146. Norton and Stephen regretted Helen's influence, seeing it as demeaning of Mill's greatness. For a sympathetic account, see Ann P. Robson, 'Mill's Second Prize in the Lottery of Life', in Michael Laine (ed.), *A Cultivated Mind: Essays on J. S. Mill presented to John M. Robson*, Toronto: University of Toronto Press, 1991, pp. 215–41.
57. Jeff Lipkes, *Politics, Religion and Classical Political Economy in Britain: John Stuart Mill and his Followers*, London: Macmillan, 1999, especially pp. 9, 77.
58. Richard Reeves, *John Stuart Mill: Victorian Firebrand*, London: Atlantic Books, 2007, 476.
59. CWJSM X (*Essays on Ethics, Religion and Society*), p. 487.
60. Taylor, *Memories*, p. 21.
61. Information kindly provided by John Tucker, Local and Family History Librarian, Torquay Library, Torquay.
62. Ernest Belfort Bax, *Reminiscences and Reflexions of a Mid and Late Victorian* (New York: Thomas Seltzer, 1920), p. 111.
63. I learned of the existence of this source from Smith, 'Feminism', pp. 27–8. The unpublished memoir of Florence Fenwick Miller is held in the archives of the Wellcome Institute, London. Dr Janet Smith generously provided me with a scan of the page that contains these comments, for which I am deeply grateful.
64. Miller was a freethinker, so this is not a case of the faithful wanting to believe there might have been a conversion.
65. There was no Roman Catholic cemetery in Torquay at this time and an Anglican clergyman and service were required for an interment in the Anglican burial grounds.

11
By Their Fruits Ye Shall Know Them

'Wherefore by their fruits ye shall know them.'

(Matthew 7:20)

John Stuart Mill burned with a white-hot passion for social and political reform. He believed that it was right and good that his own particular contribution to 'the regeneration of mankind' would be primarily philosophical, but he was convinced that even his most technical, intellectual work such as his *Logic* was in the service of social improvement. The backhanded tribute to this was Mill's surprising impatience with intellectual investigations for their own sake. In 1833, he even boasted that it was so, claiming that he had written part of a review as a manifesto, in order to declare to the world: 'I don't care one straw about premisses except for the sake of conclusions.'[1] In 1870, he put a halt to a theoretical dispute because he lost the thread that would connect it to a social issue: 'Both of us would thus spend a great deal of time for no sufficient result, since no important practical consequences depend on our convincing one another.'[2] Most tellingly of all, Mill was dismissive of the work (which would become foundational to the computer age) of the mathematician and logician George Boole:

> My impression was, that there is great ingenuity and power of consecutive thought... But you are right in supposing that I do not see, in the result attained, any value commensurate with the mental effort. I look upon it as I do upon Mr De Morgan's elaborate system of numerical definite propositions and syllogisms: as a remarkable feat of mental gymnastics, capable of being very useful in the way of a scholastic exercise, but of no considerable utility for any other purpose.[3]

The goal must not be just to understand the world, but to change it.

Therefore, Mill was always fond of the idea of being a Member of Parliament. In the House of Commons, he could both legislate for change and champion it in a place where his words would have sizeable influence. Until his retirement in 1858, however, he was not free to do so as being a politician was incompatible with being a civil servant in the India Office. In 1837, when he had high hopes for the Radical Party, Mill bolstered their cause in the *London and Westminster Review* and wistfully longed to be in the House himself: 'I often wish I were among them.'[4] In 1841, Comte praised Mill for not having stood for an election as that would result in his ending up wasting his intellectual powers in mundane parliamentary debates. Mill felt it was his duty to be candid with Comte and therefore he sheepishly confessed that far from rejecting the role as not worthy of his efforts he probably would have already tried to become a Member of Parliament if his circumstances did not forbid it.[5] Even in 1854, when Mill was in a kind of retreat of despair from the state of British politics, he confessed to Harriet that he sometimes still thought that 'it would be pleasant' to be in Parliament.[6] In 1859, Mill told Thomas Hare that he wished he was in the House of Commons so he could have answered a speech by Disraeli.[7] And it was not like there would have been no interest in him being a candidate. In 1851, Mill replied to the Roman Catholic editor Frederic Lucas—who had officially approached him on behalf of the Tenant League to stand for a seat—that he would have been 'highly gratified' to be returned but, alas, it was not possible for him to serve in Parliament.[8]

After the death of his wife, Mill began to desire to be out and about more and to engage more with the questions regarding the British political system. He wrote *Thoughts on Parliamentary Reform* (1859) in which he suggested a scheme for plural voting as a way of ensuring the political influence of the educated classes in a democratic age. He also opposed the secret ballot, despite this being a major goal of reformers speaking on behalf of the working classes. Indeed, the secret ballot had been one of the six points of Chartism. Then, in 1861, came Mill's *Considerations on Representative Government*. In it, he returned to Coleridge's insight that the forces of both permanence and progression need to be represented. There are people who incline to caution and others who incline to boldness: 'in some, the desire to avoid imperilling what is already possessed is a stronger sentiment than that which prompts to improve the old and acquire new advantages'. A good political system is one in which 'persons of both types ought to be included in it, that the tendencies of each may be tempered, in so far as they are excessive, by a due proportion of the other'.[9] Mill then put forward a fascinating claim that the Old Testament depicts a model society in this regard. The Tories of the ancient Hebrews were those who rallied around 'the sacerdotal order'. If the Conservative party has it all its own way, however, a society becomes stationary and stagnant. This had happened in places such as India and China. The Hebrews, on the other hand, are a foremost example of an ancient people who made admirable advances. The reason for this is because the forces of progress were marshalled by figures such as Isaiah and Jeremiah. In other words, Mill transposed Coleridge's scheme into a biblical key, with priests representing permanence and prophets representing progress.

Mill's moment came in 1865. He was approached to stand as a Liberal candidate for the constituency of Westminster. He won in the election of 1865, but then lost his seat in the election of 1868. Why he won in 1865 is not hard to fathom. Westminster had been a safe Liberal and Radical seat for a generation. In the previous three elections, the Conservatives had not even put forward a candidate. Mill was a well-respected, national name who would be an ornament to the constituency. There were only two Liberals standing, and it is hardly surprising that they took the two seats, leaving the lone other candidate, the Conservative, to come in third and thus lose out. Why Mill lost in 1868, however, needs more explanation. It is true that the recent Reform legislation meant that the electorate itself was differently composed and, as it would prove, the election of 1868 was the start of a move for this constituency to turn Tory. On the other hand, Mill's loss meant that a Westminster seat which was hitherto a Liberal stronghold went Conservative in a Liberal wave election: it was, in fact, the only seat in London the Tories won. Moreover, the Conservatives only ran one candidate in a constituency with two seats so, even if it is argued that the decisive factor was that Westminster was becoming Conservative (a claim which is far from established), there still needs to be an explanation for why a political, professional, and intellectual non-entity like Captain Grosvenor won the other seat rather than John Stuart Mill, a writer and thinker of international eminence.

In order to understand that, one needs to examine Mill's behaviour as a candidate and as a Member of Parliament. Mill responded to the request that he stand for Westminster with an Olympian list of conditions, including that he would not campaign or canvass for votes; that he would not donate any money to the campaign for his own election; that, if elected, he would see himself as there to pursue momentous matters and therefore he would not waste his time on any purely local issues of concern in the constituency; and that he would answer no questions about his personal religious convictions. What to make of these extraordinary stipulations? They sit uneasily between admirable and aloof. Like Shakespeare's Coriolanus as a candidate for the consulship, the populace wondered: is his insistence that he will not follow the customs for soliciting the support of the people a sign of a high-minded refusal to flatter or a proud disposition? Mill was unquestionably motivated by noble principles. He was disgusted with the bribery that was rife in parliamentary elections, both literal and in the form of telling people whatever they wanted to hear. As to the latter, the other Liberal candidate, R. W. Grosvenor, made himself momentarily a figure of fun when he promised a local physician that he would only ever receive medical treatments in line with his pet theories. It is one thing for a candidate to pledge his heart and mind, the *Daily News* quipped, but it is a bit much when a constituency even lays claim to his bowels.[10] Mill, by contrast, was bringing righteous standards into a mucky world. On one of the rare occasions he consented to explain his political positions to the electorate, the philosopher was cheered loudly for proclaiming that he would rather be honest than be elected.

More questionable was Mill's refusal to help with the finances of his election. Bribery ought not to be tolerated, but Mill was fully aware that there were legitimate expenses in a campaign: he just expected others to pay for them. Mill's refusal to make any contribution seems to have been from a sense that being a Member of Parliament should be viewed as a duty that one performed rather than a privilege which one sought. To give money to help one's own chances of being elected would be to look too much like one was pursuing a personal prize. Relatedly, Mill repeatedly insisted over these years that he did not want to be in Parliament, that losing an election would be a welcome opportunity to return to a more pleasant way of life, and the like. Such remarks were largely disingenuous: it was Mill's way of saying that politics was best thought of as service and what it means to serve is to put duty before one's own pleasure. A campaign worker hinted that the wealthy Mill's high-mindedness was somewhat exploitative of the lowly: 'none of us had a sandwich or a biscuit that was not purchased at our own expense.'[11] This was particularly galling as Mill sat out both elections being waited on by his household servants in his pleasant continental second home in Avignon. Others were sacrificially giving their time and money, while he could not even be bothered to stay in the country. By the second election, the sheen on these principled stances had worn off rather more.

Then there was Mill's actual performance as an MP. He had never been a good speaker, but given his national eminence, this came as a disappointment to many. Still, especially after a bit of trial and error, Mill did give a few effective orations over the course of his parliamentary career. He even got in a bit of gladiatorial party politics in the beloved tradition of the House. Sir John Pakington expressed indignation that Mill had called Conservatives 'the stupid party'. The philosopher rose to clarify: 'I never meant to say that Conservatives are generally stupid. I meant to say that stupid people are generally Conservative.'[12] Yet there was a more fundamental concern than that Mill was not a polished debater. As an MP, he gained an unshakeable reputation as impolitic, intemperate, and a man of crotchets. Having long adopted the radical position on a whole variety of issues, Mill repeatedly failed to calculate the sensitivities that still existed for most people on a range of subjects. He got off to a bad start with a speech on Ireland. Mill was well known as possessing one of the nation's finest logical minds, so many were bewildered by his unmeasured, impassioned hectoring. The Fenians were a current public concern in England—akin to fears today of terrorist organizations—and Mill seemed tone deaf to this context.

It is to John Stuart Mill's immortal glory that he was on the right side on almost all the major issues. He was bravely right to insist that the situation in Ireland was so unjust that only revolutionary measures would be up to what was needed. To back the story up before his time in Parliament, Mill defied a strong British wave of support for the cause of the Confederacy in the American Civil War. He was surprised and delighted that William Whewell was emphatically opposed to the South. Whewell had been the foil in *A System of Logic*, but theory only counts for so much: by their fruits ye shall know them. Whewell was all right. Only religious words could bear the weight of the strength of Mill's feelings on the American struggle. Carlyle's racist views were 'a true work of the devil'.[13] To support the South because it was in the interest of Britain's textile industry—as many did—was to be willing to make 'Satan victorious' in exchange for cotton. As for those who just wanted the North to end the war by letting the South secede, Mill said that he could not go along with those who cry 'peace, peace' when there can be no peace (Jeremiah 8:11).[14] All in one sentence on the American Civil War in his *Autobiography*, Mill referred to slavery as 'the accursed thing' (Joshua 6:18), the abolitionist William Lloyd Garrison as an 'apostle', and John Brown—who was killed for an effort to instigate a slave uprising—as a 'martyr'.[15] Throughout his life, Mill always admired and commended martyrdom as one of the highest expressions of human virtue. He was annoyed that people assumed that the hedonism of his Utilitarianism stood in contrast to such self-sacrifice: 'There is in the doctrine I maintain nothing inconsistent with the loftiest estimation of the heroism of martyrs.'[16] Most of all, this honour belonged to Abraham Lincoln who, like the greatest of all martyrs, was slain on Good Friday. Lincoln's martyrdom 'consecrates his name through all history'. The American president had received 'the crown of martyrdom' (evoking Revelation 2:10).[17]

Martyrdom, however, is usually a status conferred on someone only by their fellow partisans. In Mill's first months as a Member of Parliament, there was a disturbance in Jamaica. The black residents of the Morant Bay area rioted and the authorities lost control for a few days. The colonial governor, Edward John Eyre, declared martial law to be in force over the troubled region, and although the military regained control without meeting any resistance, the officers in charge still had 439 people killed, 600 flogged, and 1,000 houses destroyed.[18] In the midst of these excessive, unjustifiable actions, there was the haunting case of one man, G. W. Gordon. He was a prosperous Jamaican of mixed race, a member of the Jamaican Assembly, a fierce political opponent of Eyre, and through his passionate oratory, a focal figure for the mass of people who wanted something done about their grievances. When Eyre heard about the disturbances in Morant Bay, he immediately assumed that it was part of a widespread conspiracy being led by Gordon who, as a legislator, was the one Jamaican whose radical rhetoric was said in his hearing. Eyre put out an order for his arrest. Gordon, who was in undisturbed Kingston, promptly turned himself in. The governor, however, instead of having him tried in the functioning civilian courts, had Gordon transported to Morant Bay, where martial law was in force. There he was given the mere semblance of a trial by military officers—Gordon was not allowed to consult a lawyer or to call witnesses in his own defence—and within days he had been executed. The officers in charge had paused, however, between their judgment and the carrying out of the sentence. A report of the proceedings was sent to Eyre who in turn gave his personal endorsement of the decision to execute Gordon. This whole situation was a sensation in Britain. For some of the more blustering conservatives or imperialists, Eyre was a hero who had saved the white population of the island from otherwise certain death by his prompt and decisive actions. For most people, Eyre was a colonial governor who had done wrong and had been punished for it by having his actions condemned in an official report and by having been recalled from his post in disgrace. For Mill and those of his ilk, however, Gordon was a martyr and Eyre was a murderer. Mill became chairman of the Jamaica Committee when it tenaciously, unwaveringly, relentlessly exhausted every possible avenue attempting to see Eyre prosecuted. As the previous chairman of the Jamaica Committee had predicted, these efforts were not only unsuccessful, but had the effect of turning Eyre himself into a martyr in the eyes of many. Mill become the 'prosecuting philosopher', a man possessed by an unruly, vindictive passion. To the extent that we now can see how deeply the critics of the Member for Westminster were tainted by prejudices of race, class, and empire in this dispute, perhaps Mill himself counts as a third candidate for the crown of martyrdom in this narrative.

As he himself proudly proclaimed, the glory of Mill's time in Parliament was his championing of women's suffrage. Indeed, Mill's commitment to the rights of women by itself should qualify him to be considered one of the figures from nineteenth-century Britain worthy of lasting fame and honour. Mill claimed that as soon as he ever thought about the issue as a boy he had decided that gender equality was the right view and he never wavered thereafter. This is true in regard to the suffrage. When the youthful Mill first put to himself the question, 'Is there a good reason to exclude women from the electorate?', he answered himself with a 'no'. Nevertheless, it is also true that Harriet's influence led Mill towards deeper convictions regarding gender equality more generally. As he put it, 'it was she who taught me to understand the less obvious bearings of the subject'.[19] Thus one can find sexist assumptions or phrases in Mill's earlier work that he later would have seen for what they were. The clearest is a letter to John Sterling in 1831 in which Mill asserted that the 'proper sphere' of women 'is that of the private virtues'.[20] In print in the following year, he praised the 'mental powers' of Benjamin Smart for being 'clear, vigorous, and masculine'.[21] And there are, alas, even obvious ways in which his mind continued to be sexist throughout his life. His view of his mother is a prime example—and his sisters for that matter. In fact, with the obvious exceptions of Harriet and Helen, Mill was often dismissive of the women he knew well. John Austin and George Grote were forgiven, while their wives were perpetually condemned with the sexist trope that they were gossips.

This is all to bury the lede, however. Mill was in an extreme minority of men in the nineteenth century who genuinely believed in gender equality. He was also ready to sacrifice his time, energy, and reputation in the furtherance of this righteous cause. He helped to organize and presented to Parliament petitions in favour of women's suffrage. Then on 20 May 1867, Mill made the first ever motion in support of this goal, putting forward an amendment to the Reform Bill to change the word 'man' to 'person' so that women who met the other qualifications which also restricted the size of the male electorate would also have the right to vote. It failed, of course. In the most incongruous response, the *Evening Standard* decided that Mill was 'the ladies' man.'[22] He could not be laughed off, however. Women's rights became one of the causes to which Mill dedicated the last years of his life. In the year following his election defeat appeared his *The Subjection of Women* (1869). Mill intended it as dependent upon, and a piece with, what Harriet had done in her *Enfranchisement of Women* (1851), and he also credited Helen with helping him with his treatise. *The Subjection of Women* contains lucid sentences of argumentative force: 'Marriage is the only actual bondage known to our law. There remain no legal slaves, except the mistress of every house.'[23] And with perfect Utilitarian clarity: 'But it would be a grievous understatement of the case to omit the most direct benefit of all, the unspeakable gain in private happiness to the liberated half of the species.'[24] Surprisingly, especially given Mill's recent parliamentary efforts, *The Subjection of Women* is not preoccupied with women's suffrage. Instead, the focus is overwhelmingly on equality in marriage. As to Christianity, Mill retools the ancient Hebrews as progressive versus the Chinese as static motif from *Considerations on Representative Government.* In this iteration, religions such as Islam and Hinduism are stationary, whereas it is the glory of Christianity that it is progressive. Part of the greatness of the Christian faith, he observes, is that it is able to free itself from unjust social systems from the past. And here is a section on what individual women might be able to achieve:

> It cannot be inferred to be impossible that a woman should be a Homer, or an Aristotle, or a Michael Angelo, or a Beethoven, because no woman has yet actually produced works comparable to theirs in any of those lines of excellence.... But it is quite certain that a woman can be a Queen Elizabeth, or a Deborah, or a Joan of Arc...[25]

It is fascinating that when Mill wanted to list the women who had manifestly achieved great things in history, of the three he mentions, one is a biblical character (Deborah) and another a Catholic mystic and folk saint (Joan of Arc). Mill and Helen both served on the general committee of the London National Society for Women's Suffrage. Mill always maintained that his entire three years of toil in Parliament were worth it just to have been able to move the amendment for women's suffrage on 20 May 1867. When a bill to allow women who met the other legal qualifications to vote finally passed into law in 1928—sixty-three years after Mill's amendment and fifty-five years after his death—a delegation of leading suffragists remembered the first battle in this long struggle and went to lay a wreath upon Mill's statue.[26]

Mill's subscription to the campaign fund of Charles Bradlaugh was the single action of his which cost him the most votes. Bradlaugh was Britain's leading advocate of atheism. His pen name was 'Iconoclast' and he was part of a radical plebeian, infidel culture that delighted in baiting and offending Christians. During Mill's few years in Parliament, Bradlaugh had founded the National Secular Society, which quickly became the leading organization for defiant religious unbelievers. It is hard today to grasp just how visceral a reaction Iconoclast provoked. T. H. Huxley, for instance, the original 'agnostic' who was not above tweaking the orthodox in his own writings, wrote privately in 1873 that he had a 'peculiar abhorrence' for Bradlaugh and everything that he did.[27] Although atheists were barred from Parliament, Bradlaugh stood for a seat (Northampton) for the first time in the election of 1868. Giving money to Bradlaugh's campaign and, moreover, allowing this fact to be announced before the election, was so impolitic that some of Mill's supporters initially thought the report must have been a hoax. Mill was slow to realize the cost of what he had done and, when he did, he was loath to admit to himself that his own rashness might have lost him his place in Parliament.

Mill strove to explain himself. One main line of defence was that just because he had given support to an avowed atheist did not mean that he was himself an atheist. Mill was not an atheist, and he knew that such a label was not the right one for his views on religion, sceptical though they were. Nevertheless, he so danced and dogged about on this point—asserting that accusing him of being an atheist was like people who assert that William Gladstone is a Roman Catholic and the like—that Helen wrote to him in disgust, warning that Jesuitical phrasing was not the way to confront this crisis: 'Do not disgrace yourself as an open truthful man.'[28] Still, Mill's point was impeccable: supporting an atheist was not proof of being one. Mill did not want a full airing of his own religious views as he surmised that his scepticism would alienate some voters, but it is also true (as had been the case with his relationship with Harriet when she was still married to John Taylor) that there was no obvious classification or label for his eccentric mix of religious doubts, denials, conjectures, convictions, and hopes. When Bradlaugh was finally elected in 1880 the Iconoclast refused to take the standard oath which included the words 'so help me God' and therefore was not allowed to take his seat. The Secularist leader G. J. Holyoake asked Mill in 1869 why he had felt justified in swearing such an oath. Mill replied that it was not part of his own work to testify against such formalities. A passage Mill cut out of the letter is particularly revealing: 'Perhaps however your question refers to the words which I think are in the parliamentary oath "on the true faith of a Christian". On this point my answer would be that I am as much entitled to call my own opinion about Christ the true faith of a Christian, as any other person is entitled to call his so.'[29] He presumably cut it out because that would have been saying too much for such a correspondent. To be a Christian is not merely to have an opinion of Christ, but to be a follower of Christ. To have an informed view that Plato was all wrong does not make one a Platonist; to be a Platonist is to be someone who is following some lead given by Plato. Holyoake was not a follower of Christ in any sense. Mill, on the other hand, although he was most certainly not an orthodox Christian, was indeed entitled to say that his reverence for Christ and his admiration for the life and sayings of Jesus of Nazareth did give him a right to call himself a Christian.

Another argument Mill made was that a person's religious convictions were irrelevant in politics: all that matters is what legislative goals they would support. To make this point, Mill recurringly evoked his proof text of Matthew 7:20: atheists 'are entitled like other persons to be judged by their actions ("By their fruits ye shall know them" are the words of Christ) & not by their speculative opinions'.[30] Indeed, in the 1865 election he had used this text as warrant for his own refusal to be interrogated about his theological beliefs: 'I conceive that no one has any right to question another on his religious opinions; that the tree ought to be judged, and only judged by its fruits.'[31] This was also a reasonable stance to take. Mill declared repeatedly that he believed that there should be no religious tests for Parliament and that atheists should have the right to be MPs. He also remarked on multiple occasions that anyone who had read his *On Liberty* should know that he defended the right of people to express opinions even when he disagreed with them. All this was clear and cogent. Still, it did not answer the case. Mill had not merely defended the right of atheists to serve and to speak. He had supported the candidacy of the nation's most notorious, militant atheist. Mill would also defend the right of a sympathizer with the Confederacy to liberty of speech and to sit in Parliament, but to give money to the campaign of the leading pro-slavery advocate in the country would be a matter of giving support to the cause, not just refusing to allow it to be muzzled or excluded. Mill had convinced himself that Bradlaugh should be thought of as a representative of the working classes and a brave radical who supported a range of political causes unrelated to religion, and that he was supporting him only for these reasons. People generally did not see it that way. As Mill (with the help of Helen, who no longer trusted him to speak on this issue on his own) explained, 'If Mr B is only generally known for blasphemy, it must be because the facts concerning him are not generally known.... those who have done me the honour to approve of my general line of conduct & my published writings for 30 years & more, might fairly be expected to suppose that I was not likely to support any man for no other reason than that he had made himself remarkable by blasphemy.'[32] But the electorate had not been carefully reading either Bradlaugh or Mill's writings over the years and, if they had, they would have been struck by what was offensive in Iconoclast and it would never have occurred to them to notice that Mill had carefully avoided occasions to offend that had crossed his path.

Mill the parliamentarian unsettled people in other ways. The Reform League was a working-class organization campaigning for male suffrage. Its desire to meet in Hyde Park led to clashes with the government and property damage. There was a whiff of violence in the air. Mill gave money to the Reform League and addressed one of its meetings. In his mind, he was a mediating figure who was heroically steering the situation in a more lawful, orderly, and calm direction. Others saw him as mixing in low company and encouraging ruffians. There was a cumulative effect to all this. Mill was seen as too excitable, too given to startling crusades. Not only did he refuse to work on his constituents' local interests, but when they heard about what he was doing it was all too often in the service of some cause in which they did not believe; perhaps even a cause they thought was wrongheaded, dangerous, or offensive. Such a result was actually a natural outcome of how Mill viewed his vocation as a Member of Parliament. Gladstone observed that Mill's speeches were sermons. Indeed, it was because of the high moral tone that the philosopher brought to Parliament that the prime minister famously christened Mill 'the Saint of Rationalism'. Mill himself said that being in the House gave him 'a taller pulpit' and that he was there 'to preach'.[33] He deliberately saw his task as championing those worthy causes which were particularly unpopular. He was quite willing to play a long game. For instance, he had no illusions that he would be able to achieve women's suffrage; he was content to get people thinking about it, to help to advance a movement that would not come to fruition any time soon. In other words,

Mill was undertaking precisely what he had envisioned in *Considerations on Representative Government* as the progression side of the equation. He was the voice of one crying in the wilderness. He was an Old Testament prophet. The only flaw in this scheme was that Jeremiah did not need to stand for election in order to have his term of office as a prophet renewed.

One final note before we say goodbye to parliamentary politics and retreat back to Avignon. None of the causes that Mill championed had a fault line of support between orthodox Christians, on the one hand, and religious sceptics, on the other. In fact, in everything he stood for Mill stood shoulder-to-shoulder with some devout Christians. This is true even of his own election campaign. He was nominated by a church warden of St George's, a Church of England congregation in Hanover Square. The chairman of his campaign was Charles Westerton, a man who was well known as a zealous Christian and staunch Protestant. (Mill was amazed to learn that as strident a Christian as Westerton admired *On Liberty*.) The highest position in the Anglican hierarchy in the constituency was the Dean of Westminster, and Dean Stanley unwaveringly supported Mill in both elections. The same point holds true in Parliament itself. The great Christian statesman, W. E. Gladstone, worked closely with Mill and spoke well of him and his efforts. There was sometimes a fault line between Dissenters and Anglicans, with the former markedly more apt to join in Mill's crusades. Yet it was often evangelical Dissenters who were most zealous in these causes. G. W. Gordon, for instance, had been a Baptist and the evangelical Baptist community was particularly anti-Eyre. Evangelical Dissenters championed religious equality before the law and therefore were frequently actively committed to the right of atheists to become Members of Parliament. When that right was eventually secured, it was unquestionably the determination and strength of evangelical Nonconformists that brought it about. The division lists show that the evangelical Dissenting community was often where Mill could find his allies. This was even true for his early Irish vote that so rattled the House. Only four other British MPs voted with Mill on that occasion, but all of them were Dissenters, most of whom were well known for their vocal commitment to Christian causes: the Quaker John Bright; the Unitarian T. B. Potter; the Scottish

Free Churchman Duncan McLaren; and a leading evangelical Congregationalist, George Hadfield.

The cause that Mill was most proud to have supported while in Parliament, women's suffrage, particularly tilted towards being supported mostly by Christians. Mill's closest unbelieving friends and colleagues were often embarrassed by his commitment to gender equality. His father, James Mill, though bitterly anti-Christian, had disappointed his firstborn son by his refusal to include women's suffrage in his scheme for reform. Comte flatly and emphatically denied that women should be considered equals, pontificating: 'the female sex constitutes a sort of state of radical childhood'.[34] Herbert Spencer disagreed with women's suffrage and gender equality. The open agnostic, James Fitzjames Stephen, also disagreed. One of Mill's most loyal disciples, the confident unbeliever Alexander Bain, disagreed. By contrast, the Christian community was where Mill found support. For his women's suffrage amendment, seventy-two MPs voted with Mill (196 voted against). In that minority were many of the most zealous evangelical Dissenting Christians in the House, including Hadfield, the Congregationalist Edward Baines (editor of the *Leeds Mercury*), and a leading Baptist layman, Sir S. M. Peto. Mill was particularly elated to have won over the eminent Quaker and revered Christian statesman, John Bright. Outside the house, the names Mill most coveted as allies in the cause had won their fame as Christian social reformers: the evangelical Anglican Josephine Butler, the Unitarian Mary Carpenter, and the liberal Anglican Florence Nightingale. When it came to another main cause of the women's movement, the repeal of the Contagious Diseases Act, Mill even specifically and directly solicited the support of Congregational ministers. Mill was also encouraged by the theologian F. D. Maurice's support of women's suffrage. Most people read Dickens's *Bleak House* as satirizing evangelical do-gooders, but it is telling that Mill read it as an assault on the campaign for women's rights: the causes were overlapping, after all.

Avowed atheists now serve in Parliament. American slavery was abolished. Revolutionary measures did come to Ireland. Working men have the vote. Gender equality is enshrined in law. Mill's causes were so often right and true and just. By their fruits ye shall know them.

Notes

1. Francis E. Mineka (ed.), *The Earlier Letters of John Stuart Mill, 1812–1848* (Collected Works of John Stuart Mill XII), Toronto: University of Toronto Press, 1963, p. 181.
2. Francis E. Mineka and Dwight N. Lindley (eds), *The Later Letters of John Stuart Mill, 1849–1873* (Collected Works of John Stuart Mill XVII), Toronto: University of Toronto Press, 1972, p. 1721.
3. John Stuart Mill to W. S. Jevons, 15 May 1865: Marion Filipiuk, Michael Laine, and John M. Robson (eds), *Additional Letters of John Stuart Mill* (Collected Works of John Stuart Mill XXXII), Toronto: University of Toronto Press, 1991, p. 153.
4. CWJSM XII (*Earlier Letters*), p. 324.
5. Oscar A. Haac (translator and editor), *The Correspondence of John Stuart Mill and Auguste Comte*, New Brunswick, NJ: Transaction Publishers, 1995, pp. 39, 43.
6. CWJSM XIV (*Later Letters*), p. 175.
7. CWJSM XV (*Later Letters*), p. 626.
8. CWJSM XIV (*Later Letters*), p. 58.
9. John Stuart Mill, *Essays on Politics and Society*, ed. J. M. Robson (Collected Works of John Stuart Mill XIX), New York: Routledge, 1977, pp. 388–9.
10. Bruce L. Kinzer, Ann P. Robson, and John M. Robson, *A Moralist In and Out of Parliament: John Stuart Mill at Westminster, 1865–1868*, Toronto: University of Toronto Press, 1992, p. 71. (This discussion of Mill and Parliament owes a general debt to this source.)
11. Kinzer, *Moralist*, pp. 273–4.
12. W. L. Courtney, *Life and Writings of John Stuart Mill*, London: Walter Scott, n.d. (preface dated 1888), p. 147.
13. John Stuart Mill, *Essays on Equality, Law, and Education*, ed. J. M. Robson (Collected Works of John Stuart Mill XXI), Toronto: University of Toronto Press, 1984, p. 95.
14. Richard Reeves, *John Stuart Mill: Victorian Firebrand*, London: Atlantic Books, 2007, pp. 334, 337.
15. John Stuart Mill, *Autobiography and Literary Essays* (Collected Works of John Stuart Mill I), ed. J. M. Robson, Indianapolis: Liberty Fund, 2006 (reprint of Toronto: University of Toronto Press, 1981), p. 266.
16. CWJSM XVI (*Later Letters*), p. 1327.
17. CWJSM XVI (*Later Letters*), pp. 1051, 1063.
18. I have drawn on previous work of mine: Timothy Larsen, *Contested Christianity: The Political and Social Contexts of Victorian Theology*, Waco: Baylor University Press, 2004, pp. 169–88.

19. John Stuart Mill to Paula Wright Davis, 11 December 1869: CWJSM XVII (*Later Letters*), p. 1670.
20. CWJSM XII (*Earlier Letters*), p. 84. (Mill later crossed this sentence out in his copy of the letter as a kind of *ex post facto* censorship.)
21. John Stuart Mill, *Newspaper Writings (August 1831–October 1834)*, ed. Ann P. Robson and John M. Robson (Collected Works of John Stuart Mill XXIII), Toronto: University of Toronto Press, 1986, p. 431.
22. Kinzer, *Moralist*, p. 129.
23. CWJSM XXI (*Essays on Equality, Law, and Education*), p. 323.
24. CWJSM XXI (*Essays on Equality, Law, and Education*), p. 336.
25. CWJSM XXI (*Essays on Equality, Law, and Education*), p. 302.
26. Kinzer, *Moralist*, p. 148.
27. Timothy Larsen, *A People of One Book: The Bible and the Victorians*, Oxford: Oxford University Press, 2011, p. 196.
28. Michael St. John Packe, *The Life of John Stuart Mill*, London: Secker and Warburg, 1954, p. 474.
29. CWJSM XVII (*Later Letters*), p. 1631.
30. CWJSM XVI (*Later Letters*), p. 1479.
31. CWJSM XVI (*Later Letters*), p. 1069.
32. CWJSM XVI (*Later Letters*), pp. 1522–3.
33. CWJSM XVI (*Later Letters*), pp. 1165, 1234.
34. Haac, *Mill and Comte*, p. 180.

12
Spiritually Minded

'For to be carnally minded is death; but to be spiritually minded is life and peace.'

(Romans 8:6)

Standing alongside *A System of Logic* and *Principles of Political Economy*, Mill's other large, ambitious work was *An Examination of Sir William Hamilton's Philosophy* (1865). Although the *Logic* was intended to undermine the intuitionists, it was not the place to take on the metaphysical issues at stake directly. The time had now come when Mill was ready to engage that fight head on. Unlike his two other major works—let alone some of the shorter treatises such as *On Liberty* and *The Subjection of Women*—the *Examination* has not continued to be of interest to many people. On one level, it was a victim of its own success. Hamilton died in 1856. Mill advised his publisher that a posthumous volume of Hamilton's lectures would sell well: 'His reputation for learning (with everybody) and for profundity (with one of the two great divisions of the philosophical world) stands higher than that of any other Englishman of this century.'[1] Mill opened the *Examination* itself with the same tribute: 'Among the philosophical writers of the present century in these islands, no one occupies a higher position than Sir William Hamilton.'[2] Mill's demolition was so thorough and effective, however, that Hamilton's stock was permanently deflated. As no one now imagines that Sir William Hamilton will prove to be the better philosopher and thinker than John Stuart Mill, it is hard to muster up a desire to read through 560 pages of dense argumentation in order to verify afresh to one's own satisfaction such a foregone conclusion. On the other hand, there is the disincentive of the ways in which Mill failed in this book as well as the ways in which he succeeded. Mill wanted to degrade Hamilton's position because the deceased thinker was meant to serve as the 'representative of the best form of Germanism'.[3] Hamilton, however, actually had created an unstable and unsatisfactory philosophical blend all his own. Mill was effective at demonstrating Hamilton's confusions and inconsistencies, but he was mistaken in his assumption that German Idealism would thereby be vanquished in Britain as well. In the Concluding Remarks of the *Examination*, Mill gave a prediction which indicates the extent to which he had not measured where the real strength of the opposition lay: 'Kant, probably, will be finally judged to have left no noticeable contribution to philosophy which was both new and true.'[4] In the late Victorian period and beyond, there would be a thriving British Idealist movement which drew heavily and sympathetically upon the thought of both Kant and Hegel. The forces of intuitionism did not scatter in defeat and disarray when their British knight was bested on the field of combat.

Some people have also found the book a bit unpleasant because Mill does not just tackle the major disagreement with Hamilton over intuitionism, but rather relentlessly challenges everything he found assailable across Hamilton's entire oeuvre. In other words, the structure of the *Examination* is simply one Hamilton error after another. This can begin to feel personal, and this unease might be augmented by the fact that Hamilton had already been dead for almost a decade by that time and so could not defend himself. In truth, Mill knew that he needed a foil to clarify his own thoughts. He observed in a letter to the Reverend W. J. Fox in 1833: 'I have always done more justice to a subject when I have treated it controversially than when I have attempted a systematic exposition.'[5] Mill was blocked for years trying to complete his *Logic* until the unexpected gift of having Whewell to tilt against gave him the way forward. Hamilton provided the gladiatorial impetus Mill needed to pursue a major work on metaphysics. The *Examination* is heavy-going nonetheless. (This reader found light relief in the unintended comedy of Mill's insinuation that Hamilton was a Nominalist in name only.)[6] Most of all, it is a neglected work because the *Examination* is sometimes addressing issues that are no longer live ones—at least when framed in these terms—in philosophical debate; and, furthermore—because Mill was not giving a systematic presentation of his own view—the gleanings can be slim.

Even more so than with *A System of Logic*, the presence of God pervades the *Examination*. Religion is often introduced in gratuitous ways to illustrate points that are in no sense inherently religious. Here is a quotation that can serve both to make that point as well as to remind the reader of the technical nature of this treatise:

> Propositions and Reasonings may be written in Extension, but they are always understood in Comprehension. The only exception is the case of propositions which have no meaning in Comprehension, and have nothing to do with Concepts—those of which both the subject and the predicate are proper names; such as . . . St. Peter is not St. Paul.[7]

Moreover, the theological implications and applications of philosophical ideas were very much concerns of Mill's when he wrote the *Examination*, and so he often brings God into the discussion in more substantive ways in order to tease these out. At one point, for instance, he takes a general quotation of Hamilton's and inserts into it claims about the Deity in square brackets in order to show how it might be appropriated in a religious conversation:

> To disclaim this conclusion would be to bring down upon himself the language in which he criticized Reid and Stewart; it would be to maintain 'that I can know *that* I [believe] without knowing *what* I [believe]—or that I can know the [belief] without knowing what the [belief] is about: for example . . . that I am conscious of [believing in God], without being conscious of the [God believed in]'.[8]

Hamilton actually agreed with Mill's position that knowledge of God is not given to the human race 'in immediate consciousness'; that God is not 'apprehended by direct intuition'.[9] So far, so good. What troubled Mill was Hamilton's use of the category of 'the Absolute'. For Mill, the most important attribute of God is that God is good. It is said that every preacher really only has one sermon; whenever Mill found himself preaching he always proclaimed the goodness of God. The Absolute could only be read as a way of speaking about God and this was a dangerously under-defined deity:

> The Absolute—not something absolute, but the Absolute itself,—the proposition can be understood in no other sense than that the supposed Being possesses in absolute completeness *all* predicates; is absolutely good, and absolutely bad; absolutely wise, and absolutely stupid; and so forth. The conception of such a being, I will not say of such a God, is worse than a 'fasciculus of negations';. . .[10]

Moreover, Mill did not need to imagine how Hamilton's philosophy might be transposed into pernicious theology. This labour had already been performed by the Reverend H. L. Mansel.

Mansel's Bampton Lectures at the University of Oxford, *The Limits of Religious Thought* (1859), provoked Mill to an outburst which became by far the most famous passage in the *Examination*. It is worth giving a longer excerpt than is typical. Mill begins by quoting the biblical phrase 'glad tidings' (see, for instance, Luke 1:19). By this phrase Mill means that the true Gospel is Good News precisely because God is Good. Mill then protests against Mansel's inability to proclaim this full, true, biblical gospel:

> If, instead of the 'glad tidings' that there exists a Being in whom all the excellences which the highest human mind can conceive, exist in a degree inconceivable to us, I am informed that the world is ruled by a being whose attributes are infinite, but what they are we cannot learn, nor what are the principles of government, except that 'the highest human morality which we are capable of conceiving' does not sanction them; convince me of it, and I will bear my fate as I may. But when I am told that I must believe this, and at the same time call this being by the names which express and affirm the highest human morality, I say in plain terms that I will not. Whatever power such a being may have over me, there is one thing which he shall not do: he shall not compel me to worship him. I will call no being good, who is not what I mean when I apply that epithet to my fellow-creatures; and if such a being can sentence me to hell for not so calling him, to hell I will go.[11]

The *Examination* became forever defined by Mill's evocation of the everlasting fire that never shall be quenched.

It is often imagined that Mill had thereby said something defiantly irreligious. As that interpretation is decisively wrong, it is worth taking some time to show how mistaken it is. Mansel argued that as the finite cannot comprehend the infinite it should not surprise us that we are not able to offer satisfactory, rational explanations regarding God's existence, nature, and actions. This fact, he averred, does not tell against God and God's ways, but only marks human limitations and ignorance. Mansel maintained: 'In His Moral Attributes, no less than in the rest of His Infinite Being, God's judgments are unsearchable, and His ways past finding out.'[12] Fortunately, the Deity has given us revelation to guide us and we have faith by which to believe in it.

Reason can help us discern that something is a revelation of God, but once that judgement has been made then one must accept it *in toto* and not attempt to sit in judgement regarding which parts of that revelation seem more or less comprehensible, reasonable, or right.

Mansel was given credit for wishing to defend the Christian faith, but many believed that his scheme actually damaged it. Years before Mill would join in, his friend, the Reverend F. D. Maurice, one of the leading theologians of nineteenth-century Britain, led a relentless crusade against Mansel's book and the way of thinking it advocated. Maurice promptly wrote *What is Revelation? Letters to a student of theology on the Bampton Lectures of Mr. Mansel* (1859). Mansel's preface was dated 18 February 1859, and Maurice's 4 June, meaning that it had only taken Maurice around three months to respond. Moreover, Maurice's book was a 352-page attack upon a series of lectures by Mansel that amounted to only 228 pages. Then Maurice followed this with *Sequel to the Inquiry, What is Revelation?* The preface is dated January 1860 and it is 296 pages long, giving us 648 pages in total of Maurice lambasting the Bampton lecturer.

It is necessary to read these volumes through to grasp just how overheated Maurice's response to Mansel was. They are difficult books to excerpt as they consist mainly of Maurice quoting passages from Mansel and then inviting the reader to be outraged, coupled with Maurice taking a high tone about what he has stood for in his own ministry. In the second paragraph of the preface of *What is Revelation?* Maurice is already declaring that if he believed Mansel's teaching was true he would resign from the ordained ministry; indeed, he adds later, 'it would be needful for me to abandon every conviction that was most precious to me'.[13] Maurice first made the exact point that Mill would later reiterate: such a proclamation means that people 'have not understood whether we came to them with good tidings, or with ill tidings, or with no tidings at all'.[14] The second chapter of *What is Revelation?* addresses Mansel's use of Hamilton. Here are a few examples of the unmeasured way that Maurice denounces his victim: 'Of all outrages upon philosophical method, and upon ordinary English justice, which are to be found in our literature, I believe this is the most flagrant'; 'he is simply setting at nought the words of Christ, and overthrowing the whole Bible'; 'Such men, I believe, do more to lower the moral tone and moral practice of England than all sceptics and infidels together.'[15] At one point, Maurice says that if what Mansel claims is true then 'let us burn our Bibles; let us tell our countrymen, that the Agony and Bloody Sweat of Christ, His Cross and Passion, His Death and Burial, His Resurrection and Ascension mean nothing'.[16] He imagines Mansel's views finding their culmination in this statement of faith: 'We shall praise thee, O Devil, we shall acknowledge thee to be the lord.'[17] When it comes to two Anglican clerics having a theological dispute, shall we just say that such language places this one toward the less cordial side of the spectrum?

Several attempts have been made to identify a literary precursor that might have prompted Mill's 'to hell I will go' rhetorical flourish. What has not yet been noticed, however, is that there is one right here in Maurice, who quotes an account that Anselm of Canterbury had once observed that 'he would rather be in Hell if he were pure of sin, than possess the Kingdom of Heaven under the pollution of sin'.[18] Moreover, Maurice's critique is Mill's critique: Mansel has perniciously asserted that 'we are not to know anything of an Absolute Morality'.[19] By contrast, Maurice explicitly commends his philosopher-friend: 'I would exhort all clergymen to study a passage on this subject in Mr. Mill's "Liberty".'[20] In the *Sequel*, Maurice observed that Mill's seeming assumption in the *Logic* that truth was merely propositional had made him uneasy, but this burden was lifted when he read *On Liberty*: 'convincing me that in his heart of hearts the author acknowledges a substantial truth which is above all propositions—for which it is worth while to fight and suffer and die'.[21]

Mill himself credited Maurice's *What is Revelation?* and its *Sequel* with inspiring him to write *An Examination of Sir William Hamilton's Philosophy*. He wrote to Maurice himself: 'You were continually in my thoughts when I wrote the chapter against Mansel, and your controversy with him contributed much towards stirring me up to write the book.'[22] The reason why there is an assumption that Mill had said something un-Christian which had upset believers was because the *Examination* was his most recent book when he stood for Parliament, and politically conservative religious newspapers and Tory campaign workers used the 'to hell I will go' quote to insinuate that Mill was an atheist who was being sacrilegious. The quote was literally put on campaign placards as a way of trying to spook the electorate. Such is politics. It was not just Maurice, however, who was on the same side in this theological dispute with Mill. Serious theologians and respected Churchmen lined up to agree with Mill and to affirm that his 'to hell I will go' statement was a perfectly orthodox and admirable one. The Reverend Charles Kingsley said so, as did the Reverends William Henry Lyttelton and Mark Pattison. Mill's old foil, the Reverend William Whewell, was also on Mill's side in this dispute. The highest figure in the Anglican hierarchy in Mill's constituency, Arthur Stanley, the Dean of Westminster, publicly agreed with Mill. So did a member of the episcopal bench, Connop Thirlwall, bishop of St David's, who trumpeted in print that this contested passage in Mill's treatise 'breathes the purest spirit of Christian morality'.[23] The Roman Catholic theologian W. G. Ward agreed with Mill as well. Mill claimed that Ward had demonstrated that the notion that morality was based in God's arbitrary will (something in the same cluster of ideas associated with Mansel) was rejected by 'the orthodox doctrine of the Roman Catholic Church'.[24] Indeed, while they presumably must have existed, I have not come across any theologian who took Mansel's side on the issue of disagreement with Mill. On the other hand, new allies of Mill's did crop up during this research. For instance, following the question regarding the true glad tidings evoked by both Maurice and Mill, the Christian writer George MacDonald mocked Mansel's view in one of his *Unspoken Sermons*:

> Where would the good news be if John said, 'God is light, but you cannot see his light; you cannot tell, you have no notion what light is; what God means by light, is not what you mean by light; what God calls light may be horrible darkness to you, for you are of another nature from him!'[25]

Most of all, R. W. Dale, an eminent Congregational minister who was emerging as the most important evangelical theologian of his generation in Britain, explicitly and unequivocally endorsed Mill against Mansel. In an article in the evangelical *British Quarterly Review* in 1867 (when Mill was still serving in Parliament), Dale insisted that not only was Mansel entirely in the wrong on the point at issue: 'But Mr. Mill might have gone further, that the view against which he protests annihilates not only the idea of morality, but the idea of religion too.'[26] Dale expanded this to an attack on Mansel that went on for pages in *The Atonement*, his *magnum opus*. Dale's *Atonement* was not only a classic work of evangelical theology that become a widely used textbook for generations, but it was so welcomed as a defence of orthodoxy even beyond the evangelical world that it was praised by John Henry Newman and W. E. Gladstone. Dale included a block quote from Mansel in order to attack him specifically. Here is Dale's way of making the same point as Mill: 'When we do homage to Him because of His justice, goodness, and truth, we imply that if He were not just and good and true, He would have no claim to our homage.'[27] As MacDonald and Dale (in the *Atonement*) were writing after both Mill and Mansel had died, they were not trying to influence politics or personalities—they were simply trying to get the theology right. To John Stuart Mill went the honour of helping to vindicate the goodness of God, and orthodox theologians and Christian ministers were not reticent to express their agreement and gratitude.

Mill's other book which appeared in 1865 was *Auguste Comte and Positivism.* Mill had become enthusiastic about Comte's views at the end of the 1820s, and in November 1841 began a correspondence with the French thinker. The strong influence of Comte's stadial view of history upon Mill has already been noted. It is now time to address the place of Comte's Religion of Humanity in Mill's life and thought. Linda C. Raeder has argued that Mill's correspondence with Comte best expresses what he really thought on religious questions and that the Religion of Humanity was Mill's own, personal religious identity; indeed, that through his commending of the Religion of Humanity Mill saw himself as 'a religious founder'.[28] Alas, there is much that limits the utility of Raeder's study. She fails to take into account that Mill routinely bent to agree with his correspondents, and therefore just because this was a private exchange of letters it did not make it any more the best record of Mill's truest self than his letters with his best male friend, John Sterling, or Thomas Carlyle, or W. G. Ward, or his conversations with Caroline Fox, or his interactions with others. Regrettably, Raeder sometimes reveals that she did not always understand what she was discussing. For instance, Bishop Butler—the great slayer of Deism—is himself identified as a Deist in her account—as is that other leading champion of orthodoxy, William Paley.[29] Apparently unaware of the entire Unitarian tradition and denomination, she writes naively: 'one surely cannot remove the dogmatic notion that Christ is God and claim to have preserved Christianity'.[30] More to the point, she was apparently unaware that Comte's Religion of Humanity inspired the creation of actual congregations in Britain and that Mill neither founded this form of organized religion himself nor joined it. None of the key figures associated with it such as Richard Congreve, Frederic Harrison or Edward Beesly are even mentioned in Raeder's account.[31] Writing to Congreve, Mill even asked his forgiveness for his free way of critiquing Congreve's religion—the Religion of Humanity—which Mill realized must be perceived by a true Comtean believer as showing a want of 'reverence'.[32] T. R. Wright observed that some of the British devotees of the Religion of Humanity thought of Mill 'as more of an opponent than ally'.[33] Mill and the Religion of Humanity, like so much else about Mill and religion, is far from straightforward.

To return to the correspondence, Mill was clearly pleased to be interacting with a thinker who was a fellow unbeliever in traditional religion. Mill gave a more direct version of the famous statement in the *Autobiography*, informing Comte that he 'had the rare fate in my country of never having believed in God, even as a child'.[34] Comte, in turn, declared that he stood for the position that 'it is possible today not to believe in God and still not be a real atheist'.[35] There was something else at work, however, beyond mere camaraderie. Mill was persistently anxious that Comte would expect him to make some irreligious public declaration. Mill's reassuring statements of unbelief in this correspondence, therefore, were also a way to attempt to pacify Comte: 'I agree with you in your anti-dogmatic position, but it would not be prudent to address questions of religion', is an accurate summary of Mill's recurring message. Not worried about committing only himself, Mill even tried to dissuade Comte from having some of his writings translated into English on the grounds that Comte's attacks on religion were 'unsuited for an English audience'.[36] Indeed, reining in Comte's iconoclastic approach to Christianity was something of a concerted goal. Sarah Austin, who was also an admirer of the Frenchman's work, had written to Mill a few months earlier: 'I wish you could persuade Comte to be more reserved about religion. He sets it aside with a cool contempt.'[37] Positively (as it were), Mill always, emphatically, liked the *idea* of a Religion of Humanity. He commended it in his published writings over and over again across the decades. To this extent, Raeder was certainly on to something.

Mill's thinking went like this: dogmatic religion belongs to a former stage in human history and therefore the germane question is what ought to happen next. The mistake of eighteenth-century sceptics was that they pursued a path of pure negation; only tearing down what was old without endeavouring to replace it with something new. Something like a Religion of Humanity is therefore needed. It would jettison the dogmatism which made the old religions untenable while filling the void constructively with something that is tenable. Comte recognized that people would still need 'a *cultus* . . . a set of systematic observances, intended to cultivate and maintain the religious sentiment.'[38] As Mill wrote in his diary in 1854, Comte's achievement was 'the thoroughness with which he has enforced and illustrated the possibility of making *le culte de l'humanité* perform the functions and supply the place of a religion'.[39]

On the other hand, Mill always thought that the actual cult which Comte ended up devising was laughable. He expressed both views in a letter written in 1848: Comte had established 'the grounds for believing that the *culte de l'humanité* is capable of fully supplying the place of a religion, or rather (to say the truth) of *being* a religion—and this he has done, notwithstanding the ridiculousness which everybody must feel in his premature attempts to define in detail the *practices* of this *culte*'.[40] Comte had created a liturgical year with eighty-four sacred days; he developed nine sacraments; and on and on it went. Mill saw all this as 'the ludicrous side' of Comte's efforts.[41] Part of Mill's distaste was undoubtedly because Comte had a deeply Catholic sensibility, while Mill himself had a decidedly Protestant one. Comte's *cultus* is also perhaps another instance in which Mill can recognize that there is a religious devotional sense that needs to find a way to express itself, but where his lack of such instincts made it hard for him truly to understand it, let alone join it. Comte was all for science replacing the supernatural, yet he still wanted to kneel down and pray for two hours every day, and he instinctively expected others to do the same as part of his new Religion of Humanity.[42] Comte's British disciples such as Richard Congreve wanted to combine their rational views with gathering together on Sundays as a congregation for liturgical worship. In Mill's eyes, devotion should be much less regimented and prescriptive than that. Indeed, the worst part of it all for him was how dictatorial Comte became. The author of *On Liberty* found that one of his intellectual heroes, Auguste Comte, had descended to a point where he desired to create a 'spiritual despotism'. In the end, Mill lamented, the Frenchman had exalted himself into the position of 'the supreme moral legislator and religious pontiff of the human race'.[43]

Once again, it is important to realize that Mill explicitly rejected Comte's assumption that the triumphant of positivism meant that belief in God would no longer be tenable. Instead, throughout *Auguste Comte and Positivism* Mill argues that what positivism achieves is only the elimination of a god-of-the-gaps. People once attributed to the direct action of God whatever they did not understand. As scientific knowledge advances, such a god inevitably recedes, however. You do not pray for a god to act specially, in order for the sun to rise or the tide to come in, once you understand these phenomena scientifically. In a positivist age, therefore, belief in God would be confined to a God who has created natural laws and works through them. This means that religion would need to change accordingly: prayer, for instance, would shift from petition to praise. The notion of a Religion of Humanity was worth asserting because it pointed the way toward a *cultus* that was not contradicted by science.

Tellingly, 'spiritual' and 'religion' were positive words in Mill's lexicon—they generally spoke of things that were good and needed to be retained. He assumed that the goal was to purify religion, not to eliminate it. He declared in his *Autobiography* that those who deny dogmatic beliefs are sometimes 'genuinely religious, in the best sense of the word religion'.[44] Mill often used 'spiritual' as a term of approbation. In Mill's view, the human race should be striving towards 'spiritual perfection'.[45] This was true in his letters to both Carlyle and Comte, let alone his published works. Mill enthused to Comte: 'You have convincingly brought out that social regeneration depends on spiritual force.'[46] The idea of a Religion of Humanity was Mill's way of envisioning a future in which theological dogmatism would have been set aside and yet people's spiritual nature would still be cultivated and expressed and their religious needs would still be met. Let there be religion within the bounds of reason.

Notes

1. Francis E. Mineka and Dwight N. Lindley (eds), *The Later Letters of John Stuart Mill, 1849–1873* (Collected Works of John Stuart Mill XV), Toronto: University of Toronto Press, 1972, p. 519.
2. John Stuart Mill, *An Examination of Sir William Hamilton's Philosophy and of the Principal Questions Discussed in his Writings*, ed. J. M. Robson (Collected Works of John Stuart Mill IX), London: Routledge, 1996, p. 1. (The Collected Works text is based on the third edition.)
3. CWJSM XV (*Later Letters*), p. 763.
4. CWJSM IX (*Examination*), p. 493.
5. John Stuart Mill to W. J. Fox, 4 July 1833: Francis E. Mineka (ed.), *The Earlier Letters of John Stuart Mill, 1812–1848* (Collected Works of John Stuart Mill XII), Toronto: University of Toronto Press, 1963, p. 160.
6. CWJSM IX (*Examination*), p. 316.
7. CWJSM IX (*Examination*), p. 340.
8. CWJSM IX (*Examination*), p. 119.
9. CWJSM IX (*Examination*), p. 36.
10. CWJSM IX (*Examination*), p. 46.
11. CWJSM IX (*Examination*), p. 103.
12. Henry Longueville Mansel, *The Limits of Religious Thought Examined*, Boston: Gould and Lincoln, 1859, p. 202.
13. Frederick Denison Maurice, *What Is Revelation? Letters to a Student of Theology on the Bampton Lectures of Mr. Mansel*, London: Macmillan, 1859, p. viii.
14. Maurice, *What Is Revelation?*, p. 13.
15. Maurice, *What Is Revelation?*, pp. 75, 124. 244.
16. Maurice, *What Is Revelation?*, p. 308.
17. Maurice, *What Is Revelation?*, p. 311.
18. Maurice, *What Is Revelation?*, p. 81.
19. Maurice, *What Is Revelation?*, p. 320.
20. Maurice, *What Is Revelation?*, p. 349.
21. Frederick Denison Maurice, *Sequel to the Inquiry, What is Revelation?*, Cambridge: Macmillan, 1860, pp. 207–8.
22. John Stuart Mill to Frederick Denison Maurice, 11 May 1865: CWJSM XVI (*Later Letters*), p. 1047. Mill had made the same theological point decades earlier in a review in the *Monthly Repository* in October 1833: John Stuart Mill, *Essays on Ethics, Religion and Society* (Collected Works of John Stuart Mill X), ed. J. M. Robson, Indianapolis: Liberty Fund, 2006 (reprint of Toronto: University of Toronto Press, 1969), pp. 20–9.
23. CWJSM XVI (*Later Letters*), p. 1069.
24. CWJSM IX (*Examination*), p. 164–5.

25. George MacDonald, *Unspoken Sermons* (3 series in one volume), Whitethorn, California: 2004, p. 545. (This is from the third series which was originally published in 1889.)
26. [R. W. Dale], 'The Expiatory Theory of the Atonement', *British Quarterly Review*, XLVI (1867), pp. 463–504 (487).
27. R. W. Dale, *The Atonement: The Congregational Union Lecture for 1875*, 21st edition, London: Congregational Union of England and Wales, 1900 (original edition, 1875), pp. 368–9.
28. Linda C. Raeder, *John Stuart Mill and the Religion of Humanity*, Columbia, MO: University of Missouri Press, 2002, p. 6.
29. Raeder, *Mill*, p. 90.
30. Raeder, *Mill*, p. 250.
31. For this world, see T. R. Wright, *The Religion of Humanity: The Impact of Comtean Positivism on Victorian Britain*, Cambridge: Cambridge University Press, 1986.
32. John Stuart Mill to Richard Congreve, 8 August 1865: CWJSM XVI (*Later Letters*), p. 1085–6.
33. Wright, *Religion of Humanity*, p. 49.
34. Oscar A. Haac (translator and editor), *The Correspondence of John Stuart Mill and Auguste Comte*, New Brunswick, NJ: Transaction Publishers, 1995, pp. 118–19.
35. Haac, *Mill and Comte*, p. 320.
36. Haac, *Mill and Comte*, p. 317.
37. CWJSM XIII (*Earlier Letters*), p. 654.
38. CWJSM X (*Essays on Ethics, Religion and Society*), p. 341.
39. John M. Robson (ed.), *Journals and Debating Speeches* (Collected Works of John Stuart Mill XXVII), Toronto: University of Toronto Press, 1988, p. 646.
40. CWJSM XIII (*Earlier Letters*), pp. 738–9.
41. CWJSM X (*Essays on Ethics, Religion and Society*), pp. 341–2.
42. For the details of this cult, see Auguste Comte, *The Catechism of Positive Religion*, trans. Richard Congreve, third edition, London: Kegan Paul, Trench, Trübner, & Co., 1891.
43. CWJSM X (*Essays on Ethics, Religion and Society*), pp. 314, 332.
44. John Stuart Mill, *Autobiography and Literary Essays* (Collected Works of John Stuart Mill I), ed. J. M. Robson, Indianapolis: Liberty Fund, 2006 (reprint of Toronto: University of Toronto Press, 1981), p. 47.
45. CWJSM XII (*Earlier Letters*), p. 144.
46. Haac, *Mill and Comte*, p. 110.

13
The Hope That is in You

> 'Be ready always to give an answer to every man that asketh you a reason of the hope that is in you.'
>
> (1 Peter 3:15)

John Stuart Mill left his last testament on matters spiritual to be published posthumously. In accordance with his wishes, Helen Taylor arranged for this in the year after her stepfather's death. It was published as *Three Essays on Religion* (1874). The first two essays, 'Nature' and 'Utility of Religion' were composed in and around 1854, when Harriet was still alive, the last one, 'Theism', in the period 1868–70. The first two are often read as anti-Christian and the last one as disconcertingly, if not alarmingly, sympathetic to the Christian faith. It is unquestionably true that the tone of 'Theism' is much more sympathetic to aspects of traditional religion and that with some of these encouraging statements regarding certain Christian beliefs Mill goes further than he had ever gone before. Nevertheless, despite multiple claims to the contrary, Mill actually had quite a stable theological scheme which he maintained from the early 1830s until his death in 1873. This was not clear even to some of his closest collaborators simply because he never published on some of the points of his scheme or only referred to them in passing in his writings. Moreover, he varied over the course of his life or depending on who his interlocutor was in regard to whether he placed the stress upon the more sceptical or believing aspects of his thoughts. Mill's theological vision went like this: Even from a scientific point of view and without any intuitive sense or direct experience of the divine, there is still sufficient evidence to warrant the conclusion that God probably exists; God is good, but not omnipotent; the life and sayings of Christ are admirable and deserve our reverence; the immortality of the soul or an afterlife are possible but not certain; humanity's task is to co-labour with God to subdue evil and make the world a better place; the affirmations in the previous points such as that God exists and is good cannot be proven, but it is still a reasonable act to appropriate these religious convictions imaginatively on the basis of hope.

The classic problem of evil asks: If God is all-powerful and all-good, how can there be evil in the world? Would not an all-good God desire for there to be no evil, and would not an all-powerful God be able to make this desire a reality? Mill realized that any attempt to solve this problem logically was apt to do so by undermining one of the three points of its triangle. His fury at Mansel was because he read him as being willing to undermine the claim that God is good by intimating that human beings are in no position to judge the morality of God's actions, and thus implying that God might not be good in the way that we understand goodness. Mill the Moralist and Activist was even more concerned that the problem might be addressed by denying the evilness of evil: 'if therefore we maintain that an omnipotent & *good* Being tolerates these things, we must maintain them to be good in themselves, that is, we must (as I said in my former letter) affirm Evil to be Good'.[1] That only left one corner of the triangle on which to place pressure and Mill accepted that solution fully as the only one that was both logical and morally edifying: God was not omnipotent. Throughout his whole mature life Mill was a prophet of God's goodness. Already in *The Spirit of the Age* in 1831 he was developing this line of thought: 'It is a matter of common complaint, that even the Supreme Being is adored by an immense majority as the Almighty, not as the All-good; as he who can destroy, not as he who has blessed.'[2] In 'Theism' Mill made it clear that he was trading the one attribute in order to strengthen the other: 'The power of the Creator once recognized as limited, there is nothing to disprove the supposition that his goodness is complete.'[3] The concession that God the Father was not the Almighty at a stroke removed seemingly all the positive evidence against the existence of God: every 'if God exists why?' question can be answered with 'because God did not or does not have the power to do that'. In a letter written in 1861, Mill reflected that once the idea of omnipotence is removed, a belief that 'the world was made by a good & wise Being, is in itself perfectly credible'.[4] To this Mill added Manichean dualism: there are evil forces at work but the good God opposes them, even though this God is not powerful enough to eliminate them. This was a rational solution to the problem of evil but, over the years, it also increasingly became for Mill an uplifting theological vision in its own right. It is morally invigorating for people to realize that they are called to partner with the Deity to subdue the forces of evil. Already in 1841, Mill rhapsodized to his pious friend Barclay Fox about the need for people to 'feel called to what my friends the St Simonians not blasphemously call "continuing the work of Creation" i.e. cooperating as instruments of Providence in bringing order out of disorder'.[5]

In 1847, Mill and Harriet drafted a letter to the Secularist newspaper, the *Reasoner*, edited by G. J. Holyoake. This publication was part of the defiant, plebeian, infidel culture of unbelief. In other words, they were addressing an audience that would bring out Mill and Harriet's sceptical side the most forcefully. Indeed, the tone is one of attacking traditional religion. Nevertheless, even when writing to militant anti-Christian propagandists who did not believe in God at all, Mill is still so conscientious as not only to leave his theological scheme intact, but to make most of it explicit and visible. Thus, he urges that one can charge the portrait of the traditional deity with being marked by 'wickedness', but then dutifully acknowledges that if one believed that God was a being of 'extremely limited power and hemmed in by obstacles which he is unable to overcome', that concession would save God's character. Moreover, Mill affirms that as the evidence is uncertain it is legitimate for people imaginatively to appropriate belief in God. The philosopher even includes his admiration for the Gospels, while—like Bentham—recommending that these Secularists attack St Paul.[6] In other words, the ideas in 'Theism' were not a new departure for Mill. He put the side of the question most congenial to Christians particularly sympathetically at the end of his life, but even that tendency—although not always followed—was not new.

Mill completed the first essay, 'Nature', in early February 1854. It was one of the topics that Harriet had assigned to him. Although this is reputedly an irreligious essay, once again, this judgement made by some readers is primarily based on matters of tone and emphasis. Mill's wider scheme—including its theological hopes and affirmations—is evident in this essay even when it is read alone, apart from 'Theism'. Mill clearly lays out his solution to the problem of evil: 'The only admissible moral theory of Creation is that the Principle of Good *cannot* at once and altogether subdue the powers of evil.'[7] 'Nature' even includes Mill's vision of God creating human beings 'capable of carrying on the fight with vigour and with progressively increasing success'. The 'duty of man is to co-operate with the beneficent powers' to bring about a world of greater and greater 'justice and goodness'.[8] Perhaps Morley, Bain, and others read all this as just a rhetorical flourish, but it was actually a long-held theology of the coming of the Kingdom of God, Mill's millennium. Despite the reports in secondary sources, most of 'Nature' is not an attack on Christian orthodoxy at all. It is not even an essay whose theme is confined to religion. 'Nature' is a somewhat intemperate protest against the way that people attempt to rig arguments by denouncing something as 'unnatural'. Mill concedes that he is not even opposing a general conviction that people actually hold, but only a form of special pleading that they selectively deploy. His sensible claim is that the right thing to do is often to attempt to conquer nature rather than to obey it. The only correct meaning of the admonition to follow nature is to study it in order to use its laws to bring about desirable outcomes. This point prompts Mill to give a long, odd rant in which Nature is anthropomorphized in order that it might be condemned. Here is but a small fraction of it:

> Nature impales men, breaks them as if on the wheel, casts them to be devoured by wild beasts, burns them to death, crushes them with stones like the first christian martyr, starves them with hunger, freezes them with cold, poisons them by the quick or slow venom of her exhalations...[9]

Mill goes on to assert: 'That a thing is unnatural, in any precise meaning which can be attached to the word, is no argument for its being blamable.'[10] This indicates that Mill was just as much criticizing other opponents of his such as anti-Malthusians as he was engaging a specifically religious discussion. 'Nature' is a sermon by Mill the Revolutionary—Mill the Reformer taking the side of progress rather than permanence—on how what is and what ought to be are not the same thing.

'Utility of Religion' was the next assignment that Harriet gave Mill when he finished 'Nature'. He reported to her on 3 April 1854 that he had completed it. Once again, despite rumours to the contrary, it is not primarily an attack on traditional Christianity, and is not merely critical but also includes aspects of Mill's wider scheme and theological affirmations. Its main burden is to recommend the idea of a Religion of Humanity as a viable replacement for dogmatic religion. Rather than seeking to demonstrate that orthodoxy is wrong, Mill addresses those who have already reached that conclusion and seeks to reassure them that they do not need to shore up a religion they do not believe is tenable because it serves a beneficial function in society. Mill acknowledges that religion does yield benefits, and so his project is to demonstrate that a non-dogmatic religion could also produce these desirable outcomes. Mill rejects a thoroughly sceptical solution in which religion is simply rejected rather than refined or replaced: 'When the only truth ascertainable is that nothing can be known, we do not, by this knowledge, gain any new fact by which to guide ourselves.'[11] Man cannot live by logic alone.

One of the weaker parts of the essay is Mill's attempt to explain why traditional religion is such a tremendous force in so many people's lives. He argues that this is because it is inculcated and policed by authority, early education, and public opinion. As to the latter, for instance, Mill writes: 'Religion has been powerful not by intrinsic force, but because it has wielded that additional and more mighty power.'[12] Mill fails to address the deeper reality that parents have taught religion to their children because they believed it and public opinion came to reinforce it because members of the public believed it. Mill's real point seems to be that if people did sincerely believe in the Religion of Humanity, then a society could arise in which it had the same strength for good as dogmatic religion has had. Once again, Mill condemns a god-of-the-gaps, offering a Just-So story regarding the origin of religion as wrong answers being given to scientific questions out of ignorance. Mill also gives one of his father's favourite arguments against orthodoxy—that the necessity of a Creator cannot be too weighty a concern because human beings cannot know the origins of things. This, of course, is ironic given that he has just offered an unverifiable claim regarding the origin of religion. On the constructive side, Mill once again affirms that it is reasonable for people imaginatively to appropriate belief in God. Mill spends a fair amount of space praising the teaching of Christ, listing specific sayings and teachings of Jesus of Nazareth that he finds admirable (such as 'the lesson of the parable of the Good Samaritan').[13] The point of this material is that all that is good in Christianity will not be lost but rather retained in a Religion of Humanity. (Mill is rather sanguine about this. Comte himself did not even include Christ in his calendar of saints, and Mill seems unable to imagine that in just a few decades a figure such as Friedrich Nietzsche would insist that the way forward is to jettison these admonitions from Jesus.) Mill also concedes that the non-dogmatic future might mean that people will have to let go of the expectation of life after death. Having offered the Religion of Humanity for consideration, Mill also let breathe some of the other aspects of his scheme. If one forgoes the assertion that God is omnipotent, then 'belief in supernatural' religion is still rationally defensible.[14] This leads on to his glorious vision of partnering with God to usher in (as even Mill's contemporaries were apt to pun) the millennium:

> A virtuous human being assumes in this theory the exalted character of a fellow-labourer with the Highest, a fellow-combatant in the great strife; contributing his little, which by the aggregation of many like himself becomes much, towards that progressive ascendency, and ultimately complete triumph of good over evil, which history points to, and which this doctrine teaches us to regard as planned by the Being to whom we owe all the benevolent contrivance we behold in Nature.[15]

Such a faith, even though supernatural, Mill avers, can legitimately be maintained in the future, positivist age side-by-side with the Religion of Humanity.

The immortality of the soul, like so many of these topics, was, for Mill, a possibility that he never found certain but also never ruled out as impossible. How likely the possibility appeared to Mill would vary. In an entry in his diary in 1854, he is at his most sceptical. He longs for Harriet to live forever—it seems the only fitting thing to happen to a magnificent intellect like hers—but then he asks somewhat desperately: 'but where is the proof, and where the ground of hope?'[16] In 'Theism', however, with Harriet's inanimate, mortal remains now entombed, Mill insists that the possibility of life after death is no less unlikely than permanent annihilation: 'There is, therefore, in science, no evidence against the immortality of the soul but that negative evidence, which consists in the absence of evidence in its favour. And even the negative evidence is not so strong as negative evidence often is.'[17] In 1842, when writing to his pious Christian friend, Barclay

Fox, Mill went so far as to put the balance of probability on the side of the afterlife: 'What we call our bodily sensations are all in the mind & would not necessarily or probably cease because the body perishes.'[18] In a letter to John Sterling in 1840 he settled on the word 'perhaps' rather than 'probably', and that seems the best description of Mill's general view of the subject over the years—perhaps we live on after our body dies.[19] His statement on the matter to Thomas Carlyle in 1834, once again, reveals that Mill's opinions on such questions were often marked by a fundamental continuity across his mature, adult life: 'With respect to the immortality of the soul I see no reason to believe that it perishes; nor sufficient evidence for complete assurance that it survives.'[20]

Turning to the question of the Deity, across the decades Mill repeatedly observed that he wanted to believe in God and affirmed that such a belief is beneficial. This is a far cry from the kind of militant unbeliever who finds religious avowals pernicious. Also in that same letter in 1834, Mill confessed to Carlyle that he had 'the strongest wish to believe' in God's existence.[21] In his *Examination*, Mill hauntingly defined 'doubt' as 'a disposition to believe, with an inability to believe confidently'.[22] Florence Nightingale had her own theological scheme in which the Creator has set the human race on a march of progress which had affinities with Mill's own one of co-labouring with God to eliminate evil. Mill wrote to her that it would be 'a great moral improvement' for most atheists 'if they believed the world to be under the government of a Being who, willing only good, leaves evil in the world solely in order to stimulate the human faculties by an unremitting struggle against every form of it'.[23] Likewise, in a letter written in 1871, Mill insisted that even though God's existence cannot be proven, belief in the right kind of God 'is morally beneficial in the highest degree'.[24] Once again, such comments created a wide gulf between Mill and figures such as Richard Carlile (before his late religious turn), G. J. Holyoake, and Charles Bradlaugh—or even Leslie Stephen, Alexander Bain, and John Morley.

Mill never fully addressed the question of whether God's existence is sufficiently proved in the case of some people because they directly apprehend or experience the divine. In 'Theism', his response to the Argument from Consciousness was merely that it was manifestly not true that such a consciousness is universal: 'one man cannot by proclaiming with ever so much confidence that *he* perceives an object, convince other people that they see it too'.[25] What warrant, then, do those who had no internal sense or experience of God have to believe? If not in all cases, then certainly in at least such a case as that, Mill taught that God's existence, although not proven conclusively, could be accepted on the basis of probability. Once again, this is a constant from his 1834 letter to Carlyle—in which he shyly conceded that his 'probable God' would presumably not be deemed a sufficiently robust religious commitment in the eyes of the Scottish sage—right through to 'Theism'. Harry Settanni has convincingly argued that the best term for Mill's religious position and identity is not agnosticism—let alone atheism—but 'probabilist theism'.[26] In 'Theism', Mill judged that there is 'a large balance of probability' in favour of there being a Creator.[27] And, to reiterate, although it might have surprised some of his disciples, this was Mill's view all along. In 1861, he wrote in a letter that 'the world was made, in the whole or in part, by a powerful Being who cared for man, appears to me, though not proved, yet a very probable hypothesis'.[28] Although not proven, on the basis of probability, it was a rational act to accept the existence of God imaginatively. Mill made this point repeatedly across the years. For instance, in that same letter in 1861 he wrote: 'This *is* my position in respect to Theism: I think it a legitimate subject of imagination, & hope, & even belief (not amounting to faith) but not of knowledge.'[29] (Mill is apparently defining 'faith' here as entailing an unwarranted assumption of certitude.)

It is easy for us to misunderstand what Mill was saying in these repeated statements of his because in popular discourse today 'imagination' evokes make-believe. Mill, however, was using imagination in the Romantic sense as the faculty which discerns meaning. He was *not* saying that Christians are free to use their imagination to pretend there is a God, to make up a God out of their own fancies. As he made clear in his letter to the *Reasoner*, Mill believed that to be an atheist or a Secularist required no less a work of the imagination.[30] Whether one believed or disbelieved one was still obliged to attempt a vision of the whole, to discern meaning: this is a function of the imaginative faculty. Mill wrote a particularly fascinating letter in this regard in 1868. His correspondent, Henry Jones, had lost his faith. Jones had been a teacher in an Anglican school, and his change of convictions therefore necessitated that he resign his post. He was writing to Mill in the hope that the eminent man would help him find new employment. It would seem that in the zeal of his deconversion—and perhaps in an attempt to win the sympathy of the famous freethinker—Jones wrote of his discovery that God, prayer, miracles, and the afterlife all were notions that lacked proof. Far from delighting in this newfound unbelief, Mill responded by saying that Jones needed to go on to the discovery that these matters are 'as difficult to disprove as to prove'.[31] In other words, Mill wanted Jones to understand that his realization that proof was lacking did not relieve him from the task of weighing probabilities and imaginatively discerning meaning one way or the other. Most surprising of all, Mill insisted that in the case of prayer there was particularly strong evidence weighted in its favour:

> I mean the effect produced on the mind of the person praying, not by the belief that it will be granted but by the elevating influence of an endeavour to commune & to become in harmony with the highest spiritual ideal that he is capable in elevated moments of conceiving. This effect may be very powerful in clearing the moral perceptions & intensifying the moral earnestness. It may be so powerful as to leave it open to question whether it is produced solely by the internal action of human nature itself or by a supernatural influence, & this question will have to be resolved by each individual from his personal experience.[32]

In other words, Mill is suggesting that the ability of prayer to change a person might be so efficacious as to constitute weighty, presumptive evidence that God is at work. In 1862, Mill maintained that if someone believes that God exists, then 'the moral probability that a given extraordinary event (supposed to be fully proved) is a miracle, may greatly outweigh the probability of its being the result of some unknown natural cause'.[33] Imagine there's more than naturalism, it isn't hard to do.

Mill's other main term was 'hope'. John Stuart Mill taught that it is rational to put one's hope in God. In a letter written on 13 May 1872 (a little less than a year before his death) he used both terms: 'I am convinced that the cultivation of an imaginative hope is quite compatible with a reserve as to positive belief, & that whatever helps to keep before the mind the ideal of a perfect Being is of unspeakable value to human nature.'[34] The philosopher made this case at length in 'Theism'. 'The whole domain of the supernatural' could still be viable if it is 'removed from the region of Belief into that of simple Hope'.[35] Mill's 'General Results' include:

> On these principles it appears to me that the indulgence of hope with regard to the government of the universe and the destiny of man after death, while we recognize as a clear truth that we have no ground for more than a hope, is legitimate and philosophically defensible. The beneficial effect of such a hope is far from trifling.[36]

This is Mill's final word on religion: hopeful, imaginative, beneficial, probabilist theism.

Again, it is important to see that these words were more robust for Mill than they might sound to many people today. One of the most revered classic defences of the Christian faith popular in mid-Victorian Britain—a seminal textbook at the University of Oxford at that time—was Bishop Butler's *Analogy*. Mill engages with it explicitly and approvingly in 'Theism'.[37] As far as I can tell, however, no one has yet made the connection between it and Mill's probable God. Butler opens his *Analogy* with a discussion of probability. He maintains that 'probability is the very guide of life' and therefore his entire apologetic for Christianity is set in the context of probability theory.[38] Butler even asserts:

> Nay further, in questions of great consequence, a reasonable man will think it concerns him to remark lower probabilities and presumptions than these; such as amount to no more than showing one side of a question to be as supposable and credible as the other; nay, such as but amount to much less even than this.[39]

In 'Theism', Mill said this even more enthusiastically than Butler: 'it is a part of wisdom to make the most of any, even small, probabilities on this subject, which furnish imagination with any footing to support itself upon'.[40] In other words, to decide that there is some probability and to act on that conviction is all that even the great orthodox bishop and defender of the faith is requiring of you, let alone the sceptical Utilitarian philosopher. Mill lived his own life this way. His letters would mention the need to make plans based on probabilities. For instance, in February 1854 Mill became interested in an experimental medical treatment which he initially assumed was 'quackish' by Dr Francis Ramadge, author of *The Curability of Consumption.*[41] He wrote to Harriet about it several times but—in a rare act of independence—decided to undergo the treatment without waiting for her approval. Mill's rationale for risking his body in this way is the exact same one that he used when discussing his spirit: 'I thought there was ground for hope though not for faith.'[42] The hoped-for heaven indeed.

While not wishing to deflect from understanding Mill in his own times and context, it is also worth observing that his most significant departure from a traditional doctrine of God—his denial of divine omnipotence—anticipated substantial trends in twentieth-century theology. In particular, Mill's theological scheme anticipates in some ways the Process Theology movement. One of its most prominent adherents was Charles Hartshorne, whose various appointments included being a member of the Federated Theological Faculty at the University of Chicago. Hartshorne's books included *Omnipotence and Other Theological Mistakes* (1984). At a popular level, the same theological move was made in Rabbi Harold Kushner's *New York Times* bestseller, *When Bad Things Happen to Good People* (1981). The running title for chapter seven is 'God Can't Do Everything'. The Conservative rabbi reflected: 'God does not want you to be sick or crippled. He didn't make you have this problem, and He doesn't want you to go on having it. He can't make it go away. That is something which is too hard even for God.'[43] Mill once reflected that deep down he suspected that most believers sacrificed God's almightiness in order to preserve God's goodness. Scholars sometimes imagine that denying omnipotence was Mill's sneaky, irreligious plot to define God out of existence. How literal and essential is the affirmation that God is almighty, however, is a matter of theological judgement: there is nothing in Mill's scheme that would have prevented him from being an ordained minister in a range of mainline denominations and a beloved member of the faculty of a major, venerable theological seminary in the twentieth century and beyond.

Moreover, one need not wait for a church of the future after Mill's death, as there is a real sense in which Mill may be identified as a well-wisher with the Broad Church of the liberal wing of the Church of England in his own day.[44] After all, his best male friend, the Reverend John Sterling, was from this milieu. In 1831, Mill rejoiced that

Richard Whately had been elevated to the archbishopric of Dublin and Edward Maltby to the bishopric of Chichester. The former he extolled in print: 'A minister desirous of saving the Church, by the only means by which it has now any chance of being saved—by improving its spirit—could not make a more advisable appointment.'[45] In 1835, Mill expressed his confidence that 'the young and cultivated members of the English clergy' were moving in the right direction, namely, away from dogmatism.[46] Mill cheered on liberal Churchmen down the decades. In 1840, he was 'delighted' when Connop Thirlwall was elevated to the episcopal bench.[47] In 1842, Mill articulated a hope very much akin to that of liberal Anglicans that the future would not be marked by either the dogmatic belief of the Tractarians or the dogmatic unbelief of 'German Rationalists' but that a middle way between these two extremes would triumph.[48] He was pleased that the judgement in the *Essays and Reviews* meant that the latitudinarian part of the Church of England was secure. Mill tended to praise all the leading Broad Churchmen of the nineteenth century, living and dead: Thomas Arnold, S. T. Coleridge, F. D. Maurice, and so on. Canon Charles Kingsley was invited to his home; and Dean A. P. Stanley was even Mill's guest at Avignon. Mill liked the theology of the Broad Churchwoman, Florence Nightingale, and was so encouraged by the Broad Church don, the Reverend Benjamin Jowett, that he lifted his ban on the University of Oxford in the case of those who wished to enter Balliol College under Jowett's guidance. More substantially, across the decades Mill himself advocated the Broad Church vision of a national church that was truly inclusive—gathering to herself people of goodwill holding diverse views on theological matters. Most of all, in his inaugural address as Lord Rector at the University of St Andrews, the philosopher made the Broad Church argument that liberal thinkers should stay in the Church of Scotland or Church of England. It is worth quoting at length:

> Neither is it right that if men honestly profess to have changed some of their religion opinions, their honesty should as a matter of course exclude them from taking a part for which they may be admirably qualified, in the spiritual instruction of the nation.... I hold entirely with those clergymen who elect to remain in the national church, so long as they are able to accept its articles and confessions in any sense or with any interpretation consistent with common honesty, whether it be

> the generally received interpretation or not. If all were to desert the church who put a large and liberal construction on its terms of communion, or who would wish to see those terms widened, the national provision for religious teaching and worship would be left utterly to those who take the narrowest, the most literal, and purely textual view of the formularies who,...if the church is improvable, are not the most likely persons to improve it. Therefore, if it were not an impertinence in me to tender advice in such a matter, I should say, let all who conscientiously can, remain in the church. A church is far more easily improved from within than from without. Almost all the illustrious reformers of religion began by being clergymen: but they did not think that their profession as clergymen was inconsistent with being reformers.[49]

In 1872 (the year before his death), Mill wrote to John Venn reassuring him that he need not feel qualms about being ordained into the priesthood of the Church of England.[50] Relatedly, Mill always longed for the churches to be more faithful to their own highest ideals: truly to abide by the example and sayings of Christ. Writing to the Venerable Archdeacon John Allen in 1867, Mill was elated by a Congregational church which placed members who had been caught in a bribery scheme under church discipline: 'This gave me the rare satisfaction of finding an existing Church, or branch of a Church, who are actually Christians.'[51] Mill's critique of the Puritans was that they focused on the Old Testament at the expense of 'Christ and the Sermon on the Mount'.[52] Like so many other religious reformers in the nineteenth century, Mill believed that the way forward might entail returning more wholeheartedly to the teachings of Jesus.

Which leads on, finally, to Mill on Christ himself. Once again, there is a great deal of continuity across Mill's adult life. In a letter to Carlyle in 1833, Mill spoke of his high regard for Christ and his sayings. He never wavered from that position. In 1861, Mill affirmed that 'reverence for Christ' was an attitude in which 'I myself very strongly participate'.[53] He never believed that Christ performed miracles and he did not believe that he was God. On even those points, however, Mill felt on sound ground because of his conviction that Jesus himself never made such claims. In 1863, Mill made the remarkable observation: 'I cannot presume to say that Christ may not have worked miracles: & I confess if I could be convinced that he ever *said* he had done so, it would weigh a great deal with me in favour of the belief.'[54] Mill also followed Christ's example in saving the best wine for last. His tribute to Christ in 'Theism' has taken many readers by surprise. It needs to be quoted at length:

> The East was full of men who could have stolen any quantity of this poor stuff, as the multitudinous Oriental sects of Gnostics afterwards did. But about the life and sayings of Jesus there is a stamp of personal originality combined with profundity of insight, which if we abandon the idle expectation of finding scientific precision where something very different was aimed at, must place the Prophet of Nazareth, even in the estimation of those who have no belief in his inspiration, in the very first rank of the men of sublime genius of whom our species can boast. When this pre-eminent genius is combined with the qualities of probably the greatest moral reformer, and martyr to that mission, who ever existed upon earth, religion cannot be said to have made a bad choice in pitching on this man as the ideal representative and guide of humanity; nor, even now, would it be easy, even for an unbeliever, to find a better translation of the rule of virtue from the abstract into the concrete, than to endeavour so to live that Christ would approve our life. When to this we add that, to the conception of the rational sceptic, it remains a possibility that Christ actually was what he supposed himself to be—not God, for he never made the smallest pretension to that character and would probably have thought such a pretension as blasphemous as it seemed to the men who condemned him—but a man charged with a special, express and unique commission from God to lead mankind to truth and virtue . . .[55]

It is important to understand how this passage fits into Mill's unfolding argument. Already in 'Theism' he has systematically gone through the natural theology arguments used to attempt to prove the existence of God. This leads him on to the question of religious beliefs being warranted, not by natural religion, but on the basis of revelation. Mill rules out something being established as a true revelation on the grounds of claims of miracles. Does that then mean that there is no revelation of God at all? Mill's answer to that question is the passage just quoted: in a world of probabilities, there *is* evidence to warrant the possibility that Christ is a true revelation of God. In the *Examination*, Mill had already held out this possibility, gesturing toward an argument for revelation based on the testimony that a historical figure said 'words that seemed to require a greater than human wisdom'.[56]

Mill even offers a popular, orthodox Victorian apologetic argument that the Christ of the Bible is too good not to be true:

> It is of no use to say that Christ as exhibited in the Gospels is not historical and that we know not how much of what is admired has been superadded by the tradition of his followers. . . . who among his disciples or among their proselytes was capable of inventing the sayings ascribed to Jesus or of imagining the life and character revealed in the Gospels? Certainly not the fishermen of Galilee; as certainly not St. Paul . . .[57]

It is also suggestive that Mill's standard term for this historical figure was 'Christ'. It would have been perfectly acceptable and in no way offensive even to pious readers for him to have spoken of Jesus of Nazareth. There is a sense in which Mill really did accept the possibility that this Jesus from Galilee was the Christ, the Messiah, the Anointed One. Indeed, all the way back in 1833 Mill spoke with reverent approval of Jesus's messianic consciousness as recorded in the synoptic Gospels: 'How clearly one can trace in all of them the *gradual* rise of his conviction that he was the Messiah: and how much loftier & more self-devoted a tone his whole language & conduct assumed as soon as he felt convinced of that.'[58] The answer given in the synoptic Gospels to Jesus's question, 'But whom say ye that I am?', is 'Thou art the Christ'.

'Theism' was dismaying to many of Mill's followers who were unbelievers. G. W. Foote, a leading light of the militant plebeian Secularist movement, wrote *What Was Christ? A Reply to John Stuart Mill* (1887). This tract is a sexist rant throughout. Christ is condemned as 'effeminate'. Foote liked his heroes to be warriors. He praises Mohammad at length. Likewise, Cromwell 'was a more original character than twenty Christs'.[59] Most of all, he attacks Harriet, who Foote asserts made a 'victim' of Mill's 'brain': 'How different was his attitude in the vigor of manhood.' Foote even writes regarding Mill, 'We find all his greatest books were composed before he fell under her influence', apparently unware that Mill only ever wrote one book without Harriet's influence.[60] (Let alone the fact that every scholar who has looked into the matter has come to the conclusion that 'Theism' was more sympathetic to Christianity precisely because Harriet's influence was by then gone.) Foote does astutely realize that Mill had ended up adopting the Christological position of classic Unitarian Christianity.

In more elite society, the consternation was the same. It is said that the agnostic Leslie Stephen was so enraged by 'Theism' that he could not stop pacing about in his irritation. Stephen's wife chimed in gloatingly: 'I always told you John Mill was orthodox.'[61] Alexander Bain was deeply disappointed by 'Theism' and did his best to intimate—completely without warrant—that its contents should not be counted among Mill's considered views. (In direct contradiction to this insinuation, Helen testified that the three essays represented Mill's 'deliberate and exhaustive treatment of the topics under consideration'.)[62] Most of all, John Morley, a true disciple of Mill, wrote two articles critiquing 'Theism'. The editor of the *Fortnightly Review* was miffed by Mill's 'qualified rehabilitation of supernatural hypotheses', but it was Mill's suggestion that Christ was a unique, divinely inspired figure that most rankled.[63] The same man who had authored *A System of Logic* had now encouraged believers to hope that Christianity really was a supernatural revelation. How could this be? 'I am only insisting how profoundly irreconcilable it is with the scientific principles which Mr. Mill inculcated', an exasperated Morley maintained.[64] In an outburst of frustration, Morley even went so far as to say that there is little difference between believing in Mill's theological scheme and believing that most extravagant statement of orthodoxy, the Athanasian Creed (a formula that even many Anglican clergymen found so excessive and dogmatic that they wished the Church of England would formally abandon it).[65]

More positively, Bain observed that Mill had done something brave by defying everyone from his own masters such as his father and Bentham, down to disciples such as himself and Morley: 'the most signal example of his courage was the composition of the Essay on Theism'.[66] Mill had pondered religion his whole life and his death served to reveal that his conclusions were not what many had expected. As much as Mill admired and was convinced by Comte's three-part stadial scheme of history—the theological, the metaphysical, and the positivist—ironically, there is a sense in which Mill reversed it in his own life. His first book, *A System of Logic,* was his great positivist contribution. Then, two decades on, he turned to a substantial work on metaphysics, *Examination of Sir William Hamilton's Philosophy*. Finally, he reached the theological stage with 'Theism'.

Notes

1. Francis E. Mineka and Dwight N. Lindley (eds), *The Later Letters of John Stuart Mill, 1849–1873* (Collected Works of John Stuart Mill XV), Toronto: University of Toronto Press, 1972, p. 759.
2. John Stuart Mill, *Newspaper Writings (December 1822–July 1831)*, ed. Ann P. Robson and John M. Robson, Collected Works of John Stuart Mill XXII, Toronto: University of Toronto Press, 1986, p. 290.
3. John Stuart Mill, *Essays on Ethics, Religion and Society* (Collected Works of John Stuart Mill X), ed. J. M. Robson, Indianapolis: Liberty Fund, 2006 (reprint of Toronto: University of Toronto Press, 1969), p. 487.
4. CWJSM XV (*Later Letters*), p. 754.
5. John Stuart Mill to Barclay Fox, 6 May 1841: Francis E. Mineka (ed.), *The Earlier Letters of John Stuart Mill, 1812–1848* (Collected Works of John Stuart Mill XIII), Toronto: University of Toronto Press, 1963, pp. 473–4.
6. CWJSM XXIV (*Newspaper Writings*), pp. 1082–4. (The letter was never sent.)
7. CWJSM X (*Essays on Ethics, Religion and Society*), p. 389.
8. CWJSM X (*Essays on Ethics, Religion and Society*), pp. 389, 402.
9. CWJSM X (*Essays on Ethics, Religion and Society*), p. 385.
10. CWJSM X (*Essays on Ethics, Religion and Society*), p. 400.
11. CWJSM X (*Essays on Ethics, Religion and Society*), p. 405.
12. CWJSM X (*Essays on Ethics, Religion and Society*), p. 411.
13. CWJSM X (*Essays on Ethics, Religion and Society*), p. 417.
14. CWJSM X (*Essays on Ethics, Religion and Society*), p. 425.
15. CWJSM X (*Essays on Ethics, Religion and Society*), p. 425.
16. John M. Robson (ed.), *Journals and Debating Speeches* (Collected Works of John Stuart Mill XXVII), Toronto: University of Toronto Press, 1988, p. 654.
17. CWJSM X (*Essays on Ethics, Religion and Society*), p. 462.
18. John Stuart Mill to Barclay Fox, 10 May 1842: CWJSM XIII (*Earlier Letters*), p. 520.
19. John Stuart Mill to John Sterling, 22 April 1840: CWJSM XIII (*Earlier Letters*), p. 428.
20. John Stuart Mill to Thomas Carlyle, 12 January 1834: CWJSM XII (*Earlier Letters*), p. 207.
21. John Stuart Mill to Thomas Carlyle, 12 January 1834: CWJSM XII (*Earlier Letters*), p. 206.
22. John Stuart Mill, *An Examination of Sir William Hamilton's Philosophy and of the Principal Questions Discussed in his Writings*, ed. J. M. Robson (Collected Works of John Stuart Mill IX), London: Routledge, 1996, p. 129.

23. John Stuart Mill to Florence Nightingale, 23 September 1860: CWJSM XV (*Later Letters*), p. 709. (Mill observes that this scheme would be an improvement for most Christians and Deists as well. The point here is that he thinks that even most atheists would be better off believing in the right kind of God than not believing in God at all.)
24. CWJSM XVII (*Later Letters*), p. 1829.
25. CWJSM X (*Essays on Ethics, Religion and Society*), p. 444.
26. Harry Settanni, *The Probabilist Theism of John Stuart Mill*, New York: Peter Lang, 1991.
27. CWJSM X (*Essays on Ethics, Religion and Society*), p. 450.
28. CWJSM XV (*Later Letters*), p. 754.
29. CWJSM XV (*Later Letters*), p. 755.
30. CWJSM XXIV (*Newspaper Writings*), p. 1083.
31. John Stuart Mill to Henry Jones, 13 June 1868: CWJSM XVI (*Later Letters*), p. 1414.
32. John Stuart Mill to Henry Jones, 13 June 1868: CWJSM XVI (*Later Letters*), p. 1414.
33. CWJSM XV (*Later Letters*), p. 814.
34. John Stuart Mill to Edwin Arnold, 13 May 1872: CWJSM XVI (*Later Letters*), pp. 1893–4.
35. CWJSM X (*Essays on Ethics, Religion and Society*), pp. 482–3. See also Karl W. Britton, 'John Stuart Mill on Christianity', in John M. Robson and Michael Laine (eds), *James and John Stuart Mill: Papers of the Centenary Conference*, Toronto: University of Toronto Press, 1976, pp. 21–34.
36. CWJSM X (*Essays on Ethics, Religion and Society*), p. 485.
37. CWJSM X (*Essays on Ethics, Religion and Society*), p. 469.
38. Joseph Butler, *The Analogy of Religion*, London: Religious Tract Society, n.d. (originally 1736), p. 5.
39. Butler, *Analogy*, p. 5.
40. CWJSM X (*Essays on Ethics, Religion and Society*), p. 483.
41. CWJSM XIV (*Later Letters*), p. 171.
42. CWJSM XIV (*Later Letters*), p. 199.
43. Harold S. Kushner, *When Bad Things Happen to Good People*, New York: Schocken Books, 1981, p. 129.
44. For an account of this wing, see Tod E. Jones, *The Broad Church: A Biography of a Movement*, Lanham: Lexington Books, 2003.
45. CWJSM XXIII (*Newspaper Writings*), p. 356.
46. CWJSM XII (*Earlier Letters*), pp. 264–5.
47. CWJSM XIII (*Earlier Letters*), p. 442.
48. CWJSM XIII (*Earlier Letters*), p. 497.

49. John Stuart Mill, *Essays on Equality, Law, and Education*, ed. John M. Robinson and Stefani Collini (Collected Works of John Stuart Mill XXI), Toronto: University of Toronto Press, 1984, p. 251.
50. John Stuart Mill to John Venn, 14 April 1872: CWJSM XVII (*Later Letters*), p. 1881. Venn did receive ordination, but his qualms recurred later and he resigned his clerical office.
51. CWJSM XVI (*Later Letters*), p. 1274.
52. CWJSM XXV (*Newspaper Writings*), p. 1174.
53. CWJSM XV (*Later Letters*), p. 754.
54. CWJSM XV (*Later Letters*), p. 895.
55. CWJSM X (*Essays on Ethics, Religion and Society*), pp. 487–8.
56. CWJSM IX (*Examination*), p. 193.
57. CWJSM X (*Essays on Ethics, Religion and Society*), p. 487. For this argument among orthodox Victorian Christians, see Timothy Larsen, *Crisis of Doubt: Honest Faith in Nineteenth-Century England*, Oxford: Oxford University Press, 2006.
58. CWJSM XII (*Earlier Letters*), p. 182.
59. G. W. Foote, *What Was Christ? A Reply to John Stuart Mill*, London: Progressive Publishing Company, 1887, p. 13.
60. Foote, *What Was Christ?*, p. 5.
61. Alan P. F. Sell, *Mill on God: The Pervasiveness and Elusiveness of Mill's Religious Thought*, Aldershot: Ashgate, 2004, p. 158.
62. Helen Taylor, 'Introductory Notice', in John Stuart Mill, *Three Essays on Religion*, second edition, London: Longmans, Green, Reader, and Dyer, 1874, p. [vii].
63. [John Morley], 'Mr. Mill's Three Essays on Religion' (Concluded), *Fortnightly Review*, n.s. 17 (1875), pp. 103–31 (113).
64. Morley, 'Mill's Essays' (Concluded), p. 118.
65. For other reactions, see Alan P. F. Sell (ed.), *Mill on Religion: Contemporary Responses to Three Essays on Religion*, Bristol: Thoemmes Press, 1997. This is even true in the secondary literature. 'Theism' goes too far in affirming the supernatural for Alan Millar, for instance: Alan Millar, 'Mill on Religion', in John Skorupski (ed.), *The Cambridge Companion to Mill*, Cambridge: Cambridge University Press, 1998, pp. 176–202 (especially 198).
66. Alexander Bain, *John Stuart Mill: A Criticism: with personal recollections*, London: Longmans, Green, and Co., 1882, p. 158.

14
The Night Cometh When no Man can Work

'I must work the works of him that sent me, while it is day:
the night cometh, when no man can work.'

(John 9:4)

With the exception of his time in parliament, after Harriet's death Mill mainly settled down with his stepdaughter Helen to a quiet, retired, domestic way of life. As if a character straight out of Bunyan's *Pilgrim's Progress*, Mill hired an additional servant for their English home at Blackheath who was named Mrs Goodenough. Helen decided that she wanted a firearm and eventually purchased a revolver: feminist get your gun. They owned a cat whom Mill usually referred to as 'puss' but whose Christian—or, more aptly, pagan—name was Phidia. When he wrote to Helen, Mill would include feline salutations. In one letter, he reported that he had read in a newspaper about a cat show and loyally expressed his confidence that, if Phidia had been entered, she would have won a prize. Even when writing to his friend and old India House colleague, W. T. Thornton, Mill proudly reported that they had recently improved the Avignon property by adding a 'Puss-House'.[1] And more and more of the year was spent at their home in France. Mill observed that he and Helen were introverts who were trying to get far away from the tiresome crowd: 'To most people, I believe, society is a relaxation; we, on the contrary, need relaxation *from society*; & to pass our time in the virtual solitude in which we live here is not merely a luxury but a necessity to us.'[2] Some thought he had pushed this preference to the point of rudeness in the case of the Crown Princess of Prussia and the Princess Alice. These royal princesses were so keen to meet the eminent philosopher that they were willing to travel all the way to the south of France for the privilege, but Mill put a stop to any such plan by bluntly informing them he would not receive them. Mill's best male friend in his Avignon life was the pastor of the Protestant church there, the Reverend Louis Rey. Going so little into society, Mill was often taken aback by his own fame. In 1859 he observed: 'I really had no idea of being so influential a person as my critics tell me I am.'[3] Despite the continuing growth of his reputation thereafter, this idea only ever intermittently sank in. Frequently a generous correspondent—even with complete strangers of no particular influence or standing—it was hard for Mill to get used to the fact that these pronouncements—which he assumed to be private communications—would so often end up being published. To take just one instance, an American wrote to Mill in 1869 asking for his thoughts on Chinese immigration to the United States. The political economist dutifully wrote back all of the pros and cons he could think of on the question. His correspondent, however, of course, was an activist seeking ammunition: he cut out of the letter everything that Mill said on the favourable side and published the rest as a leading British thinker's denunciation of Chinese immigration. This led to angry letters from advocates for immigration and it took a long time and much bother for Mill to figure out what had happened and to try to set it right. Most of all, in his final years Mill kept writing, chipping away at treatises intended for publication.

At the time of his death, he was at work on a volume on socialism. In the last part of his life Mill became more sympathetic towards both organized religion and organized labour.[4] He saw it as his duty to write down his best thoughts for the benefit of posterity. Throughout his life, John Stuart Mill had a Christian-inflected—even providentially tinged—sense of vocation. It is easy today not to hear that word in its original meaning. The first definition in the *Oxford English Dictionary* is: 'The action on the part of God of calling a person to exercise some special function, especially of a spiritual nature, or to fill a certain position; divine influence or guidance towards a definite (esp. religious) career; the fact of being so called or directed towards a special work in life; natural tendency to, or fitness for, such work.'[5] Beginning in the early 1830s, Mill often spoke of discerning his vocation. In 1834 he informed Carlyle: 'if I have any *vocation* I think it is exactly this, to translate the mysticism of others into the language of Argument'.[6] By contrast, the philosopher rejected the notion of trying to become the leader of a political party on the specific grounds that it was not a part of his vocation. Most of all, Mill knew that recording his ideas lucidly in prose was his vocation. He reminisced to W. T. Thornton that when he had completed the first draft of *A System of Logic*: he had, 'for the first time, the feeling that I had now actually accomplished something—that one certain portion of my life's work was done'.[7] At the time, he wrote: 'I do not expect to find many readers for this book, but I had things to say on the subject, & it was part of my task on earth to say them & therefore having said them I feel a portion of my work to be done.'[8] Mill had an almost Calvinist sense of his duty to fulfil his vocation to write. He wrote to Harriet in 1854: 'I have been feeling much (I must have been incapable of feeling anything if I had not) about the shortness & uncertainty of life & the wrongness of having so much of the best of what we have to say, so long unwritten & in the power of chance—& I determined to make a better use of what time we have.'[9] Mill himself would reach for additional words of resonant, religious import in order to express his convictions on this subject. He wrote in his diary, for instance: 'I feel bitterly how I have procrastinated in the sacred duty of fixing in writing, so that it may not die with me, everything that I have in my mind which is capable of assisting the destruction of error and prejudice and the growth of just feelings and true opinions.'[10] In addition to 'vocation' and his 'sacred' duty, Mill also spoke of his work in terms of 'calling'. Once again, to use such language is to summon the power of a religious charge. 'Calling' only makes literal sense if there is another being doing the calling—namely God. It evokes scripture. To take just one example: 'the Lord called Samuel: and he answered, Here am I' (1 Samuel 3:4). If God's calling a prophet seems a farfetched connection to make when discussing the life of a religious sceptic, Mill himself would speak of his ideas as those which he was 'under a special obligation to preach'.[11] Mill so highly approved of the work of the Land Tenure Reform Association that he even left it the substantial sum of £500 in his will. Nevertheless, when he was invited to become a leading officeholder he declined on the basis of his calling in life: 'It would be impossible for me to undertake a prominent position in the Assn without giving it an amount of time and labour which I do not feel called upon to give.'[12] Mill never imagined that he was free to do whatever he found pleasing that would not violate the harm principle.

He was driven throughout his life with the sense of a task that had been given to him to do. His advice to young people was that they should endeavour to discern what their particular work in this world is. To be a faithful steward of the gift's one has been given is all.

Throughout his adult life, Mill frequently quoted the Bible and reflected on its contents. This was typical of his time and place.[13] Mill was not doing this in a way that was exceptional in relation to his contemporaries, but as it is not typical today—especially for lifelong religious sceptics—it is important to grasp this feature in order to understand Mill, his mind, and the culture of which he was a part. It is hard today to grasp just how scripture-saturated a culture the nineteenth century was. Even when in France—a country which struck Mill as much less religious than Britain—when as a young man he took a course there in modern Greek, he found that it was taught by studying the New Testament in the original and then comparing and contrasting its ancient, *Koine* Greek with the contemporary version of the language. Not only did Mill often include a relevant verse of scripture when making a point in his letters and publications but, as Alexander Bain himself observed, given Mill's own description of his early education, this can be contrasted with the surprising rarity of classical quotations in Mill's writings.[14] Moreover, Mill was not evoking scripture as mere window-dressing: he was keenly interested in the field of biblical hermeneutics—the correct way to interpret scripture—and often reflected on it or other people's contributions to this subject. Here, for instance, is a passage in which one might assume that Mill was just quoting scripture incidentally, were it not that this citation then leads him into a long meditation on the proper method of biblical interpretation:

> I have long since renounced any hankering for being happier than I am; and only since then have I enjoyed anything which can be called well-being. How few are they who have discovered the wisdom of the precept, Take no thought of the morrow [Matthew 6:34]; when considered as all the sayings of Christ should be, not as laws laid down with strict logical precision for regulating the details of our conduct; since such must be, like all other maxims of prudence, *variable*: but as the bodying forth in words of the *spirit* of all morality, right self-culture, the principles of which cannot change, since man's nature changes not, though surrounding circumstances do. I do not mean by using the word

> self-culture, to prejudice any thing as to whether such culture can come from man himself, or must come directly from God: all I mean is that it is culture of the man's self, of his feelings and will, fitting him to look abroad and see how he is to act, not imposing upon him by express definition, a prescribed mode of action; which it is clear to me that many of the precepts of the Gospels, were never intended to do, being manifestly unsuited to that end: witness that which I have just cited; or the great one of doing all men as you desire that they should do to you; or of turning the left cheek &c. which last the Quakers have made themselves ridiculous by attempting to act upon a very little more literally than other people. All these would be vicious as moral statutes, binding the tribunal, but they are excellent as instruction to the judge in the *forum conscientiae*, in which spirit he is to look at the evidence; what posture he must assume in order that he may see clearly the moral bearings of the thing which he is looking at.[15]

As Mill's habit of quoting scripture to make points has been demonstrated throughout this book, there is no need to belabour it here. *The Collected Works of John Stuart Mill* identifies many of these quotations—but it also misses others. Mill's tendency to proof text—to quote a verse that made his point for him triumphantly—has already been well established in this volume. The one final point to underline here is that in his letters it is clear that he is often recalling these passages from memory and thus demonstrating that he possessed deep biblical literacy. To take a typical instance, Mill wrote to the author, thinker, and Member of Parliament Auberon Herbert in 1872 (the year before Mill died): 'The only point in which I do not agree with you is the impression that the present is a time of crisis. I have always felt very strongly the truth of St. Paul's saying, "Behold *now* is the acceptable time: behold now is the time of salvation"'[16] (2 Corinthians 6:2). The second 'time' is 'day' in the Authorized Version (and the Douai–Rheims translation), demonstrating that Mill did not look it up but had it very close to word perfect from memory. There are numerous such incidents in his letters. Mill often thought and communicated through texts of scripture.

Mill even had what some devout Christians call a 'life verse'. Bain refers to it as Mill's 'favourite text'.[17] It is John 9:4: 'I must work the works of him that sent me, while it is day; the night cometh, when no man can work.' As was observed earlier, leading scholars, not being themselves biblically literate, have repeatedly claimed that Thomas Carlyle crafted this phrase rather than Jesus of Nazareth according to a canonical Gospel. John 9:4 is a verse that, for Mill, underlined his sense of vocation, of duty, of calling. He quoted it throughout his adult life. In 1840, Mill wrote to his friend Barclay Fox about the death of Mill's favourite brother, Henry. The philosopher reflected that everyone should benefit from such a loss by finding a moral in it: 'with me that moral is, "work while it is called today—the night cometh in which no man can work"'.[18] In 1854, Mill berated himself in his private diary: 'I seem to have frittered away the working years of life in mere preparatory trifles, and now "the night when no one can work" has surprised me with the real duty of my life undone.'[19] He wrote to Bain in 1867: 'I have so little time now that I must keep it for the few things which it is my special duty to do before the night cometh when no man can work.'[20] In the last full year of his life, Mill heard of the deaths of the Italian patriot Giuseppe Mazzini and his old friend, the Reverend F. D. Maurice. He mused: 'The best consolation is that the essential part of their work was done.'[21] Mill cannot be said to have made a bad choice in pitching on this saying of Christ from the Gospels as his guide in life.

The family curse was 'consumption' (tuberculosis). Mill had it, leading to debilitating episodes throughout much of his adult life. The family patriarch, James Mill, had died from it at the age of sixty-three. Harriet died from it at the age of fifty-one. (Some secondary sources suggest that Mill himself had infected her with the disease.) Mill's brother Henry lost his struggle with tuberculosis at the age of nineteen. While this favourite brother was dying at such a young age in Cornwall, Mill thought he could see his own end: 'After an expressive pause, John Mill quietly said, "I expect to die of consumption".'[22] It did dog him his entire adult life, provoking leaves of absence on medical grounds from his India House work and continental trips to try to improve his health. From 1836—the year of his father's death—Mill suffered from an almost continual twitching of his right eye. Contemporaries found it disconcerting and assumed that it was but a surface manifestation of Mill not being a well man. Yet he lived on longer than he thought he would. John Stuart Mill died of erysipelas at his home in Avignon on 7 May 1873.[23] He was sixty-six years old.

The Victorians were fascinated by deathbed pronouncements. Helen gave to the world as Mill's official last words: 'My work is done.' Bain himself saw this as an allusion to John 9:4.[24] The philosopher had worked while it was day and now the night could come. It was also perhaps one last attempt at the imitation of Christ, evoking the last words from the cross: 'It is finished.' The closest that Mill ever came as an adult to having a home church was the Protestant one in Avignon in these final years. He gave a large, annual, financial contribution to help with the expenses of this Christian congregation.[25] In 1858, Mill had declared that he always refused on principle to give any money to schools that were organized on a confessional basis, but in these final years of his life he frequently donated money to a range of religious schools. The very last public meeting that Mill attended was at the Protestant church in Avignon. It was held on Sunday 27 April 1873. It was a meeting of an organization to promote Protestant elementary schools. Mill even accepted a position as an honorary member of its executive committee.[26] As Mill lay dying, the Reverend Louis Rey rushed to the house, but he was too late. The Protestant pastor led Helen and the others in the house in prayer.

When George Grote died in 1871 he was buried in Westminster Abbey. Mill consented to be a pallbearer at Grote's funeral. He remarked to Bain on that occasion: 'In no very long time, I shall be laid in the ground with a very different ceremonial from that.'[27] It is possible Mill meant that he found distasteful the pomp of it all or a private life becoming a national spectacle. Bain took the comment to mean that he disliked the religious nature of the ceremony and that is certainly a reasonable interpretation. A plan was floated to recognize Mill's significance to the nation by also having him buried in Westminster Abbey. Abraham Hayward, who had been nursing a grudge against Mill for decades from a clash in a debate, embarked on an energetic campaign to smear Mill's reputation. He wrote a snide obituary for *The Times*. Contacting numerous influential people directly, he spooked figures such as William Gladstone, who had been sympathetic to the idea, by digging up Mill's youthful arrest for distributing birth control literature. This malicious campaign was enough to rule out the Abbey, although many came to Mill's defence. Stopford Brooke, one of the most popular liberal Anglican preachers of the day, even condemned Hayward's attacks from the pulpit.[28]

In any event, Mill had made his wishes clear in his will: 'Lastly I desire and direct that my mortal remains may be buried in the said tomb of my dear wife in the said Cemetery at Avignon and that the same shall on no account or pretext whatsoever be buried in any other place whatsoever.'[29]

In the end, Mill's funeral was a small and quiet affair in Avignon. Less than a dozen people were present. All of his friends who were religious sceptics being in England, it is possible that everyone who attended Mill's funeral was a Christian. The Reverend Louis Rey conducted the service. Fittingly, he spoke of Mill's 'moral vocation' to 'fulfil his duty'. The pastor then reminded his hearers of the religious meaning of the word vocation, taking Mill's funeral oration in a decidedly religious and Christian direction:

> I connected this vocation back to God who is the Father and the Guarantor of Duty. From this, I lifted out faith and immortality, which are necessary for remuneration and for the reign of justice; and, gathering these grand postulates of the soul, I showed them realized, guaranteed, and offered in the sacrifice of Jesus Christ as the consolation and the hope of a mourning humanity.[30]

Rey also once again led Helen and the few other mourners in prayer.

Again and again, those who have approached the subject of John Stuart Mill and religion have been struck by the paradox that he was a religious sceptic who nevertheless was surprisingly religious. Linda C. Raeder observed: 'From beginning to end, religious themes abound, implicitly and explicitly, in his books, articles, correspondence, and diary.'[31] Similarly, Alan Sell declared: 'It is part of my purpose to show that, far from being confined to the *Three Essays*, Mill's religious thought pervades his writings.'[32] Most startling of all, Nicholas Capaldi, writing a comprehensive intellectual biography of Mill, was led to conclude: 'In the end, Mill's philosophy of history is supplemented by theology.' Aware of how jarring this would sound, Capaldi added in an endnote: 'I know of no satisfactory alternative to this resolution. Hence it is important to see that Mill's theism plays an important intellectual role in his mature thought.'[33] Thomas Carlyle's first word on Mill was that he was a mystic and, in a sort of *inclusio*, John Morley's final word was that Mill ended up appealing to 'a mystic sentiment'.[34] His close friend Louis Rey also judged Mill to be a 'mystic'. The Protestant pastor moreover insisted that Mill's 'was a soul religious by nature' and—in a fine attempt to grasp the paradox—that the philosopher possessed 'a scepticism which might be called religious'.[35] Mill did not tend to show his spiritual side to Alexander Bain, but even that unbeliever was driven to concede: 'It has been said by his opponents, with some show of plausibility, that Mill was at bottom a religious man.'[36] As we have seen, this observation was also made by some of his friends as well.

In a letter to an unknown recipient apparently written in late 1855, Mill gave this charge: 'I rely on you for taking care that nothing whatever admitting of a religious interpretation shall be inscribed on my tomb.'[37] As we have seen, Mill took a more sympathetic attitude towards religion in his final years so there is no reason to assume that this was still his wish by the 1870s. Nevertheless, ironically, the reason why this wish was not fulfilled was because what was written on Mill's tomb was composed and ordered to be affixed there by Mill himself. In accordance with the strict instructions in his will, Mill's mortal remains joined those of his wife Harriet and thus the inscription on his tomb included his own allusion to Matthew 6:10 (from the Lord's Prayer) and its evocative longing for 'the hoped-for heaven'. His work on earth was done.

Notes

1. Francis E. Mineka and Dwight N. Lindley (eds), *The Later Letters of John Stuart Mill, 1849–1873* (Collected Works of John Stuart Mill XVII), Toronto: University of Toronto Press, 1972, p. 1549.
2. CWJSM XV (*Later Letters*), p. 855.
3. CWJSM XV (*Later Letters*), p. 640.
4. Jeff Lipkes has documented these changes and put forward the case for these two trends being connected: Jeff Lipkes, *Politics, Religion and Classical Political Economy in Britain: John Stuart Mill and his Followers*, London: Macmillan, 1999.
5. 'Vocation' in the *Oxford English Dictionary*, accessed at www.oed.com
6. Francis E. Mineka (ed.), *The Earlier Letters of John Stuart Mill, 1812–1848* (Collected Works of John Stuart Mill XII), Toronto: University of Toronto Press, 1963, p. 219.
7. Alexander Bain, *John Stuart Mill: A Criticism: with personal recollections*, London: Longmans, Green, and Co., 1882, p. 158.

8. CWJSM XIII (*Earlier Letters*), p. 496.
9. CWJSM XIV (*Later Letters*), p. 141.
10. John M. Robson (ed.), *Journals and Debating Speeches* (Collected Works of John Stuart Mill XXVII), Toronto: University of Toronto Press, 1988, p. 644.
11. CWJSM XIII (*Earlier Letters*), p. 411.
12. CWJSM XVII (*Later Letters*), p. 1644.
13. Timothy Larsen, *A People of One Book: The Bible and the Victorians*, Oxford: Oxford University Press, 2011.
14. Bain, *John Stuart Mill*, p. 142.
15. CWJSM XII (*Earlier Letters*), pp. 100–1. (I have added the reference in square brackets.)
16. John Stuart Mill to Auberon Herbert, 29 January 1872: Marion Filipiuk, Michael Laine, and John M. Robson (eds), *Additional Letters of John Stuart Mill* (Collected Works of John Stuart Mill XXXII), Toronto: University of Toronto Press, 1991, p. 235.
17. Bain, *John Stuart Mill*, p. 159.
18. CWJSM XII (*Earlier Letters*), p. 425.
19. CWJSM XXVII (*Journals and Debating Speeches*), p. 665.
20. CWJSM XVI (*Later Letters*), p. 1324.
21. CWJSM XVII (*Later Letters*), p. 1880.
22. Horace N. Pym (ed.), *Memories of Old Friends: being extracts from the Journals and Letters of Caroline Fox of Penjerrick, Cornwall*, London: Smith, Elder, and Co., 1882, p. 79.
23. Jose Harris, 'Mill, John Stuart (1806–1873)', *Oxford Dictionary of National Biography* (accessed online at www.oxforddnb.com).
24. Bain, *John Stuart Mill*, p. 159.
25. Letter by Louis Rey printed in 'John Stuart Mill au Point du Vue Religieux', *La Critique Philosophique: Politique, Scientifique, Littéraire*, 18 (5 June 1873), pp. 283–5. (I am grateful to Morgan Rawlinson for providing all the French translations that are used in this chapter.)
26. Rey, 'John Stuart Mill au Point du Vue Religieux', pp. 283–5.
27. Bain, *John Stuart Mill*, p. 133.
28. Richard Reeves, *John Stuart Mill: Victorian Firebrand*, London: Atlantic Books, 2007, p. 481.
29. John Stuart Mill, *Miscellaneous Writings*, edited by John M. Robson (Collected Works of John Stuart Mill XXI), Toronto: University of Toronto Press, 1989, p. 336.
30. Louis Rey, *John Stuart Mill en Avignon*, Vaison, n.p., 1921, pp. 158–9. (This source is a reprint or rebound from an article in *Annales de l'Ecole palatine d'Avignon* and the pagination was retained from that source.)

31. Linda C. Raeder, *John Stuart Mill and the Religion of Humanity*, Columbia, MO: University of Missouri Press, 2002, p. 1.
32. Alan P. F. Sell, *Mill on God: The Pervasiveness and Elusiveness of Mill's Religious Thought*, Aldershot: Ashgate, 2004, p. 21.
33. Nicholas Capaldi, *John Stuart Mill: A Biography*, Cambridge: Cambridge University Press, 2004, pp. 137, 382.
34. [John Morley], 'Mr. Mill's Three Essays on Religion', *Fortnightly Review*, n.s., 16 (1874), pp. 634–51 (here 637).
35. Louis Rey, 'The Romance of John Stuart Mill', *Nineteenth Century*, Vol. LXXIV, No. 439 (September 1913), pp. 502–26 (here pp. 524–5).
36. Bain, *John Stuart Mill*, p. 139.
37. CWJSM XIV (*Later Letters*), p. 501.

Selected Bibliography

General Sources

John Stuart Mill, *The Collected Works of John Stuart Mill*, ed. J. M. Robson and others, 33 volumes, Toronto: University of Toronto Press, 1965–91. Use has also been made of reprints of some of these volumes by the Liberty Fund and by Routledge. The short citation used is CWJSM.

The volumes are as follows:
I *Autobiography and Literary Essays* (1981)
II, III *Principles of Political Economy* (1965)
IV, V *Essays on Economics and Society* (1967)
VI *Essays on England, Ireland and the Empire* (1982)
VII, VIII *System of Logic: Ratiocinative and Inductive* (1973)
IX *An Examination of Sir William Hamilton's Philosophy* (1979)
X *Essays on Ethics, Religion, and Society* (1969)
XI *Essays on Philosophy and the Classics* (1978)
XII, XIII *Earlier Letters, 1812–1848* (1963)
XIV, XV, XVI, XVII *Later Letters, 1848–1873* (1972)
XVIII, XIX *Essays on Politics and Society* (1977)
XX *Essays on French History and Historians* (1985)
XXI *Essays on Equality, Law, and Education* (1984)
XXII, XXIII, XXIV, XXV *Newspaper Writings* (1986)
XXVI, XXVII *Journals and Debating Speeches* (1977)
XXVIII, XXIX *Public and Parliamentary Speeches* (1988)
XXX *Writings on India* (1990)
XXXI *Miscellaneous Writings* (1989)
XXXII *Additional Letters* (1991)
XXXIII *Indexes* (1991)

Oxford Dictionary of National Biography, accessed online at oxforddnb.com
Oxford English Dictionary, accessed online at www.oed.com

Unpublished Materials

Mill–Taylor Collection, London School of Economics, London.
The Library of John Stuart Mill, the Archives, Somerville College, Oxford.
Keynes Papers, Archives Centre, King's College, Cambridge.
Smith, Janet, 'The Feminism and Political Radicalism of Helen Taylor in Victorian Britain and Ireland', unpublished PhD thesis, London Metropolitan University, 2014.

Published Works

Austin, Sarah (ed.), *Selections from the Old Testament: or the Religion, Morality, and Poetry of the Hebrew Scriptures, arranged under heads*, London: Effingham Wilson, 1833.

Bain, Alexander, *James Mill: A Biography*, London: Longmans, Green, and Co., 1882.

Bain, Alexander, *John Stuart Mill: A Criticism: with personal recollections*, London: Longmans, Green, and Co., 1882.

Bax, Ernest Belfort, *Reminiscences and Reflexions of a Mid and Late Victorian*, New York: Thomas Seltzer, 1920.

Bebbington, D. W., *Evangelicalism in Modern Britain: A History from the 1730s to the 1980s*, London: Unwin Hyman, 1989.

Bentham, Jeremy, *Not Paul, But Jesus*, London: John Hunt, 1823.

Bentham, Jeremy, *The Influence of Natural Religion on the Temporal Happiness of Mankind*, introduction by Delos McKown, Amherst, New York: Prometheus Books, 2003. (Originally published as Philip Beauchamp [Jeremy Bentham and George Grote], *Analysis of the Influence of Natural Religion on the Temporal Happiness of Mankind*, 1822.)

Bicknell, John W. (ed.), *Selected Letters of Leslie Stephen: Volume 1: 1864–1882*, London: Macmillan, 1996.

Bonner, Hypatia Bradlaugh, *Charles Bradlaugh: His Life and Work*, 2 vols, London: T. Fisher Unwin, 1895.

Bowring, John (ed.), *Matins and Vespers: with Hymns and Occasional Devotional Pieces*, second edition, London: Printed for the Author (sold by G. and W. B. Whittaker), 1824.

Brett, R. L. (ed.), *Barclay Fox's Journal*, Fowey: Cornwall Editions, 2008.

Butler, Joseph, *The Analogy of Religion*, London: Religious Tract Society, n.d. (originally 1736).

Capaldi, Nicholas, *John Stuart Mill: A Biography*, Cambridge: Cambridge University Press, 2004.

Carlyle, Thomas, *Sartor Resartus*, London: Chapman & Hall, n.d. (originally serialized in 1833–4).

Comte, Auguste, *The Catechism of Positive Religion*, trans. Richard Congreve, third edition, London: Kegan Paul, Trench, Trübner, & Co., 1891.

Conway, Moncure D., *Centenary History of the South Place Society*, London: Williams and Norgate, 1894.

Courtney, W. L., *Life and Writings of John Stuart Mill*, London: Walter Scott, n.d. (preface dated 1888).

Cox, Catherine Morris, *Genetic Studies of Genius: Volume II: The Early Mental Traits of Three Hundred Geniuses*, Stanford: Stanford University Press, 1926.

Crimmins, James E., *Secular Utilitarianism: Social Science and the Critique of Religion in the Thought of Jeremy Bentham*, Oxford: Clarendon Press, 1990.

Dale, R. W., 'The Expiatory Theory of the Atonement', *British Quarterly Review*, XLVI (1867), pp. 463–504.

Dale, R. W., *The Atonement: The Congregational Union Lecture for 1875*, 21st edn, London: Congregational Union of England and Wales, 1900 (original edition, 1875).

Devigne, Robert, *Reforming Liberalism: J. S. Mill's Use of Ancient, Religious, Liberal, and Romantic Moralities*, New Haven: Yale University Press, 2006.

Dickens, Charles, *Hard Times: For These Days*, London: Bradbury & Evans, 1854.

Eisenach, Eldon, J., *Mill and the Moral Character of Liberalism*, University Park, PA: Pennsylvania State University Press, 1998.

Elliot, Hugh S. R. (ed.), *The Letters of John Stuart Mill*, 2 vols, London: Longmans, Green, and Co., 1910.

Flower, Eliza (ed.), *Hymns and Anthems. The Words chiefly from Holy Scripture and the Writings of the Poets. The Music by Eliza Flower*, Vol. I, London: Cramer Addison & Beale, 1842.

Foote, G. W., *What Was Christ? A Reply to John Stuart Mill*, London: Progressive Publishing Company, 1887.

Fox, W. J., *Christian Morality: Sermons on the Principles of Morality inculcated in the Holy Scriptures*, Boston: Leonard C. Bowlers, 1833.

Galt, John ('The Rev. Micah Balwhidder'), *Annals of the Parish*, Edinburgh: William Blackwood, 1821.

Garnett, Richard with Edward Garnett, *The Life of W. J. Fox: Public Teacher and Social Reformer*, London: John Lane, 1909.

Gaskell, E. C., *The Life of Charlotte Brontë*, New York: D. Appleton, 1862.

Gibbon, Edward, *The Decline and Fall of the Roman Empire*, with notes by the Rev. H. H. Milman, 5 vols, vol. 5, New York: The Kelmscott Society, n.d. (the final part was originally published in 1789).

Gibson, Richard Hughes and Timothy Larsen, 'Nineteenth-century spiritual autobiography: Carlyle, Newman, Mill', in Adam Smyth (ed.), *A History of English Autobiography*, Cambridge: Cambridge University Press, 2016, pp. 192–206.

Grote, Harriet, *The Personal Life of George Grote*, second edition, London: John Murray, 1873.

Haac, Oscar A. (translator and editor), *The Correspondence of John Stuart Mill and Auguste Comte*, New Brunswick, NJ: Transaction Publishers, 1995.

Hare, Julius Charles (ed.), *Essays and Tales by John Sterling, With a Memoir of His Life*, 2 vols, London: John W. Parker, 1848.

Hindmarsh, D. Bruce, *The Evangelical Conversion Narrative: Spiritual Autobiography in Early Modern England*, Oxford: Oxford University Press, 2005.

Jacobs, Jo Ellen, *The Voice of Harriet Taylor Mill*, Bloomington: Indiana University Press, 2002.

Jacobs, Jo Ellen (ed.), *The Complete Works of Harriet Taylor Mill*, Bloomington: Indiana University Press, 1998.

Jones, Tod E., *The Broad Church: A Biography of a Movement*, Lanham: Lexington Books, 2003.

Kelly, Bernard W., *Historical Notes on English Catholic Missions*, London: Kegan Paul, Trench, Trübner & Co., 1907.

Kinzer, Bruce L., Ann P. Robson, and John M. Robson, *A Moralist In and Out of Parliament: John Stuart Mill at Westminster, 1865–1868*, Toronto: University of Toronto Press, 1992.

Kushner, Harold S., *When Bad Things Happen to Good People*, New York: Schocken Books, 1981.

Laine, Michael (ed.), *A Cultivated Mind: Essays on J. S. Mill presented to John M. Robson*, Toronto: University of Toronto Press, 1991.

Larsen, Timothy, *Friends of Religious Equality: Nonconformist Politics in Mid-Victorian England*, Woodbridge: Boydell, 1999.

Larsen, Timothy, 'Charles Bradlaugh, Militant Unbelief, and the Civil Rights of Atheists', in Caroline Litzenberger and Eileen Groth Lyon (eds), *The Human Tradition in Modern Britain*, Lanham: Rowman & Littlefield, 2006, pp. 127–38.

Larsen, Timothy, *A People of One Book: The Bible and the Victorians*, Oxford: Oxford University Press, 2011.

Larsen, Timothy, 'The Catholic Faith of John Stuart Mill's Stepdaughter: A Note on the Diary and Devotional Life of the Feminist Activist Helen Taylor (1831–1907)', *Catholic Historical Review*, 103, 3 (Summer 2017), pp. 465–81.

Leader, Robert Eadon, *Life and Letters of John Roebuck*, London: Edward Arnold, 1897.

Lipkes, Jeff, *Politics, Religion and Classical Political Economy in Britain: John Stuart Mill and his Followers*, London: Macmillan, 1999.

Macaulay, Thomas Babington, Review of James Mill, *Edinburgh Review*, 49, 97 (March 1829), pp. 159–89.

Macaulay, Thomas Babington, Review of James Mill (Cont.), *Edinburgh Review*, 50, 99 (October 1829), pp. 99–125.

MacDonald, George, *Unspoken Sermons* (3 series in one volume), Whitethorn, CA: Johannesen, 2004 (originally published in 1867, 1885, and 1889).

MacMinn, Ney, J. R. Hainds, and James McNab McCrimmon (eds), *Bibliography of the Published Writings of John Stuart Mill, edited from his Manuscript with Corrections and Notes*, Bristol: Thoemmes, 1990 (originally published in 1945).

Mansel, Henry Longueville, *The Limits of Religious Thought Examined*, Boston: Gould and Lincoln, 1859.

Martineau, Harriet (trans. and ed.), *The Positive Philosophy of Auguste Comte*, 3 vols, London: George Bell & Sons, 1896.

Maurice, Frederick Denison, *What Is Revelation? Letters to a Student of Theology on the Bampton Lectures of Mr. Mansel*, London: Macmillan, 1859.

Maurice, Frederick Denison, *Sequel to the Inquiry, What is Revelation?*, Cambridge: Macmillan, 1860.

Mazlish, Bruce, *James and John Stuart Mill: Father and Son in the Nineteenth Century*, London: Hutchinson, 1975.

Mill, James, 'The Church, and Its Reform', *London Review*, Vol. I, No. II (1835), pp. 257–95.

Mill, James, 'Religion', in *James Mill's Common Place Books*, Robert A. Fenn (ed.), vol. II, ch. 5 (2010) accessed at http://www.intellectualhistory.net/mill/cpb2ch5.html.

Morley, John, 'Mr. Mill's Three Essays on Religion', *Fortnightly Review*, n.s., 16 (1874), pp. 634–51.

Morley, John, 'Mr. Mill's Three Essays on Religion' (Concluded), *Fortnightly Review*, n.s., 17 (1875), pp. 103–31.

Norton, Sara, and M. A. De Wolfe Howe (eds), *The Letters of Charles Eliot Norton*, 2 vols, Boston: Houghton Mifflin, 1913.

Packe, Michael St. John, *The Life of John Stuart Mill*, London: Secker and Warburg, 1954.

Peart, Sandra J. (ed.), *Hayek on Mill: The Mill–Taylor Friendship and Related Writings* (The Collected Works of F. A. Hayek XVI), Chicago: University of Chicago Press, 2015.

Pickering, Mary, *Auguste Comte: Volume II: An Intellectual Biography*, Cambridge: Cambridge University Press, 2009.

Pyle, Andrew, *Liberty: Contemporary Responses to John Stuart Mill*, South Bend, IN: St. Augustine's Press, 1994.

Pym, Horace N. (ed.), *Memories of Old Friends: being extracts from the Journals and Letters of Caroline Fox of Penjerrick, Cornwall*, London: Smith, Elder, and Co., 1882.

Raeder, Linda C., *John Stuart Mill and the Religion of Humanity*, Columbia, MO: University of Missouri Press, 2002.

Ratcliffe, S. K., *The Story of South Place*, London: Watts & Co., 1955.

Reeves, Richard, *John Stuart Mill: Victorian Firebrand*, London: Atlantic Books, 2007.

Rey, Louis, in 'John Stuart Mill au Point du Vue Religieux', *La Critique Philosophique: Politique, Scientifique, Littéraire*, 18 (5 June 1873), pp. 283–5.

Rey, Louis, 'The Romance of John Stuart Mill', *Nineteenth Century*, Vol. LXXIV, No. 439 (September 1913), pp. 502–26.

Rey, Louis, *John Stuart Mill en Avignon*, Vaison, n.p., 1921, pp. 158–9.

Robson, John M., and Michael Laine (eds), *James and John Stuart Mill: Papers of the Centenary Conference*, Toronto: University of Toronto Press, 1976.

Russell, Bertrand, and Patricia Russell, (eds), *The Amberley Papers: The Letters and Diaries of Lord and Lady Amberley*, 2 vols, London: Hogarth Press, 1937.

Sell, Alan P. F., *Mill on God: The Pervasiveness and Elusiveness of Mill's Religious Thought*, Aldershot: Ashgate, 2004.

Sell, Alan P. F. (ed.), *Mill on Religion: Contemporary Responses to Three Essays on Religion*, Bristol: Thoemmes Press, 1997.

Settanni, Harry, *The Probabilist Theism of John Stuart Mill*, New York: Peter Lang, 1991.

Skorupski, John (ed.), *The Cambridge Companion to Mill*, Cambridge: Cambridge University Press, 1998.

Smith, William, *A Discourse on Ethics of the School of Paley*, London: William Pickering, 1839.

Spencer, Herbert et al., *John Stuart Mill: His Life and Work*, Boston: James R. Osgood, 1873.

Stephen, James Fitzjames, *Liberty, Equality, Fraternity*, London: Smith, Elder, & Co., 1873.

Stephen, Leslie, 'Mill, John Stuart (1806–1873)', in *Dictionary of National Biography*, Vol. XIII, Sidney Lee (ed.), New York: Macmillan, 1909, pp. 390–9.

Taylor, Algernon, 'Gregory of Nazianzum', *Westminster Review*, LVI, CX (October 1851), pp. 53–65.

Taylor, Algernon, *Convent Life in Italy*, London: Charles J. Skeet, 1862.

Taylor, Algernon, *Scenes in French Monasteries*, London: Charles J. Skeet, 1864.

Taylor, Algernon, *Memories of a Student, 1838–1888*, privately printed, n.d. [1892].

Villers, Charles, *An Essay on the Spirit and Influence of the Reformation of Luther*, Translated and Illustrated with Copious Notes, by James Mill, Esq., London: C. and R. Baldwin, 1805.

Ward, W. G., 'Mill's *Logic*', *British Critic and Quarterly Theological Review*, XXXIV, LXVIII (October 1843), pp. 349–427.

Ward, W. G., *The Ideal of a Christian Church*, London: James Toovey, 1844.

Wright, T. R., *The Religion of Humanity: The Impact of Comtean Positivism on Victorian Britain*, Cambridge: Cambridge University Press, 1986.

Index